50% OFF CCM Certification Prep Course!

Dear Customer,

We consider it an honor and a privilege that you chose our CCM Study Guide. As a way of showing our appreciation and to help us better serve you, we have partnered with Mometrix Test Preparation to offer **50% off their online CCM Prep Course.** Many CCM courses are needlessly expensive and don't deliver enough value. With their course, you get access to the best CCM prep material, and you only pay half price.

Mometrix has structured their online course to perfectly complement your printed study guide. The CCM Certification Prep Course contains **in-depth lessons** that cover all the most important topics, **video reviews** that explain difficult concepts, over **750 practice questions** to ensure you feel prepared, and more than **350 flashcards** for studying on the go.

Online CCM Prep Course

Topics Include:

- Care Delivery and Reimbursement Methods
  - Models of Care
  - Continuum of Care
- Psychosocial Concepts and Support Systems
  - Behavioral Change Therapy
  - Wellness and Illness Prevention
- Quality and Outcomes Evaluation and Measurements
  - Data Interpretations and Reporting
  - Health Care Analytics
- Rehabilitation Concepts and Strategies
  - Adaptive Technologies
  - Vocational Aspects of Disabilities
- Ethical, Legal, and Practice Standards
  - Legal and Regulatory Requirements
  - Risk Management

Course Features:

- CCM Study Guide
  - Get content that complements our best-selling study guide.
- Full-Length Practice Tests
  - With over 750 practice questions, you can test yourself again and again.
- Mobile Friendly
  - If you need to study on the go, the course is easily accessible from your mobile device.
- CCM Flashcards
  - Their course includes a flashcard mode consisting of over 350 content cards to help you study.

To receive this discount, visit their website at mometrix.com/university/ccm or simply scan this QR code with your smartphone. At the checkout page, enter the discount code: **TPBCCM50**

If you have any questions or concerns, please contact them at universityhelp@mometrix.com.

FREE Test Taking Tips Video/DVD Offer

To better serve you, we created videos covering test taking tips that we want to give you for FREE. **These videos cover world-class tips that will help you succeed on your test.**

We just ask that you send us feedback about this product. Please let us know what you thought about it—whether good, bad, or indifferent.

To get your **FREE videos**, you can use the QR code below or email freevideos@studyguideteam.com with "Free Videos" in the subject line and the following information in the body of the email:

    a. The title of your product

    b. Your product rating on a scale of 1-5, with 5 being the highest

    c. Your feedback about the product

If you have any questions or concerns, please don't hesitate to contact us at info@studyguideteam.com.

Thank you!

CCM Certification
Test Prep 2023-2024
3 Practice Exams and Case Management
Study Guide Book [8th Edition]

Joshua Rueda

Written and edited by TPB Publishing.

TPB Publishing is not associated with or endorsed by any official testing organization. TPB Publishing is a publisher of unofficial educational products. All test and organization names are trademarks of their respective owners. Content in this book is included for utilitarian purposes only and does not constitute an endorsement by TPB Publishing of any particular point of view.

Interested in buying more than 10 copies of our product? Contact us about bulk discounts:
bulkorders@studyguideteam.com

ISBN 13: 9781637758465
ISBN 10: 1637758464

Table of Contents

Quick Overview

As you draw closer to taking your exam, effective preparation becomes more and more important. Thankfully, you have this study guide to help you get ready. Use this guide to help keep your studying on track and refer to it often.

This study guide contains several key sections that will help you be successful on your exam. The guide contains tips for what you should do the night before and the day of the test. Also included are test-taking tips. Knowing the right information is not always enough. Many well-prepared test takers struggle with exams. These tips will help equip you to accurately read, assess, and answer test questions.

A large part of the guide is devoted to showing you what content to expect on the exam and to helping you better understand that content. In this guide are practice test questions so that you can see how well you have grasped the content. Then, answer explanations are provided so that you can understand why you missed certain questions.

Don't try to cram the night before you take your exam. This is not a wise strategy for a few reasons. First, your retention of the information will be low. Your time would be better used by reviewing information you already know rather than trying to learn a lot of new information. Second, you will likely become stressed as you try to gain a large amount of knowledge in a short amount of time. Third, you will be depriving yourself of sleep. So be sure to go to bed at a reasonable time the night before. Being well-rested helps you focus and remain calm.

Be sure to eat a substantial breakfast the morning of the exam. If you are taking the exam in the afternoon, be sure to have a good lunch as well. Being hungry is distracting and can make it difficult to focus. You have hopefully spent lots of time preparing for the exam. Don't let an empty stomach get in the way of success!

When travelling to the testing center, leave earlier than needed. That way, you have a buffer in case you experience any delays. This will help you remain calm and will keep you from missing your appointment time at the testing center.

Be sure to pace yourself during the exam. Don't try to rush through the exam. There is no need to risk performing poorly on the exam just so you can leave the testing center early. Allow yourself to use all of the allotted time if needed.

Remain positive while taking the exam even if you feel like you are performing poorly. Thinking about the content you should have mastered will not help you perform better on the exam.

Once the exam is complete, take some time to relax. Even if you feel that you need to take the exam again, you will be well served by some down time before you begin studying again. It's often easier to convince yourself to study if you know that it will come with a reward!

Test-Taking Strategies

1. Predicting the Answer

When you feel confident in your preparation for a multiple-choice test, try predicting the answer before reading the answer choices. This is especially useful on questions that test objective, factual knowledge. By predicting the answer before reading the available choices, you eliminate the possibility that you will be distracted or led astray by an incorrect answer choice. You will feel more confident in your selection if you read the question, predict the answer, and then find your prediction among the answer choices. After using this strategy, be sure to still read all of the answer choices carefully and completely. If you feel unprepared, you should not attempt to predict the answers. This would be a waste of time and an opportunity for your mind to wander in the wrong direction.

2. Reading the Whole Question

Too often, test takers scan a multiple-choice question, recognize a few familiar words, and immediately jump to the answer choices. Test authors are aware of this common impatience, and they will sometimes prey upon it. For instance, a test author might subtly turn the question into a negative, or he or she might redirect the focus of the question right at the end. The only way to avoid falling into these traps is to read the entirety of the question carefully before reading the answer choices.

3. Looking for Wrong Answers

Long and complicated multiple-choice questions can be intimidating. One way to simplify a difficult multiple-choice question is to eliminate all of the answer choices that are clearly wrong. In most sets of answers, there will be at least one selection that can be dismissed right away. If the test is administered on paper, the test taker could draw a line through it to indicate that it may be ignored; otherwise, the test taker will have to perform this operation mentally or on scratch paper. In either case, once the obviously incorrect answers have been eliminated, the remaining choices may be considered. Sometimes identifying the clearly wrong answers will give the test taker some information about the correct answer. For instance, if one of the remaining answer choices is a direct opposite of one of the eliminated answer choices, it may well be the correct answer. The opposite of obviously wrong is obviously right! Of course, this is not always the case. Some answers are obviously incorrect simply because they are irrelevant to the question being asked. Still, identifying and eliminating some incorrect answer choices is a good way to simplify a multiple-choice question.

4. Don't Overanalyze

Anxious test takers often overanalyze questions. When you are nervous, your brain will often run wild, causing you to make associations and discover clues that don't actually exist. If you feel that this may be a problem for you, do whatever you can to slow down during the test. Try taking a deep breath or counting to ten. As you read and consider the question, restrict yourself to the particular words used by the author. Avoid thought tangents about what the author *really* meant, or what he or she was *trying* to say. The only things that matter on a multiple-choice test are the words that are actually in the question. You must avoid reading too much into a multiple-choice question, or supposing that the writer meant something other than what he or she wrote.

2

5. No Need for Panic

It is wise to learn as many strategies as possible before taking a multiple-choice test, but it is likely that you will come across a few questions for which you simply don't know the answer. In this situation, avoid panicking. Because most multiple-choice tests include dozens of questions, the relative value of a single wrong answer is small. As much as possible, you should compartmentalize each question on a multiple-choice test. In other words, you should not allow your feelings about one question to affect your success on the others. When you find a question that you either don't understand or don't know how to answer, just take a deep breath and do your best. Read the entire question slowly and carefully. Try rephrasing the question a couple of different ways. Then, read all of the answer choices carefully. After eliminating obviously wrong answers, make a selection and move on to the next question.

6. Confusing Answer Choices

When working on a difficult multiple-choice question, there may be a tendency to focus on the answer choices that are the easiest to understand. Many people, whether consciously or not, gravitate to the answer choices that require the least concentration, knowledge, and memory. This is a mistake. When you come across an answer choice that is confusing, you should give it extra attention. A question might be confusing because you do not know the subject matter to which it refers. If this is the case, don't eliminate the answer before you have affirmatively settled on another. When you come across an answer choice of this type, set it aside as you look at the remaining choices. If you can confidently assert that one of the other choices is correct, you can leave the confusing answer aside. Otherwise, you will need to take a moment to try to better understand the confusing answer choice. Rephrasing is one way to tease out the sense of a confusing answer choice.

7. Your First Instinct

Many people struggle with multiple-choice tests because they overthink the questions. If you have studied sufficiently for the test, you should be prepared to trust your first instinct once you have carefully and completely read the question and all of the answer choices. There is a great deal of research suggesting that the mind can come to the correct conclusion very quickly once it has obtained all of the relevant information. At times, it may seem to you as if your intuition is working faster even than your reasoning mind. This may in fact be true. The knowledge you obtain while studying may be retrieved from your subconscious before you have a chance to work out the associations that support it. Verify your instinct by working out the reasons that it should be trusted.

8. Key Words

Many test takers struggle with multiple-choice questions because they have poor reading comprehension skills. Quickly reading and understanding a multiple-choice question requires a mixture of skill and experience. To help with this, try jotting down a few key words and phrases on a piece of scrap paper. Doing this concentrates the process of reading and forces the mind to weigh the relative importance of the question's parts. In selecting words and phrases to write down, the test taker thinks about the question more deeply and carefully. This is especially true for multiple-choice questions that are preceded by a long prompt.

9. Subtle Negatives

One of the oldest tricks in the multiple-choice test writer's book is to subtly reverse the meaning of a question with a word like *not* or *except*. If you are not paying attention to each word in the question, you can easily be led astray by this trick. For instance, a common question format is, "Which of the following is...?" Obviously, if the question instead is, "Which of the following is not...?," then the answer will be quite different. Even worse, the test makers are aware of the potential for this mistake and will include one answer choice that would be correct if the question were not negated or reversed. A test taker who misses the reversal will find what he or she believes to be a correct answer and will be so confident that he or she will fail to reread the question and discover the original error. The only way to avoid this is to practice a wide variety of multiple-choice questions and to pay close attention to each and every word.

10. Reading Every Answer Choice

It may seem obvious, but you should always read every one of the answer choices! Too many test takers fall into the habit of scanning the question and assuming that they understand the question because they recognize a few key words. From there, they pick the first answer choice that answers the question they believe they have read. Test takers who read all of the answer choices might discover that one of the latter answer choices is actually *more* correct. Moreover, reading all of the answer choices can remind you of facts related to the question that can help you arrive at the correct answer. Sometimes, a misstatement or incorrect detail in one of the latter answer choices will trigger your memory of the subject and will enable you to find the right answer. Failing to read all of the answer choices is like not reading all of the items on a restaurant menu: you might miss out on the perfect choice.

11. Spot the Hedges

One of the keys to success on multiple-choice tests is paying close attention to every word. This is never truer than with words like almost, most, some, and sometimes. These words are called "hedges" because they indicate that a statement is not totally true or not true in every place and time. An absolute statement will contain no hedges, but in many subjects, the answers are not always straightforward or absolute. There are always exceptions to the rules in these subjects. For this reason, you should favor those multiple-choice questions that contain hedging language. The presence of qualifying words indicates that the author is taking special care with their words, which is certainly important when composing the right answer. After all, there are many ways to be wrong, but there is only one way to be right! For this reason, it is wise to avoid answers that are absolute when taking a multiple-choice test. An absolute answer is one that says things are either all one way or all another. They often include words like *every*, *always*, *best*, and *never*. If you are taking a multiple-choice test in a subject that doesn't lend itself to absolute answers, be on your guard if you see any of these words.

12. Long Answers

In many subject areas, the answers are not simple. As already mentioned, the right answer often requires hedges. Another common feature of the answers to a complex or subjective question are qualifying clauses, which are groups of words that subtly modify the meaning of the sentence. If the question or answer choice describes a rule to which there are exceptions or the subject matter is complicated, ambiguous, or confusing, the correct answer will require many words in order to be expressed clearly and accurately. In essence, you should not be deterred by answer choices that seem

4

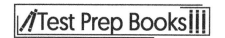

excessively long. Oftentimes, the author of the text will not be able to write the correct answer without offering some qualifications and modifications. Your job is to read the answer choices thoroughly and completely and to select the one that most accurately and precisely answers the question.

13. Restating to Understand

Sometimes, a question on a multiple-choice test is difficult not because of what it asks but because of how it is written. If this is the case, restate the question or answer choice in different words. This process serves a couple of important purposes. First, it forces you to concentrate on the core of the question. In order to rephrase the question accurately, you have to understand it well. Rephrasing the question will concentrate your mind on the key words and ideas. Second, it will present the information to your mind in a fresh way. This process may trigger your memory and render some useful scrap of information picked up while studying.

14. True Statements

Sometimes an answer choice will be true in itself, but it does not answer the question. This is one of the main reasons why it is essential to read the question carefully and completely before proceeding to the answer choices. Too often, test takers skip ahead to the answer choices and look for true statements. Having found one of these, they are content to select it without reference to the question above. Obviously, this provides an easy way for test makers to play tricks. The savvy test taker will always read the entire question before turning to the answer choices. Then, having settled on a correct answer choice, he or she will refer to the original question and ensure that the selected answer is relevant. The mistake of choosing a correct-but-irrelevant answer choice is especially common on questions related to specific pieces of objective knowledge. A prepared test taker will have a wealth of factual knowledge at their disposal and should not be careless in its application.

15. No Patterns

One of the more dangerous ideas that circulates about multiple-choice tests is that the correct answers tend to fall into patterns. These erroneous ideas range from a belief that B and C are the most common right answers, to the idea that an unprepared test taker should answer "A-B-A-C-A-D-A-B-A." It cannot be emphasized enough that pattern-seeking of this type is exactly the WRONG way to approach a multiple-choice test. To begin with, it is highly unlikely that the test maker will plot the correct answers according to some predetermined pattern. The questions are scrambled and delivered in a random order. Furthermore, even if the test maker were following a pattern in the assignation of correct answers, there is no reason why the test taker would know which pattern he or she was using. Any attempt to discern a pattern in the answer choices is a waste of time and a distraction from the real work of taking the test. A test taker would be much better served by extra preparation before the test than by reliance on a pattern in the answers.

FREE Videos/DVD OFFER

Doing well on your exam requires both knowing the test content and understanding how to use that knowledge to do well on the test. We offer completely FREE test taking tip videos. **These videos cover world-class tips that you can use to succeed on your test.**

To get your **FREE videos**, you can use the QR code below or email freevideos@studyguideteam.com with "Free Videos" in the subject line and the following information in the body of the email:

   a. The title of your product

   b. Your product rating on a scale of 1-5, with 5 being the highest

   c. Your feedback about the product

If you have any questions or concerns, please don't hesitate to contact us at info@studyguideteam.com.

Thanks again!

Introduction to the CCM Exam

Function of the Test

The Certified Case Manager (CCM) exam is part of the Commission for Case Manager Certification's (CCMC's) certification process. CCMC is the largest case management certification program in the United States and has certified over 60,000 case managers. CCMC encourages case managers to get CCMC certification in order to gain access to jobs with employers that require certification for case managers and to gain access to promotions and pay raises from employers who value certification.

CCMC requires that individuals taking the CCM exam have at least twelve months of full-time case management experience while supervised by a certified case manager, or twenty-four months of full-time case management experience without such supervision. Accordingly, individuals who take the CCM exam are adults who are already working in the case management profession. Most have bachelor's and/or graduate degrees in social work, nursing, or another health and human services field. Some employers reimburse the cost of case management continuing education for the purpose of preparing for the CCM exam.

Test Administration

The application fee is $210, and the exam fee is $185, a total of $395 will be paid when you apply. The exam may be taken three months out of the year—April, August, and December—with applications needing to be submitted at least five months before the test date.

The test may be taken at hundreds of Prometric test centers across the United States. However, it is not necessarily offered at every Prometric location, so test takers should check to see where the closest center offering the test is located.

If a test taker fails the exam, he or she can schedule a retake during the next testing cycle by contacting CCMC and paying a $185 retake fee. If a retake is not scheduled during the next testing cycle, the test taker will have to re-apply and pay the full first-time application and examination fee.

Students with documented disabilities may submit requests for accommodations to CCMC. If CCMC approves accommodations, they will be arranged between the test taker and Prometric.

Test Format

The CCM exam is delivered by computer at the Prometric testing center. It covers five major domains of "essential knowledge" for case managers. The test consists of 180 multiple-choice questions, 150 of which are official and scored, and are divided as follows:

Domain	Approx % of test	Approx # of questions
Care Delivery and Reimbursement Methods	28	42
Psychosocial Concepts and Support Systems	25	38
Quality and Outcomes Evaluation and Measurements	19	29
Rehabilitation Concepts and Strategies	11	16
Ethical, Legal, and Practice Standards	17	25

For a $30 fee, a prospective test taker may arrange a "test drive" appointment with Prometric, for the purpose of gaining experience with the look and feel of the test, the testing center, and the process of taking the test.

Scoring

Test takers' raw scores are based simply on the number of correct answers given, with no penalty for incorrect answers or guesses. The raw scores are scaled to equalize difficulty and compared to a required passing score, which is determined based on a panel of experts' estimates of the probability that a minimally qualified candidate would have answered the questions correctly.

Upon completion of the computer-based examination, test takers will receive an e-mail from Prometric with their test results. CCMC says this immediate score is "99% accurate," and that the official result will come four to six weeks after the last exam of the testing month is given. Test takers who pass will receive a passing certificate, while those who fail will receive a detailed scoring report.

Recent/Future Developments

The content of the CCM exam was updated as of the December 2020 exam. The new content reflects changes to the profession with the tested material organized into five major domains.

Study Prep Plan for the CCM Exam

1 **Schedule** - Use one of our study schedules below or come up with one of your own.

2 **Relax** - Test anxiety can hurt even the best students. There are many ways to reduce stress. Find the one that works best for you.

3 **Execute** - Once you have a good plan in place, be sure to stick to it.

One Week Study Schedule		
Day 1	Care Delivery and Reimbursement Methods	
Day 2	Psychosocial Concepts and Support Systems	
Day 3	Rehabilitation Concepts and Strategies	
Day 4	CCM Practice Test #1	
Day 5	CCM Practice Test #2	
Day 6	CCM Practice Test #3	
Day 7	Take Your Exam!	

Two Week Study Schedule			
Day 1	Care Delivery and Reimbursement...	Day 8	CCM Practice Test #1
Day 2	Insurance Principles	Day 9	Answer Explanations #1
Day 3	Physical Functioning and Behavioral...	Day 10	CCM Practice Test #2
Day 4	Psychosocial Concepts and Support Systems	Day 11	Answer Explanations #2
Day 5	Quality Outcomes Evaluation and...	Day 12	CCM Practice Test #3
Day 6	Rehabilitation Concepts and Strategies	Day 13	Answer Explanations #3
Day 7	Ethical, Legal, and Practice Standards	Day 14	Take Your Exam!

9

One Month Study Schedule						
Day 1	Care Delivery and Reimbursement...	Day 11	Health Literacy	Day 21	CCM Practice Test #1
Day 2	Coding Methodologies	Day 12	Psychosocial Aspects of Chronic Illness and...	Day 22	Answer Explanations #1
Day 3	Goals and Objectives of Case...	Day 13	Quality Outcomes Evaluation and Measurements	Day 23	Take a Break!
Day 4	Insurance Principles	Day 14	Sources of Quality Indicators	Day 24	CCM Practice Test #2
Day 5	Management of Clients with Acute...	Day 15	Types of Quality Indicators	Day 25	Answer Explanations #2
Day 6	Models of Care Delivery	Day 16	Rehabilitation Concepts and Strategies	Day 26	Take a Break!
Day 7	Public Benefit Programs	Day 17	Rehabilitation Post Hospitalization...	Day 27	CCM Practice Test #3
Day 8	Roles and Functions of Other Healthcare...	Day 18	Job Analysis, Job Accommodation, and...	Day 28	Answer Explanations #3
Day 9	Psychosocial Concepts and Support Systems	Day 19	Ethical, Legal, and Practice Standards	Day 29	Take a Break!
Day 10	Community Resources	Day 20	Legal and Regulatory Requirements...	Day 30	Take Your Exam!

Build your own prep plan by visiting:

testprepbooks.com/prep

Care Delivery and Reimbursement Methods

Accountable Care Organizations

Since the Affordable Care Act (ACA) introduced Accountable Care Organizations (ACOs) over a decade ago, ACOs have been working to meet the healthcare industry's "Triple Aim": decreasing costs, improving patient satisfaction, and providing quality healthcare. ACOs are groups of hospitals, physicians, and other providers that work together to coordinate patient care for financial incentives. ACOs are most often able to receive their financial incentives by saving money when they are working with a large group of providers for various services that are committed to high quality healthcare.

Traditionally, under the fee-for-service model, more care provided to a patient would equal more profit for the provider, even in some cases where the care may not have been the best or most appropriate treatment. Under ACO care, earnings can be made by taking care of a population of patients preventatively, rewarding the ACO with financial incentives for keeping patients out of hospitals, and minimizing procedures, if minimum savings rate benchmarks are met. For example, most Medicare ACO benchmarks are set at about 4 percent.

Case managers working in ACOs can look for trends in the diagnosis and treatment of patients with commonly treated disease processes, and then advocate for evidenced-based protocols for treatment regarding each patient with that disease. By doing this, ACOs can make sure that quality healthcare is received and that the correct and appropriate tests and services are done for patients. Case managers can use data from these selected patient populations, including money saved and reimbursements received, to justify the cost of case managers. Case managers can be an integral part of helping patients navigate their ACO network efficiently, as they help to reduce the cost of care. Tracking patients as they move between services and transitions of care can help ACOs have a holistic view of the patient and improve patient experiences.

Since their inception a little over a decade ago, the number of ACOs has grown each year, and their impact on the healthcare system has already changed the traditional pay-for-service model. Case managers can add value to this new and developing model by bringing the skills they already use in other areas, including collaboration and coordination.

Adherence to Care Regimen

Adherence to care, a phrase that is sometimes confused with the term "compliance," is an essential component of case management and positive patient outcomes. Adhering to a care regimen is a collaborative effort—one that requires both the patient and the treating provider to be engaged in the process of establishing a treatment plan. This is somewhat different from that of compliance, in which the physician dictates priorities and the patient is expected to comply. **Compliance** refers to patients following the physician's orders without giving any input as it relates to their ability to adhere to the plan of care or identify their own priorities.

Adherence to care includes keeping scheduled appointments, taking medication as prescribed, and following the overall treatment plan as determined by the interdisciplinary healthcare team.

There are a number of causes of nonadherence among individuals as it relates to their physical or mental care, including:

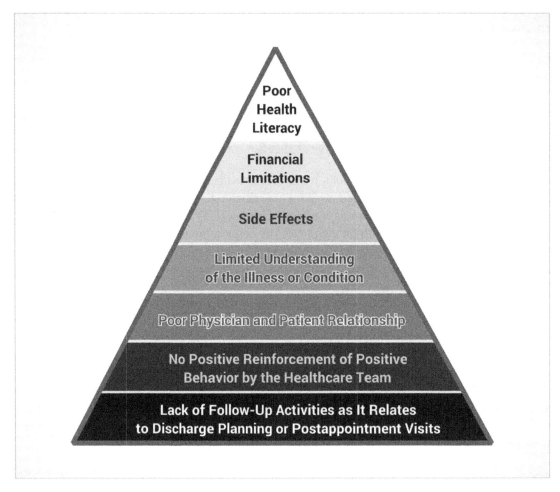

Studies have shown that up to 50% of treatment plan failures are related to a patient's inability to adhere to the prescribed treatment. These poor outcomes are known to contribute to rising healthcare costs, and more than 125,000 deaths are related to medication nonadherence each year.

A **case manager** must understand the influence they have and constantly assess the patient's consistency in adhering to the care regimen and any ongoing barriers they might encounter along the way. In order to improve the likelihood of adherence, case managers must possess a unique set of skills, with communication at the top of the list. They have to be able to ask the patient the right questions and listen for critical cues that indicate if a goal is being met or if a barrier is creating a risk for nonadherence.

Next, case managers must establish a comprehensive approach, connecting the dots between interventions, adherence, and outcomes. In addition, they have to function as an educator who is capable of informing and/or reinforcing the purpose of the treatment plan that has been agreed upon by the patient and the treating provider.

Finally, a case manager must get to know the patient and quickly learn to identify the patient's readiness and ability to adhere to a treatment plan.

Differences in and Application of Age Specific Care

Working with patients of various ages requires specific considerations. For example, pediatric cancer in a child will be treated differently than that same cancer in an adult. While many adults may receive chemotherapy in outpatient settings, children may have to be admitted for that same type of care.

When working with children, the case manager must also include the child's caregivers. Case managers may find themselves focusing on the needs of the patient's caregiver so that the caregiver can give adequate support to their child. When interviewing young children, parental consent is needed, but when possible and age appropriate, children should be actively involved in their own healthcare. Case managers should be aware of state laws concerning age of consent and sharing of information between the adolescent and parent. With children, issues such as divorce and custody agreements should be considered in care plans.

Life Span Considerations

When caring for elderly patients, case managers should provide them with as much autonomy as is safe and appropriate. Elderly patients may also be educated about making advance directives or about selecting a surrogate decision maker if they are declining. As patients get older, many prefer to age in place, and case management for geriatric patients entails considerations to make the patient's home safe and to meet common needs. Case managers for geriatric patients may need to evaluate patient's in-home needs, identify social programs for a patient, and help coordinate services and transportation to appointments.

Alternative Care Facilities

Case managers may provide their services in a variety of settings. Acute care, ambulatory care, home health, long-term care, and wellness programs are just a few examples of settings that a patient may experience along the continuum of care. Involvement in this integrated system of care is a life-long journey for most patients in which they move through a rather extensive and comprehensive array of services related to physical, behavioral, and mental health.

Continuing Care Retirement Communities

Continuing Care Retirement Communities (CCRC) provide the aging population with a plethora of services, from independent-living facilities to assisted-living facilities to skilled-nursing facilities—often all on the same campus. This structure allows residents to transition between facilities or move to a different tier as their health declines.

There are three financial models commonly made available to residents.

- **All-Inclusive Model**: Residents receive both long-term care services and healthcare services.
- **Fee-for-Service Model**: The level of care received is based on the payment for care.
- **Modified Coverage Model**: Residents qualify for long-term care based on a predetermined maximum amount.

Assisted-Living Facilities

Assisted-Living Facilities (ALFs) are a form of long-term care that is available to seniors, also known as an alternative level of care. ALFs enable seniors to remain independent, providing services only as they

are needed. It is a level of care that bridges the gap between residing in one's own home and living in a nursing facility. They are favorable because they are less expensive than nursing homes.

In some states, room, board, and amenities (e.g., housekeeping, laundry, transportation) may be covered by the Medicaid Waiver program. For most individuals, these amenities are not covered, funded, or regulated by Medicare or Medicaid. ALFs are predominantly operated by for-profit companies. The cost to reside in an assisted-living facility is related to the amount of care needed by the individual. In 2015, the median annual cost to rent a one-bedroom apartment in an assisted-living facility was estimated at $43,200.

Case managers may serve as a liaison between the facility staff, the patient, and the family throughout the patient's residency, whether it is a short-term or long-term stay.

Not only are ALFs used as a permanent solution for aging adults as their functional dependence increases, but they also serve as a resource for temporary respite care. This can be beneficial for caregivers who still have full-time jobs or are planning to take a vacation.

Types of Assisted-Living Facilities

Group Homes

Group homes come in the form of single-room residences, board and care homes, apartments, or even domiciliary care. These for-profit businesses are available for children (nineteen years or younger) or adults. In some instances, group homes are licensed by states, offering individuals an alternative living environment. Group homes may also be set up for a variety of purposes, such as to care for people with disabilities, those who suffer from chronic mental illness, or elderly dementia patients.

Staffing varies depending on the type of group home. While some homes are staffed twenty-four hours a day, others may have "house parents" on the premises who take on a parenting role.

Adult Foster Care

Adult foster care offers support for the activities of daily living and provides room and board. Managed by sponsoring families or paid caregivers living onsite, adult foster care gives aging residents the opportunity to live in an environment that mimics a home-based setting. In some states, adult foster care may be used as an alternative to long-term care or institutionalized living.

Residential Treatment Facilities

Residential treatment facilities provide access to fully integrated, long-term, intensive treatment for individuals suffering from mental illness, substance abuse, or other behavioral-health issues. This structured environment not only gives patients access to qualified staff but also to peers who can help effectively support ongoing treatment.

Individuals who require such assistance may reside in a residential treatment facility for up to a year. Residential treatment facilities provide participants with access to services that are more intensive than is commonly provided in an outpatient setting.

In a residential setting, the case manager serves as an advocate when the patient is unable to advocate for themselves. The case manager supports activities such as care coordination between various members of the interdisciplinary team and activities associated with discharge planning, so that the patient is able to make a safe transition back into the community and into outpatient services. Even

14

Case Management Models, Process, and Tools

after discharge, the case manager will need to maintain ongoing contact with the member and/or family.

The **case-management process** is a collaborative interaction between case manager and patient. According to CCMC, the case-management process consists of a wide range of activities that include:

- Assessment
- Planning
- Implementation
- Coordination
- Monitoring
- Evaluation
- Outcomes

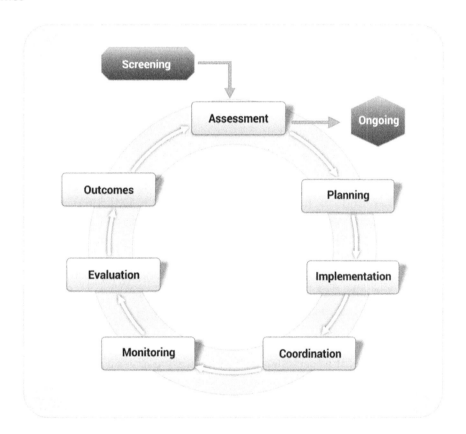

Assessments

The first action a case manager takes during the case-management process is to obtain information about the patient. This is also known as the **assessment**. The assessment process includes gathering information from charts, patients, caregivers, providers, and other members of the healthcare-delivery team where applicable. Health-risk assessments are commonly used to identify the physical and psychosocial health status of the patient. This includes assessing the patient's health-literacy status and deficits as well. The assessment tool used to gather information can vary from organization to organization, though they have similar content. Assessments can provide case managers with a complete view of the patient's current state, along with potential issues and risk factors. They allow case

managers to gather relevant information about not only the patient's health and/or psychosocial status but also historical insight into the patient's financial and familial history.

In complex cases, a home assessment may be warranted to ensure that the home environment is stable and safe.

Assessments are not a one-time event. They may be repeated more than once to establish and/or monitor ongoing needs throughout the case-management process. Assessments form the foundation for activities associated with planning, implementation, care coordination, evaluation, and outcomes management.

Planning

During the **planning** process, case managers work in a collaborative fashion with the patient, family, or caregiver, and members of the healthcare-delivery team to develop a plan of care that is cost-effective for the payer or healthcare-delivery system and promotes access to quality care with the best possible outcomes.

As a component of the plan of care, short- and long-term goals are created alongside the patient. These goals must be specific, realistic, and measurable. The patient collaborates with the case manager to prioritize these goals so that they are specific to their needs. Goals may be modified during the case-management process due to barriers or complications that arise, but they should remain individualized and specific to the patient and monitored closely, with a secondary or alternative plan in place. For each goal, interventions are identified to support its achievement.

Implementation

Once the plan of care has been created and approved by the patient, payer, treating physician, and any others indicated, **implementation** of that care plan takes place. During the implementation phase of the case-management process, the interventions are facilitated to support the achievement of those goals that were established during the planning process. Examples of interventions carried out by the case manager might include education, daily or weekly follow-ups with the patient, treating provider or caregiver, or care-coordination activities such as referrals or authorization of services. It is during the implementation phase that case managers document the progress of their client and any barriers they are encountering that may cause nonadherence.

Care Coordination

The **care-coordination** phase of the case-management process involves a coordination of activities and services that support the execution of the overall case-management plan. The case manager becomes the nucleus of activity, working with or on behalf of the member, promoting communication, putting services into place, and removing duplicate services or inefficiencies that may impede progress. Case managers provide the patient not only with a connection to the healthcare system but also to community resources.

Monitoring

Case managers must **monitor** the progress of the plan of care and anticipate when modifications may be required to ensure overall effectiveness and the achievement of expected outcomes. Monitoring may also require the case manager to revisit certain phases of the case-management process, such as assessment. In this case, the case manager will need to conduct a reassessment of the patient's overall

health or home environment and reprioritize goals in the order of those most critical to the patient or caregiver.

Reassessments might be initiated for a variety of reasons, including changes in the patient's medical or psychosocial status or a need for changed goals.

Evaluation

During the **evaluation** phase of the case-management process, case managers should review the plan of care to determine if the goals and desired outcomes have been achieved. Evaluation is not a one-time event; it should be repetitive and continuous, with the case manager not only looking to determine if goals are being achieved but also evaluating the patient's quality of life. Other things to be evaluated are cost savings, overall effectiveness, and outcomes associated with case-management activities.

Documentation during the evaluation and case-management process should always be objective when identifying whether or not goals were met.

Outcomes

Outcome tracking is an essential activity of case management. The value of case management is documented by the measurement of outcomes, requiring case managers to collect various forms of outcome data. This may include information such as patient satisfaction, core measures, HEDIS measures, return to work, quality of care, utilization of services, cost, cost savings, and clinical information. Outcomes information allows organizations, departments, and case managers to make decisions about the validity of programs and the best practices that can ultimately impact the population's health.

Case managers can use outcome data to demonstrate the relationship between case-management interventions to the overall results achieved. Ideally, case managers will have documented a baseline assessment of the patient's condition at the time they entered case management, so that any improvement is apparent when the case manager or organization begins a look-back period of the progress of the case. Results achieved should demonstrate an improvement in health status, as well as self-care abilities for a complex patient with multiple comorbidities and changes in the functional status of individuals with behavioral-health conditions.

Case Closure

Once it has been determined that the patient has achieved their best level of functioning, the case manager will make the decision to close the case. Additional factors that must be considered for **case closure** include but are not limited to:

- Risk for readmission
- Services in place or sufficiently delivered to meet the needs of the patient
- The patient's ability to adequately administer self-care
- The patient's ability to adhere to care
- The patient's support system
- The patient's action plan in place for an urgent or emergent event
- The patient's demonstrated understanding of how to seek healthcare support through the appropriate channels

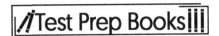

On occasion, case managers may close cases in which the following occurs:

- The patient dies.
- Benefits or eligibility for services are terminated.
- The patient or caregiver declines case-management services.
- Services are no longer available.

Coding Methodologies

Diagnosis-Related Groups

Diagnosis-Related Groups (DRGs) are used to categorize patients based on their diagnoses, types of treatment—including surgical procedures—and the presence or absence of comorbidities or complications. Clinicians and organizations such as hospitals and managed care organizations use DRGs to help with determining what constitutes an acceptable duration or length of stay based on a patient's diagnosis. Hospital stays are also assigned a DRG. Diagnosis-related groups additionally relate the case mix (the variety of cases handled) of a healthcare organization to the expense of providing medical care and are used to help healthcare providers receive appropriate financial reimbursement from health insurance organizations like Medicare. A patient's DRG is determined using ICD-11 diagnostic codes.

Diagnostic and Statistical Manual of Mental Disorders (DSM)

The **Diagnostic and Statistical Manual of Mental Disorders** (DSM-5) functions as the standard system of classification of mental disorders. Comprising three major components—the diagnostic classification, the diagnostic criteria sets, and the descriptive text—the DSM is used by mental-health professionals and other healthcare professionals, including case managers, to classify mental illness. The DSM contains diagnoses that include a diagnostic code typically used by individual providers, institutions, and agencies for data-collection and billing purposes.

International Classification of Diseases (ICD)

Under the **International Classification of Diseases** (ICD), Eleventh Revision, or ICD-11, codes are assigned to help classify individuals into manageable categories that have clinical meaning. The ICD-11 is a standard diagnostic tool that is leveraged to track epidemiology, support health management, and guide clinical activities. Healthcare professionals and organizations alike find the ICD-11 tool to be beneficial it allows for the ability to closely track both the incidence and prevalence of diseases, along with other health problems that may impact various populations.

The ICD-11 is used in more than a hundred countries and operates as a means for identifying health trends and statistics all over the world, and it allows for countries to compare and exchange health information using a common language.

The ICD-11, released in 2022, allows providers to gain a deeper level of detail about a patient's condition. The ICD is updated periodically to reflect advances in health and medical science.

Current Procedural Terminology

Current Procedure Terminology, commonly referred to as CPT, is a medical code that is utilized along with ICD numerical diagnostic coding as a component of the billing process. CPT codes are used to identify medical, surgical, and diagnostic procedures and services for entities such as physicians, health-insurance companies, and accreditation organizations.

Continuum of Care/Continuum of Health and Human Services/Social Services

The **continuum of care** (CoC) requires integrated case management for patients in multiple settings, over a period of time. It happens from birth to the start of an illness to the point in which the patient is either no longer ill or the patient is no longer eligible for medical or case-management services.

The continuum of care encompasses a wide range of services, including acute care, ambulatory care, home care, extended care, and wellness programs. The CoC supports the goal of providing integrated health services that are cost-effective for complex patients with chronic conditions, providing them with greater access to services.

Given the multiple settings in which a patient may reside, case managers may be required to communicate with other case managers in meeting physical or psychosocial needs.

In case management, patients are at greatest risk during the transition between points of care; specifically, when they are transitioning from one level of care to another. Case managers play a critical role in ensuring that these transitions are as seamless as possible. This is only achievable with effective discharge planning or, in some instances, end-of-life planning. Case managers must anticipate the needs of a patient as they move between various levels of care.

Case Managers as Advocates

Throughout the continuum of care, case managers must function as advocates and place the needs of the patient ahead of their own beliefs or, in some instances, that of the organization for which they work. This can put case managers in a precarious position in which they are working against their company's vision for the good of the patient.

Case Managers as Educators

Case managers also spend a great deal of time educating patients and families, not only about the complexity of a patient's condition but also about the various services for which they are eligible.

Patient and Family Empowerment

Throughout the CoC, case managers will find that they must also empower patients and/or caregivers so they eventually attain independence by demonstrating decision-making and self-care skills.

Case Managers as Communicators and Collaborators

Case managers must demonstrate good written and verbal skills throughout the CoC. Case managers are often the liaison between the patient and the provider, thus making effective communication a necessity. While a good case manager knows when and how to be assertive, they must be careful not to appear too aggressive. Instead, they serve as an ambassador of good will who has the best interests of both the patient and provider at heart.

Case managers are also required to function as collaborators. Although this can prove to be a time-consuming task, the long-term benefits of establishing trust with various stakeholders are well worth the energy.

Cost-Containment Principles

Case managers have a role in cost containment, which essentially means keeping treatment costs to a minimum. While they act as advocates to get the best treatment for their patients, case managers must also find the treatment option that is most financially feasible for the patient and, in some instances, the insurance organization. Case management can support efforts to reduce costs and reduce spending, moving toward the ultimate goal of cost containment and/or reduction. When deployed in the right manner, case-management activities can:

- Identify barriers to care.
- Prevent hospital readmissions.
- Support care optimization.
- Stabilize patients.

Cost savings are not always obvious or easy to document. Any cost savings that are documented must be accurate and defensible when presenting the effectiveness of case management.

Cost containment is an effort to ensure that the medical coverage provided through insurance is as comprehensive yet inexpensive as possible. Depending on the goal of cost containment, sometimes the result is a greater cost for the patient and sometimes for the insurance company, medical provider, or employer. Some cost containment strategies are used by insurance companies, such as **co-pays**, which are the fixed fees patients have to pay for different services, like a doctor's visit. Another strategy that insurance companies use for cost containment is **deductibles**, or the minimum amount that must be paid by the patient before the insurance kicks in. **Co-insurance** is another important aspect of cost

containment and refers to the percentage of treatment costs paid by the insurance company and the percentage that has to be paid by the patient. While organizations and insurance companies are attempting to keep their own costs to a minimum by placing more of the cost burden on the patient, the case manager should work to find the option that will best achieve cost containment for the patient.

Healthcare providers usually have agreements with specific insurance companies and utilize different types of insurance, which must be considered when the patient is seeking treatment. **Preferred provider organizations** (PPOs) are those medical providers that have contracts with specific insurance companies. As a result, these providers usually have better rates and lower costs for the patient when it comes to co-pays and deductibles. Similarly, **health maintenance organizations** (HMOs) function on a prepaid basis, covering a fixed amount for treatment for the year. HMOs seek the lowest costs by approving only those treatments they deem necessary and by encouraging preventative care. Medicare and Medicaid, along with other health plans, reimburse hospitals depending on a patient's Diagnosis-Related Group (DRG). This provides incentive for the hospital to keep costs lower. Navigating the system and understanding which insurance and treatment options are most cost-effective can often be a significant challenge for the patient. Case managers should assist with this process and help their patients obtain the best possible insurance option and find appropriate service providers within their coverage area.

Factors Used to Identify Client's Acuity or Severity Levels

Case-managed patients are generally assigned an **acuity level rating** that indicates the severity of an illness or disability. Acuity levels assist case managers in identifying how sick a patient is at the time of case-management engagement. Acuity levels are generally assigned using a set of criteria that has been established by the organization for which they work. Data gained during the initial intake screening coupled with the level of services required by the patients over a short-term period can aid in establishing the assigned acuity level for a patient.

Currently, there is no standing acuity model or program that is utilized by all healthcare-delivery systems, but rather there are various models, software, tools, and resources used by various agencies to determine acuity. They do share a common core of criteria, however, that may be utilized to define the acuity of a case-management patient.

Acuity levels can assist both case managers and departments in monitoring a case manager's caseload and ensuring the case manager maintains a proper caseload mix. Ultimately, there should be an equal distribution of cases per acuity level.

In addition, acuity levels can inform decisions made regarding the case-management model used by an organization, as well as the staffing levels maintained to support their programs.

Acuity measures can be helpful in predictive modeling within an organization, such as a managed care organization. Predictive modeling analyzes data received from health-insurance claims, service authorizations, pharmacy utilization, and health-risk assessments to identify the potential risk an individual might have for over utilization of services or facing a catastrophic event.

Most predictive-modeling programs generate risk scores that enable case managers and organizations to prioritize patients and identify the level of care required to achieve stabilization.

Financial Resources

The **financial resources** used to pay for healthcare expenses may vary to include waiver programs, special needs trusts, and viatical settlements.

Waiver Programs

Many states offer Medicaid Waiver Programs, which allow for the provision of long-term care services in the home and community. **Waiver programs** are a combination of standard medical and nonmedical services. Examples of the services provided by waiver programs include case management, home health aide, personal-attendant care services, adult day health services, respite care, and residential care. On occasion, states may choose to include additional value-added services.

Special Needs Trusts

Special-needs trusts (SNTs) are managed by one individual on behalf of someone else. Specifically, they are designed to benefit the disabled or mentally ill. SNTs are designed to support those who lack the mental capacity to manage their own finances. They can greatly assist with preventing loss of government benefits. Trustees of special needs trusts may be family members or third parties who are appointed by the court.

Special-needs trusts can benefit the recipient because they keep disabled individuals from being disqualified from receiving Supplemental Security Income (SSI), Medicaid, vocational rehabilitation, and subsidized housing. A special-needs trust protects the individual from being disqualified.

A trustee may seek support from a case manager so that they can provide an initial and annual assessment. The case manager may be asked to function as a liaison between the patient/family and the provider or to help educate the trustee about those services or programs available to the patient.

Viatical Settlements

Viatical settlements take place when an individual elects to sell their life-insurance policy for more than the cash surrender value, in order to immediately obtain cash. Viatical settlements are available in all fifty states and may be sold by individuals facing a terminal illness to relieve their financial burdens. There are viatical companies that will offer to buy policies directly while others may purchase the policy from another funding source. For example, someone with less than six months to live might be offered 80% of the policy's face value. Case managers can assist their clients in obtaining accurate information related to viatical settlements.

Goals and Objectives of Case-Management Practice

Case management has a set of goals at the core of its practice, and they are as follows:

- Support and facilitate improved access to care.
- Provide service and care coordination.
- Promote care that is medically necessary and cost-effective.
- Create a pathway to functional stability.
- Empower the client to engage in self-directed care.

Case managers should diligently work to assess high-risk conditions and behavior, partner with the patient or caregiver to formulate a collaborative and effective treatment plan, and monitor for outcomes. The goal for case managers is for clients to achieve and maintain optimal levels of physical

22

and mental health and functioning. This is primarily accomplished as the case manager works on behalf of the client and plays a supportive role in the client's treatment.

Case managers usually serve in a coordination capacity, connecting the client to a variety of services to meet their physical, medical, psychological, and social needs. The case manager is responsible for managing the overall plan of treatment and care, which may include involvement with multiple providers, physicians, and community resources. The case manager does not directly provide all the services that a client may need but is responsible for ensuring the client receives quality care and any necessary treatment through the appropriate resources.

Another important objective of case management is the empowerment of the client. Rather than making decisions on their behalf, a case manager collaborates with the client on treatment plans and goals and seeks to empower the client in self-directed care. The goal of case management is not to cause the client to become dependent on the case manager, but rather to help the client become independent, fully involved in their own treatment process, and able to engage in self-advocacy. This includes providing education for the client around their own illness or disability and equipping the client with the information necessary to take charge of their care and treatment.

Healthcare Delivery Systems

The United States' **healthcare-delivery system** comprises several subsystems. Access to quality healthcare is strongly driven by health-insurance coverage, location, and technology-driven systems. Legal risks can often influence the behavior of healthcare professionals.

Healthcare-delivery systems in the United States can be categorized in the following way:

Managed Care

Managed care is considered to be the dominant healthcare-delivery system in the United States. Managed care seeks to:

- Control costs by managing utilization of services.
- Regulate provider reimbursement.
- Establish efficiency with integrated healthcare practices.

Managed care organizations (MCOs) are financed by employers or government agencies by way of a contract. Through the contract, MCOs provide a set of healthcare services to members who are enrolled in the health plan. Members, also known as enrollees, are covered by the contracted health plan for a wide spectrum of services.

MCOs negotiate with providers to accept a capitation rate (in most instances) and provide members with a discounted rate. Providers agree to join a network of treating physicians and treat MCO members.

Military

Active-duty military personnel in the United States Army, Navy, Air Force, and Coast Guard, along with other uniformed nonmilitary services, receive medical care that is free of charge. The **military healthcare system** is integrated and provides comprehensive health treatment. In many instances, medical services are provided by individuals who are also in the military or in other uniformed services.

Families and dependents of active-duty or retired career military personnel may also receive care at facilities like hospitals or clinics through TRICARE coverage. **TRICARE** is an insurance plan that enables enrollees, also known as beneficiaries, to receive medical or mental-health treatment in nonmilitary facilities.

The **VA** or **Veterans Administration** healthcare system makes healthcare available to retired veterans with previous military service. Disabled veterans are given priority under this system and have access to hospital care, mental-health services, and long-term care.

Vulnerable Populations
Those who are poor, uninsured, or reside in geographic locations with economic disadvantages are identified as being among the most vulnerable population. **Vulnerable populations** receive care from settings that are specially designed to support their needs and include health centers. Additionally, physician's offices, hospitals, outpatient clinics, and emergency departments provide a "safety net" of providers who are equipped to provide comprehensive medical treatment.

Medicare
Medicare serves approximately 39 million people. Those who qualify for Medicare are 65 years of age or older or have been diagnosed with end-stage renal disease or a disability.

Medicare is composed of three parts:

Part A. **Medicare Part A** provides coverage to Medicare recipients for healthcare that is received at hospitals, hospice care, or nursing facilities, as well as some home healthcare services. There are no monthly premiums.

Part B. **Medicare Part B** provides coverage at an additional monthly premium for physician services and some outpatient services that are not included with Part A.

Part D. The **Medicare Prescription Drug Plan** provides Medicare recipients with coverage for brand-name and generic prescription drugs at participating pharmacies, which helps to reduce the cost of ordinarily high-cost drugs or medications that would otherwise prove burdensome for the recipient.

Medicaid
Medicaid provides health insurance to the disabled, children, the elderly, and low-income people. Some Medicaid recipients (older adults and those with disabilities) may qualify for long-term care services.

SCHIP
Established in 1997, the **State Children's Health Insurance Program** (SCHIP) provides coverage for those children whose families do not qualify for Medicaid due to income levels. Services covered include:

- Physician visits
- Hospital stays
- Emergency room visits

There are communities in which the number of available "safety net" providers are limited or not available, which results in a greater risk for vulnerable populations.

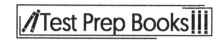

Integrated Service Delivery

Integrated delivery systems (IDSs) have become a gold standard in the United States because of their ability to establish and maintain a strong and strategic network of hospitals, physicians, and insurers.

Hospice, Palliative, and End-of-Life Care

End-of-life issues refer to the treatment and care people receive when they have a terminal or chronic illness or are approaching the end of their lives. It is the goal of health professionals and all those providing end-of-life care to ensure that the patient's last days of life are as painless and comfortable as possible. One focus is on physical care, especially pain management and dealing with common symptoms of terminal illness, such as fatigue, constipation, sleep and appetite issues, and nausea. The other aspect is psychosocial care: addressing spiritual or existential concerns, relationship problems, fears about the process of dying, loss of independence, and mental health matters, such as anxiety or depression. Palliative care and hospice care are carried out by collaborative interdisciplinary teams of doctors, nurses, social workers, clinicians, and others.

Hospice Care

Hospice care is typically administered as a component of end-of-life care to those who are suffering from terminal illness with less than six months to live. It is estimated that approximately 1.5 million people receive hospice care in a single year. Individuals who receive hospice care typically have received a diagnosis for a condition that has no cure. A component of hospice care may include palliative care. The goal in providing hospice care is not to provide a cure but to ensure that the patient's remaining days are as comfortable as possible.

Both the patient and the family should be considered clients of a hospice organization. Hospice is available to provide support for both the family and the patient. Families may receive grief counseling.

Studies have shown that some patients improve with hospice services. Recipients of hospice services may stay in their home environment or services may also be provided in a nursing-home setting.

Hospice patients and their families can receive care for six months or longer and, most importantly, they have the option of keeping their treating physician involved with the care that is being provided.

Coverage through Medicare or other insurance providers usually covers the last six months of a person's life. This can hinder access to treatment because a time-specific prognosis is very difficult, so people usually receive care for a shorter time frame than the six months for which they qualify.

Palliative Care

Palliative care is comprehensive care provided for symptoms and illnesses exacerbated by chronic conditions, including cancer, liver failure, dementia, and chronic obstructive pulmonary disease. Palliative care is delivered by a multidisciplinary team of physicians, nurses, nutritionists, pharmacists, social workers, case managers, and a number of specialists in a collaborative manner.

The characteristic that distinguishes palliative care from hospice care is the time at which palliative care may be offered. Case managers may advocate for palliative care to be administered at any stage of an illness or at any age. Ideally, palliative care should be initiated upon diagnosis for conditions like cancer and continue for the duration of therapy, follow-up care, and end-of-life care, as indicated.

Palliative care has the ability to improve one's quality of life, addressing physical, behavioral, spiritual, and practical needs. Palliative care delivers a variety of options to patients that go far beyond pain assessments.

Palliative care may be delivered in the patient's home as long as they are under the supervision of a physician, or it may be a component of hospice or provided in a long-term facility. It is typically covered by health insurance and in some instances may be covered by Medicare and Medicaid. Those who do not qualify for palliative care by any of the identified entities may need further assistance from their case manager and/or social worker to identify potential resources that can provide the necessary support to receive services.

End-of-Life Care

Patients should be encouraged to discuss **end-of-life** wishes with their family members early on in the process when possible. The decision-making process can be complex, intense, and stressful for those left to make the decision for the patient. Having a plan in place that makes the patient's wishes clear can reduce the level of stress for both the family and the patient.

It is helpful for the patient to establish a plan that outlines specifically what their wishes are related to end-of-life care. A healthcare proxy can assist with ensuring such wishes are honored. Core topics and/or decisions a healthcare proxy can assist with include the location of healthcare (e.g., at home or in a facility) and resuscitation expectations.

Case managers may need to provide guidance in pointing their patients in the right direction to complete an advanced directive and/or living will. Advanced directives and living wills are two additional resources that should be kept on file to assist with the documentation and communication of a patient's wishes.

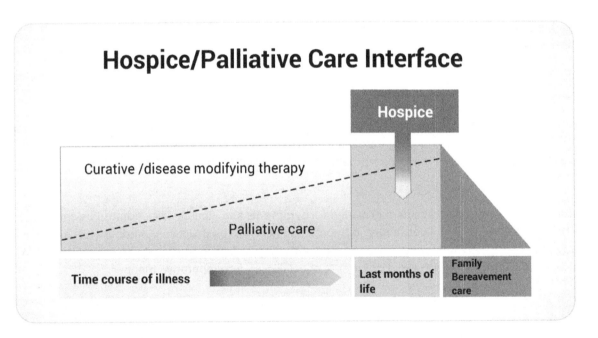

A **Do Not Resuscitate** (DNR) order prevents health workers from administering CPR on an individual whose heart has stopped or who has stopped breathing. A person may choose to have a DNR order if they have a late-stage terminal illness and the attempts to resuscitate could decrease quality of life or

be unlikely to succeed. **Withdrawal of care** happens when a decision is made to stop the life-sustaining support that is being provided, such as a ventilator. This decision is often made when life is being artificially sustained but there is no chance of improvement or recovery. These difficult decisions are made by the patient, or by the family, if the patient is incapable of making the decision. When case managers are discussing this issue with patients, it is important to ensure that patients make the decision based on their own values and wishes. While the medical facts should be fully presented to contribute to an informed decision-making process, there should be no coercion or undue influence. Ultimately, it is the decision of the patient, or the family.

Insurance Principles

Insurance can be broken down into four subcategories: health, disability, long-term, and workers' compensation.

Health Insurance

Health insurance provides individuals with access to healthcare in a variety of healthcare settings. Health insurance covers those costs associated with medical and surgical expenses as well as treatments. It may pay a portion or all of those costs. The insured individual may be required to pay for costs out-of-pocket and be later reimbursed. Healthcare insurance can protect the insured from high medical costs.

Most people in the United States receive health insurance through their employer. However, some individuals purchase health insurance on their own or have to seek health coverage through government-funded programs like Medicaid and Medicare. The Affordable Care Act has assisted in extending health insurance to individuals in the United States who may not have qualified previously.

Disability Insurance

Disability insurance is typically distributed as a form of health insurance when an individual is unable to work due to injury or illness. Disability insurance is available in two forms—short term and long term— and is plan specific. **Short-term disability** (STD) is a set of benefits leveraged to provide coverage for an individual during a time in which they are deemed disabled. Unless otherwise indicated, STD is administered over a period of time to not exceed two years.

Long-term disability (LTD) is generally issued to a group or to an individual. LTD is used to replace income lost as a result of a chronic condition or illness.

Long Term Care

Long-term care insurance is insurance that covers care received in a nursing home, home health setting, or assisted living facility due to a chronic health condition. Certain patients may not qualify for long-term care insurance if they have pre-existing conditions. While the ACA prohibits other types of insurance from denying patients due to preexisting conditions, this does not apply to long-term care insurance. Most research advocates for the mid-50s being the best age to buy long-term care insurance, as premiums for long-term care insurance rapidly increase with each year of life. Long-term care insurance is most needed by middle-class Americans, as high-income families can often afford care and low-income families qualify for Medicaid.

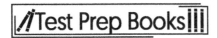

Workers' Compensation

Established with the enactment of the Workers' Compensation Act in 1911, **Workers' Compensation** is a state-governed insurance that manages work-related injuries.

With the evolution of managed care and case management has come the evolution of workers' compensation, which now often takes on a medical-management model. The distinction between traditional medical-management case management and that of workers' compensation, however, is directly driven by state laws. Case managers for workers' compensation must abide by state laws. While the statutes associated with workers' compensation may vary from state to state, the general framework associated with the practices of workers' compensation is the same.

In addition, workers' compensation does not carry a deductible or co-pay. Patients are able to see their physician of choice, and there is no limit on medical coverage; these cases can be rife with litigation.

Wage-Loss Benefits Coordination

Employers may play a role in coordinating **wage-loss payments** under workers' compensation with Social Security Disability Income (SSDI) or long-term disability insurance. The carrier is required to educate employees of their benefits under SSDI should it be determined that there is some potential for eligibility.

Role of Case Managers in Workers' Compensation

Case managers are responsible for understanding and explaining the most beneficial services to qualifying individuals. While many cases do not require case management intervention, the ones that do should begin case management activities at the initial report. Ultimately, case managers for workers' compensation should aim to monitor demonstrated progression toward returning to work, adherence and compliance with the agreed-upon treatment plan, and avoidance of activities by the client that would prevent them from returning to work. In addition to evaluating workers, the CCM in workers' compensation cases would also be responsible for assessing each situation, arranging procedures for compensation, and implementing these procedures, while acting as an intermediary among employers, employees, and attorneys. They advocate for clients but still ensure the amount paid out for compensations is fair for all parties involved.

Case managers with a background in medical surgical settings have the ability to function as a strong advocate for both workers' compensation organizations and injured parties as they are more knowledgeable about the costs and procedures of caring for different types of work related injuries. Case managers also have a role in improving the communication channels between the multiple stakeholders involved in each case. These include the injured worker, specialists, primary-care physicians, the carrier, the employer, and other members of the healthcare-delivery team. If it is determined that an employee is using drugs/alcohol at the time an injury occurs, workers' compensation claims may be denied.

Reinsurance

Reinsurance, also known as stop-loss insurance, is a method used to reduce risk or net liability. It is intended to prevent loss in catastrophic cases that could put an insurance company at risk for losing an amount of money that is so significant it could cause them to go bankrupt. Reinsurance is purchased by insurance companies from designated reinsurance carriers.

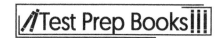

For example, a company may set aside $500,000 per covered life and set a limit of $50,000 with the reinsurer insurance company. The health insurer would cover claims of up to $50,000 and anything over the $50,000 limit would be reimbursed by the stop-loss carrier for up to a total dollar amount of $500,000.

Long-Term Care

Long-term care services become necessary when individuals are unable to take care of their functional needs as a direct result of a disabling chronic illness or injury. These activities may include but are not limited to bathing, meal preparation, shopping, getting into a chair, or getting into bed. Individuals with developmental disabilities or mental illnesses may also require long-term care services.

Long-term care insurance covers services that are not usually covered by health insurance. It is administered when clinical deficits are present—such as an inability to complete activities of daily living (ADLs) or cognitive impairment.

While some policies offer long-term care insurance for as long as an individual lives, many policies do have limits in place as it relates to the duration for which they will cover services. For example, some will only provide long-term care services over a period of two to five years. A set of criteria must be met in order to qualify for the services, including a deficiency in the following areas:

- Activities of daily living to a specified degree
- Cognitive impairments including short-term or long-term memory orientation and judgment

Those who do not qualify for long-term care services under the ADL or cognitive-impairment umbrellas may qualify to receive them as a result of a medical-necessity clause in their contract.

Forty-one percent of those who access long-term care services are under the age of sixty-five. Case managers providing services to individuals with access to long-term care services can assist their patients in ensuring that they have and/or maintain the appropriate level of services so that they are able to remain in the community and/or in their homes.

Potential long-term services covered may include:

- Home modifications
- Ramp installations
- Emergency response systems
- Respite care
- Home safety assessments
- Skilled-nursing facilities
- Hospice
- Adult day care
- Transitional living centers

Interdisciplinary/Interprofessional Care Team

The **interdisciplinary care team** (ICT) is a collaborative group of healthcare professionals from different backgrounds, disciplines, and professions with the common goal of establishing an effective plan of care. Patients and families should be integral members of the care team and fully involved in the decision-making process. The ICT may include doctors, nurses, psychologists, social workers, dieticians, and

family members. Case managers have a role in this team in that they can provide critical information that may lend itself to the shared decision-making process in establishing the best treatment plan for a patient.

ICTs are becoming more and more of a necessity for a variety of reasons, including but not limited to the following:

- Aging adults with chronic, complex, comorbid conditions

- The need for a team with varying skill sets, knowledge, and abilities to manage patient populations with complex needs

- New policies and evidence-based best practices for managing chronically-ill and disabled populations

- The trend of increased specialization among healthcare professionals

It is important to reinforce that the ICT is a collaborative group that conducts shared decision-making. Power should be distributed among individual team members when formulating a plan of care to meet the needs of the patient. However, the distribution of power may create some challenges in those instances where the client has a set of comorbid conditions in both the medical and behavioral domains. Conflict may arise between different professionals as to the best course of action. Despite the potential challenges, these teams tend to be more effective and comprehensive, as well as more cost-effective over the long term.

Levels of Care and Care Settings

Acute Care

Acute care is accessed in an effort to resolve an immediate and unanticipated health event or complex health issue, avoid death, and prevent disability, while simultaneously improving health and promoting wellness. Acute care services are provided in a hospital setting but may also be delivered in other settings based on the acuity of the patient.

Acute care encompasses the following types of services:

- **Emergency care** consists of medical care provided to those experiencing symptoms, illness, or injuries that require immediate attention and may become life threatening if left untreated.

- **Urgent care** is provided to those with an illness or condition that requires immediate attention but does not necessitate an emergency care visit.

- **Critical care** is provided to those with an illness or injury that is detrimental to life and requires constant monitoring.

- **Trauma care** and **acute-care** surgery provide emergency operative care for life-threatening health issues that require surgery within twenty-four hours of admission.

- **Short-term stabilization** provides immediate acute-care services to those in distress so that they can be transferred to another level of treatment.

Long-Term Care Services

Long-term care services offer a variety of options to those who require services that are designed to provide ongoing support for complex conditions that impact their ability to care for themselves and function independently.

Long-term care encompasses the following types of services:

- **Residential** facilities provide support and/or custodial care to those who are unable to live independently and may have a mental or physical condition.

- **Nursing homes** provide services for those who do not require hospitalization but are unable to remain in their homes to receive care.

- **Assisted living** provides housing for seniors who require minimal assistance with their activities of daily living such as bathing, dressing, and eating.

- **Adult/pediatric day health services** provide social engagement for participants as well as caregiver respite services.

- **Subacute care facilities** and **skilled nursing** provide complex care to patients who are medically stable but no longer require acute hospital care, providing them with additional time to improve their ability to function independently and safely prior to being discharged to home. Examples of the type of care provided in this setting include wound care, intravenous therapy, and rehabilitation services.

- **Long-term acute care (LTAC)** provides care to patients following an inpatient acute-care stay with an average length of stay ranging from twenty-five to thirty days.

- **Hospice care** provides end-of-life care to those who have been given a prognosis of six months or less.

It is critical to conduct effective assessments and provide ongoing evaluation so that patients are always provided with the level of care that they need. Thorough discharge and transitional planning at each stage must also be done to ensure a patient is adequately prepared for a less intense level of care.

Managed Care Concepts

About Managed Care Organizations (MCOs)

The role of **managed care organizations** (MCOs) is to manage the financing and delivery of medically necessary health services. MCOs connect patients to providers that can give them the treatment they need.

Their responsibilities include:

- Facilitation of healthcare delivery to health-plan members
- Appropriate reimbursement for services delivered
- Ensuring members have access to appropriate services

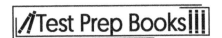

MCOs promote cost control and are designed to make healthcare more affordable and accessible. The result is lower out-of-pocket expenses and lower premiums. Payers determine which providers their members may access by establishing a network.

Members are encouraged to see primary-care physicians for their routine care and to only seek specialists under the referral of their primary-care physician. Urgent care centers are the preferred place of treatment for urgent care needs, as opposed to visits to the emergency room.

Managed care organizations utilize case-management services to ensure that members of the MCO are receiving the right services, in the right location, at the right time. MCOs take it a step further to ensure that those services are medically necessary by using industry-recognized national criteria like InterQual and Milliman. These criteria sets enable organizations to determine if a member's illness or condition warrants the level of service being received. Again, the ultimate goal is to not only ensure the member is receiving the appropriate level of care but to also keep costs down.

MCO Case Managers

MCO case managers play a vital role in their organization. They oversee the care that members receive and closely monitor the dollars spent. Case managers collaborate with others within the organization to arrange for authorization of services and validate whether or not the treatment plans in place are adequate.

MCOs may carry out services in a variety of ways. Many MCOs provide case management that is targeted in nature, focusing on those populations that pose the greatest risk due to complexity or risk for catastrophic outcomes. Case managers within the MCO have the unique responsibility of balancing the needs of the payer, physician, and patient to achieve the best possible results. Case managers operate as generalists, but some MCOs elect to use specialist case managers when possible.

NCQA, the **National Commission for Quality Assurance**, influences MCO strategies and the methods by which these organizations facilitate case-management services. NCQA challenges MCOs to implement programs such as disease-management programs that demonstrate a real improvement in health status, using industry-recognized guidelines and best practices.

The evaluation of an MCO program can be done using a variety of tools, including internal audits, documentation of best practices that demonstrate positive trends within the populations that are being managed, and those activities that lead to a reduction in inpatient bed days, admissions, and ER visits.

Health Maintenance Organization (HMO)

Health maintenance organizations (HMOs) provide access to healthcare services in a select region to individuals enrolled in a health plan. HMOs collect payments for each of their members and provide access to standard inpatient and ambulatory care services.

Some HMOs have open-access models in which members are allowed to access any provider in the network without needing to seek care from their PCP, either using a self-referral or the standard PCP referral. Other HMOs have open panels in which physicians obtain and maintain contracts through Independent Practice Associations. In the staff model, HMOs hire physicians themselves, and providers are only allowed to care for members within the health plan. Finally, some HMOs follow a group model, sometimes referred to as a closed model. In this case, the HMO has a contract with a group of doctors. These doctors can then divide profits.

Independent Practice Association (IPA)

IPAs or **Independent Practice Associations** consist of a group of physicians who are organized to support HMOs and provide services to those enrolled. IPAs are favorable for doctors because they provide a degree of independence. Despite having an exclusive contract in place with the HMO, IPAs can see patients who are not enrolled with the HMO, therefore giving them access to patients from a variety of sources and settings, and from multiple contract agreements. Under the IPA model, HMOs can establish a relationship with all the physicians in the group even if there is a single contract in place. IPAs receive reimbursement through a capitated payment or fee-for-services model.

Preferred Provider Organization (PPO)

Preferred provider organizations or PPOs are more flexible than the HMO model. PPOs permit out-of-network provider visits and patients can obtain a degree of coverage for these visits. The PPO referral process is also a bit easier because it does not require referral to see a specialist nor is there a requirement to choose a primary-care physician.

Point of Service Plans (POS)

A **point of service** plan is a fusion of the best characteristics of the HMO and PPO plans in managed care. While participants have an in-network provider who functions as their primary-care provider (PCP), they can access care outside of their network with a referral from the PCP, at a cost.

POS plans may be upwards of fifty percent cheaper than PPOs. However, they are not able to provide the same robust network of healthcare providers as commonly seen with a PPO or HMO. Deductibles can be expensive with this model, and the administrative burden is incredibly frustrating to those who dare to venture out of network. This leads to longer wait times for reimbursement, increased delays associated with some referrals, and a higher rate of co-pays.

Management of Clients with Acute and Chronic Illness(es)

It is not uncommon for individuals to have more than one chronic illness. These are sometimes referred to as **comorbid conditions** because they exist at the same time and may or may not have a direct relationship with one another. For example, someone who is a "brittle diabetic," currently struggling to manage their health condition may also have other diagnoses that are occurring at the same time, including depression or cardiovascular disease. Case managers who are providing services to clients with multiple chronic illnesses must be consistent in their application of the case-management process. Chronic conditions tend to go through cycles of stability and exacerbation, in some instances with irreversible disease progression.

Case managers who provide services to the chronically ill and disabled require an increased level of awareness, education, and support because these conditions significantly impact the client's overall and long-term well-being, especially among those who are suffering from multiple chronic illnesses. Chronic illnesses may stabilize but may not necessarily be resolved. For example, someone who has a diagnosis of diabetes may very well stabilize and control blood sugar, but their condition always has the potential to become unstable if not managed appropriately. In the case of multiple chronic conditions, all the challenges and complications of long-term illness are exacerbated. The patient will have even more difficulty managing the social, emotional, vocational, and physical domains of life.

Case managers must be aware, educated, and able to provide meaningful support in these ways:

- Identify the complications associated with different chronic conditions.
- Demonstrate an awareness of proper diagnostic testing and procedures.
- Demonstrate an understanding of current treatment options for all diagnoses.
- Verbalize an awareness of expected outcomes.
- Encourage client self-management, empowerment, and self-directed care.

Case managers may be required to play a role in helping clients understand their conditions and the potential impact those conditions have on the client's physical, behavioral, and social well-being. Case managers will also need to be prepared to assist in empowering patients to work towards self-management. A client with multiple conditions will have even more providers involved in their care, so it is imperative that the client is able to engage in self-advocacy and treatment coordination. **Self-management** is when the client takes an active role in care-coordination activities, which can ultimately reduce the risk of disorganized healthcare experiences and unnecessary healthcare costs.

Self-management can only be effective, however, if healthcare providers understand what self-management entails and demonstrate consistent support of the patient's efforts to take control of their physical and behavioral health. Case managers can influence the success of self-management activities by bridging gaps between the patient, providers, and managed care organizations facilitating the patient's benefits package.

Finally, it is important to recognize the unique struggle for those with multiple chronic illnesses. The risk of mental illness is greater, as they battle feelings of isolation, loneliness, fatigue, and hopelessness. Having multiple conditions means more doctors' visits to attend, more medications to manage, and more treatment options to consider. All of these things can be overwhelming to someone who is already struggling with the daily symptoms of illness. The job of case managers is to make sure the client has adequate social and emotional support, including support groups, therapists, and family support.

Management of Clients with Disability(ies)

The main difference between acute and chronic illnesses is duration; acute illnesses are short term and chronic illnesses are long term. **Acute illness** or disability has specific symptoms or areas of focus and can often be treated and recovered from within a limited period of time, if survived. Chronic illnesses, on the other hand, may have less definable and more varied symptoms. It is not easily treated or cured. Those with chronic illnesses or disabilities will need more comprehensive and longer-term care, often throughout the course of their lives. Typically, a chronic illness has a more gradual onset, whereas acute illness is a more sudden onset; however, a chronic illness may come as the result of an acute illness.

In managing patients with an acute illness or disability, the focus is on the cure and on treating the specific symptoms. Along with supporting the patient throughout the process of treatment, the case manager should focus on what happens after treatment or hospitalization. This includes any follow-up physical therapy or rehabilitation that needs to be arranged, as well as living arrangements, short-term living adjustments, etc. Generally, once the disease has been treated, and the patient has successfully readjusted to normal life, little follow-up will be needed, and the case manager's job may be done.

For those dealing with chronic illness or disability, the case manager will have a different role. In this situation, more emphasis needs to be placed on finding long-term providers and resources for the patient, including nursing care, if necessary. Chronic illness does not just entail short-term adjustments

but requires a lifestyle change that accommodates the limitations of the illness. Chronic illness impacts every area of a person's life, including their living environment, ability to work, sense of identity, social support system, and level of everyday functioning. The case manager's job is to encourage patient empowerment and self-directed care so that the patient will be able to maintain the best level of health and well-being that is possible. The adjustment to living with a chronic illness can also impact a person's mental health and lead to depression or anxiety.

Case managers should focus on holistic care for the patient, making sure their physical, social, and emotional needs are all being met. It is also critical to ensure that the family and caregivers are receiving adequate support, so that they are better able to take care of the patient. In order to make sure the patient has a comprehensive network of resources and support, the case manager must emphasize coordination and effective communication between the patient, family, and all service providers.

Advancements in healthcare have improved the ability to manage and treat acute illnesses and conditions in a timely and cost-effective way that is least devastating to the patient. This has enabled the system to focus more on how to best deliver case management to the chronically ill and disabled.

Medication Safety Assessment, Reconciliation, and Management

Proper medication-therapy management (MTM) and medication reconciliation helps to reduce the risk of medication errors inside and outside of the hospital, facility, or home settings. Patients with chronic conditions, or even those who develop acute conditions, are regularly prescribed new medications. Whether these new medications are based on the need to increase the dosage to alleviate symptoms or to provide relief for new ones, there is a risk of duplicating medications or inadvertently prescribing incorrect dosages.

Medication-therapy management has to do with the patient obtaining and properly taking the medications that are needed. There are various reasons why this does not occur, such as inadequate treatment, lack of finances, or neglecting to take medications that have been prescribed. The case manager's job is to identify any barriers that may exist in the patient's medication-therapy management and help the client to overcome them. **Medication Therapy Management Programs** (MTMP) were established with the US Medicare Modernization Act of 2003 for the primary purpose of promoting medication adherence among Medicare Part D beneficiaries through the use of education and counseling. MTMPs are designed to support those taking medications for chronic conditions. In addition, patients have access to self-management education and two-way communication with the MTM service provider.

Medication reconciliation is the process of documenting the patient's medication regimen, including the name of the medication, dosage, frequency, and route, and then comparing it with the prescribed medication regimen received during the transition of care (i.e., discharge, admission, or transfer). Medication reconciliation provides the opportunity to identify discrepancies and inconsistencies between what the caregiver and/or patient understands to be their treatment regimen and what the healthcare provider has documented as the treatment regimen. Medication reconciliation can identify gaps in the understanding of prescription changes and actual medication-therapy management.

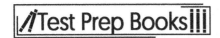

Military and Veteran Benefit Programs

TRICARE

TRICARE is a healthcare management program that operates under the Department of Defense (DoD) and provides coverage to millions of beneficiaries, including active-duty service members of the following:

- Army
- Navy
- Air Force
- Marine Corp
- US Coast Guard
- National Guard/Reserve Members
- National Oceanic and Atmospheric Administration
- Public Health Service
- Survivors
- Former spouses
- Medal of Honor recipients and their families

This program was previously known as CHAMPUS and only provided for eligible persons in limited categories. TRICARE offers a variety of health plans based on the region in which the beneficiary resides and their eligibility, and it exceeds the requirements of the Affordable Care Act.

TRICARE Prime

TRICARE Prime is available to active-duty uniformed service members and their families, activated National Guard and Reserve members, families that become eligible under the Transitional Assistance Management Program, survivors, Medal of Honor recipients and their families, and qualified former spouses. Retired service members and their families may also qualify for TRICARE Prime, unless they are eligible for TRICARE for Life.

Under TRICARE Prime, recipients are assigned a primary-care manager (PCM) who is a network or military provider that provides most of the beneficiaries' care. They are responsible for coordinating referrals, accepting copayments, and filing claims on the recipient's behalf.

While active-duty service members do not pay anything out-of-pocket, and active-duty family members only pay if they use a point-of-service option, all other beneficiaries are required to pay annual enrollment fees and network copayments.

ECHO

The **Extended Care Health Option** (ECHO) provides active-duty family members who have a qualifying mental or physical disability with financial assistance. Services provided under this program may include but are not limited to:

- Special education
- Sixteen hours per month of ECHO Respite Care with other authorized ECHO benefits
- Up to forty hours per week of ECHO Respite Care if the family member is homebound
- Durable medical equipment

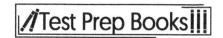

- Assistive services including interpreter or translation services
- Transportation

Children continue to qualify for ECHO benefits beyond the age of twenty-one or twenty-three as long as a parent remains on active duty or is unable to provide support due to their mental or physical disability.

TRICARE Standard and Extra

Beneficiaries who are enrolled in the Defense Enrollment Eligibility Reporting System (DEERS) are automatically enrolled in **TRICARE Standard**, if eligible. Activated National Guard and Reserve members and their families who become eligible under the Transitional Assistance Management Program, survivors, Medal of Honor recipients and their families, and qualified former spouses are eligible to participate in this program.

TRICARE Reserve Select

TRICARE Reserve Select is a premium-based plan. It is accessible all over the world for Selected Reserve members and their families. Beneficiaries of this program can visit any TRICARE-authorized provider. They do not require a referral to receive care, but some services may require authorization for services from a regional contractor. Members of the Individual Ready Reserve (IRR) do not qualify for TRICARE Reserve Select.

This plan does require beneficiaries to pay monthly premiums, annual deductibles, or a percentage for those services with coverage.

TRICARE Retired Reserve

TRICARE Retired Reserve is another premium-based plan that is available all over the world for those retired Reserve members who, along with their families or survivors, qualify. Much like TRICARE Reserve Select, this health plan does not require qualifying beneficiaries to obtain a referral for care. However, they may still be required to obtain authorization for services from their regional contractor.

TRICARE for Life

The Department of Defense (DoD) changed the TRICARE program in 2001, granting coverage to those military beneficiaries who were also eligible for Medicare and those who had purchased Medicare Part B. This program became known as the **TRICARE for Life** (TFL) program, functioning as a secondary payer to Medicare.

TRICARE-eligible beneficiaries who receive Medicare Part A and Part B are eligible to receive TFL as a Medicare-wraparound coverage. TRICARE is secondary payer after Medicare in the United States and US territories, but TRICARE for Life is the first payer in overseas areas.

TFL participants can visit any provider they choose. However, out-of-pocket expenses may be higher for those who seek care from VA providers or those providers who do not accept Medicare. VA providers are not permitted to bill Medicare.

TRICARE Young Adult

Young, unmarried adults between the ages of twenty-one and twenty-six years of age can continue to participate in TRICARE based on their sponsor's service status. The program is known as the **TRICARE Young Adult** program.

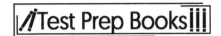
US Family Health Plan

Another option for beneficiaries is the **US Family Health Plan**. Recipients of this program receive care at a designated community-based, not-for-profit health system. The plan also provides prescription-drug coverage. Physicians treating these beneficiaries must be affiliated with at least one of the US Family Health Plan healthcare systems to provide care. Beneficiaries under this plan would not be able to receive care at military hospitals or clinics within the TRICARE network of providers.

VA

The **Veterans' Administration** (VA) provides eligible veterans access to services that closely relate to their military history, disability rating, and classification at the time of discharge. The VA is perhaps the largest healthcare system in the nation.

CHAMPVA

The CHAMPVA Center in Denver, Colorado administers the **CHAMPVA** program. CHAMPVA is not the same entity as CHAMPUS. The Department of Defense manages CHAMPUS, now known as TRICARE. Dependents (children and spouses) who meet one or more of the following eligibility requirements may qualify for CHAMPVA:

- Veteran has a permanent and total disability that is a service-related disability.
- Veteran died from a VA-related service-connected disability.
- Veteran met the definition of total disability from a service-related disability at the time of death.
- The military member died in the line of duty, and their death was not the result of misconduct.
- Note: These individuals will typically qualify for TRICARE and not CHAMPVA.

Due to their veteran status, CHAMPVA sponsors may be entitled to medical treatment through the VA system.

For those who receive Medicare, CHAMPVA is a secondary payer. Those eligible for Medicare must enroll in both Medicare Part A and Medicare Part B to maintain their CHAMPVA benefits.

Models of Care Delivery

There is a wide array of models used to provide care for patients across the continuum of care.

Patient-Centered Medical Home (PCMH)

The **Patient-Centered Medical Home** (PCMH) model provides patients access to comprehensive care. Patients receive access to a well-rounded team of providers ranging from physicians to advanced-practice nurses to physician assistants to nurses, pharmacists, nutritionists, social workers, and care coordinators. The patient is treated as an individual and families are members of the care team, supporting the development and implementation of plans of care.

The PCMH can become a major ally of not only the patient but the case manager as well. The PCMH can assist a patient and their family with navigating a complex healthcare-delivery system. They typically provide services that are accessible and offer a variety of communication methods with or on behalf of the patient. This helps patients establish a healthy relationship with their provider and ultimately feel supported during and after business hours.

A physician's practice must pass a set of nine standards and ten must-pass elements to become a designated PCMH. Once a practice achieves recognition, it is viewed as being an organization that follows a core set of principles.

Accountable Care Organization

An **accountable care organization** (ACO) is a network of physicians, hospitals, and other healthcare professionals that purposefully work together to provide adequate care to meet the needs of beneficiaries at a reasonable rate. These organizations are yet another way to assist in managing inefficient payment systems. ACOs can be hospital-led, physician-led, or joint-led.

Currently there are more than 550 Medicare ACOs that serve more than 12 million beneficiaries. There are almost 1000 ACOs currently active and almost half of those are physician-led.

ACOs that are unable to keep costs down or meet performance expectations place themselves at risk for paying penalties or being saddled with additional spending.

Case managers may have a role within ACOs to help keep costs down, but poor performance on the part of the case manager can lead to excessive costs, including the investment made to have them on staff.

The Medicare Shared Savings Program

The Affordable Care Act created the **Medicare Shared Savings Program**. It requires ACOs to hold providers mutually accountable for the health of their patients. They receive financial incentives to cooperate and save money by avoiding services such as diagnostic tests and medical procedures that are not medically necessary.

Pioneer Program

The **Pioneer Program** is another program created by the Centers for Medicare and Medicaid Services (CMS) in which high-performing health systems can keep expected savings as a direct result of accepting greater financial risk.

ACOs may resemble HMOs slightly with respect to the expected outcomes for patients. There are, however, a few differences. For example, ACO patients are not required to remain in-network, and ACOs have an obligation to meet a set of quality measures to ensure they are not blocking medically necessary care.

Health Home

Health Home was created as a result of the Affordable Care Act of 2010. It is a program that assists in coordinating care for those who suffer from chronic conditions. It is important to note that the Health Home program, a Medicaid program, should not be confused with the Patient-Centered Medical Home (PCMH) model. The PCMH model is sometimes referred to as the "medical home," reflecting that the coordination of care requires a collaborative process between the physician and the individual in need.

Conversely, providers who participate in the Health Home program provide a service that correlates to an integrated clinical approach. Health Homes are responsible for not only coordinating both primary and acute care, but they also must address behavioral health, including substance use disorders and long-term service needs, thus managing and treating the patient holistically. Patients are included in the planning process as required.

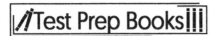

The Health Home program delivers care coordination, health promotion, and a comprehensive transition program that includes a care-management package of services. Not only does Home Health identify those services that are available throughout the healthcare-delivery system, but they also seek and make referrals to the community and other social support services.

Health Home providers may be licensed to operate in a variety of settings, including but not limited to a rural health clinic, a community mental-health center, or a home health agency. Also, they may be specialized in a variety of fields; they may be an OB/GYN, or the health home provider may be a group or clinical practice.

Health Homes may consist of a team of varied professionals, including nurses, pharmacists, social workers, or behavioral-health professionals, to name a few. Regardless of background, according to the Centers for Medicaid and Medicare Services, the Home Health team itself should be well-rounded and include medical specialists, nurses, pharmacists, nutritionists, dieticians, social workers, behavioral-health providers, chiropractic professionals, and licensed complementary and alternative practitioners.

Special Needs Plan (SNP)

Special needs plans (SNPs) serve those individuals who suffer from chronic conditions and are recipients of Medicare Part A and Part B. To qualify for an SNP, candidates must reside in the assigned service area.

SNP programs are tailored to meet the needs of those with certain conditions and improve the coordination-of-care process, providing access to hospital care, and medical and prescription-drug benefits, merging them into a single plan.

CMS identifies three groups of SNP recipients:

- **Dual Eligible** (D-SNP). D-SNP recipients have both Medicare and Medicaid.
- **Institutional** (I-SNP). Recipients of I-SNP reside in a nursing home or require nursing care in their home.
- **Chronic Condition** (C-SNP). C-SNP recipients suffer from a severe or disabling condition.

Medicare SNPs have limits on who can participate in their program. A plan may elect only to provide services to those who suffer from diabetes and, thus, build a network of providers who demonstrate a capability of caring for this population in an efficient manner. Also, drug formularies are established in a manner such that they support treatment of those with diabetes.

Under the SNP model, care coordinators may be assigned to support patients along their journey to wellness and to encourage adherence to agreed-upon treatment plan. Support may include education, monitoring of adherence to taking medication, patient empowerment, or providing access to community resources.

Chronic-Care Model (CCM)

More than 130 million people who currently live with a chronic illness live with comorbid conditions. The **chronic-care model** (CCM) is used to support the care given to those suffering from chronic disease. It is a widely accepted and adopted model that is used to improve ambulatory care, and it is a vital player in the Patient-Centered Medical Home model.

CCM consists of four core-strategy concepts: clinical information systems, decision support, delivery-system design, and organizational support. There are two patient-centered concepts in the CCM that form the foundation of this model: self-management support and community resources.

Self-Management Support

Self-management entails empowering the patient to solve problems, make decisions about their healthcare, identify potential resources, take actionable steps, and maintain the patient-provider relationship.

Community Resources

It is important that patients gain access to **community resources**. These resources may consist of peer groups that provide support or community partners, such as service organizations, that can provide educational, financial, and medical/behavioral-health resources.

The CCM has been shown to improve outcomes, particularly among individuals who participate in disease-management-based programs. Organizations who participate in CCM-based programs may find there are up-front costs for implementing a CCM program. However, the outcomes and improvement, as they relate to the number of both days hospitalized and ER visits, is visible as a direct result of this model.

Population Health

Population health is an approach to healthcare that focuses on improving the health of an entire population of patients, as opposed to the traditional model which focuses on individual care. Population health spends much of its resources on high-risk patients and preventive and wellness strategies. The goal is to keep high-risk patients healthy and out of hospitals for as long as possible. Disease management is combined with adherence to treatment plans and managed by a population health case manager who helps steer patients through the healthcare continuum. Case managers can proactively check in with patients to understand the reasons why medications are not being taken or appointments are missed. With the rise in Accountable Care Organizations that receive reimbursement based on keeping patient populations healthy, there is a subsequent rise in the need for population health case managers who are willing to advocate for patients and help them transition efficiently through the healthcare system.

Case managers should work to build a referral network for the potential needs of the population of patients that are serviced. Case managers should endeavor to assure that agencies that will be referred to are appropriate and have a contact person. Post referral, case managers should evaluate the referral to see if patients were satisfied and treatment plans were met using that agency.

Negotiation Techniques

Case managers play a critical role within each of the programs identified in that they not only help to coordinate care and treatments to ensure that the patient remains stable, but they also serve as the liaison between the patient and the community or providers. For a patient to be successful with these programs, the case manager has to have a clear understanding of what the objective is for each of these programs and then advocate on behalf of the client.

Depending on the provider and managed-care contracts, negotiation may be necessary when it comes to costs or treatment. The case manager may be responsible for negotiating on behalf of the client in

order to get the best treatment possible, as well as to lower costs. Negotiation can also be useful in working with patients, families, and/or providers in developing an appropriate treatment plan.

Negotiation is the process of discussion and cooperation in order to get the best possible solution for all parties. This will likely involve compromise on both sides, but the case manager should compromise as little as possible when it comes to the health of the patient. Therefore, it is important that the case manager knows exactly what they are pursuing in the negotiation. This means thorough preparation and a clear knowledge of the client's needs for treatment and reasonable costs to bring to the negotiation table. Being prepared ahead of time will help the case manager know what to settle for as the bottom line.

When it comes to negotiation, the case manager will be more successful pursuing cooperative or collaborative negotiation rather than competitive or aggressive negotiation. Cooperative negotiation starts with building a relationship of trust with all those involved in the discussion. This emerges through clear, honest, and responsive communication. Communication is not just speaking, but also involves active listening and appropriate body language.

While case managers should be firm in getting what the client needs, they should always conduct the negotiation with respect and a desire to collaborate. Creating an emotionally hostile environment is never helpful, so the case manager should remain calm and de-escalate volatile situations when possible. It is also important to start with areas of common ground and agreement, before moving on to the areas of disagreement. The goal is not to create a situation where one person wins, and one loses. Rather, everyone should come away from the negotiation having gained something.

Physical Functioning and Behavioral-Health Assessment

Physical functioning refers to basic activities of daily life (ADLs), such as eating and bathing. ADLs also include activities that help a person maintain independence, like driving, shopping, or cooking. **Behavioral-health assessments** evaluate a person's level of functioning regarding their mental/emotional health, substance abuse, or behavioral needs. These assessments usually use a variety of measures and interview strategies, with both close-ended and open-ended questions that are intended to gather information about the client. While physical functioning and behavioral health may seem unrelated at first glance, they are closely connected to one another.

When it comes to a person's level of physical functioning, there are many factors involved beyond a physical condition or illness. Social and emotional support, mental-health issues such as depression, and a person's cognitive functioning can all contribute to physical functioning. Research has found a correlation between physical functioning and mental health. Many different forms of mental illness can include physical symptoms, such as changes in appetite, sleep disorders, fatigue, and even pain. Though these physical symptoms all contribute to impaired physical functioning, the root cause may be behavioral or mental, rather than physical. When evaluating a client with low physical functioning, it is important to also assess their behavioral health. Something like depression may point to a nonphysical cause, such as a lack of motivation or lack of enjoyment in daily activities, which may be hindering the ADLs.

Both physical and mental limitations can have a significant impact on one's quality of life and can lead to an increased risk of falls, bone fractures, depression, and increased healthcare costs. Assessments can help to reveal inadequacies among support systems and allow case managers the opportunity to

collaborate with other members of the healthcare-delivery team to address these limitations, whether by way of implementing services, coordinating care, or adjusting treatment plans.

Private Benefit Programs

Consumers have the option to pursue a variety of **private-based benefit programs**.

Pharmacy Benefits Management

Pharmacy-benefits management (PBM) consists of third-party administrators (TPAs) whose primary responsibilities are associated with prescription-drug programs. PBMs work strategically with self-insured companies and government programs to maintain formularies and establish pharmacy contracts. PBM also has a role in negotiating discounts and rebates with pharmaceutical companies. These TPAs earn their revenue as a direct result of service fees that result from large contracts for processing prescription-drug claims. PBM influences more than eighty percent of drug coverage, therefore giving them a significant voice in the healthcare decision-making process.

Indemnity

Indemnity insurance, known as a fee-for-service plan, allows consumers to direct their own healthcare. Customers are able to visit physicians, including specialists, of their choice and are permitted to seek care at the hospital of their choice. A portion of the "total charges" are covered by the insurance company.

Most consumers of this program are required to pay their deductible first, and after this is met the insurance company will pay the claims at a percentage of UCR, also known as the usual, customary, and reasonable rate. Indemnity plans work well for those looking to have the freedom to choose which doctors provide their care and the ability to see the specialist of their choice.

Employer-Sponsored Health Coverage

Many companies offer their employees private health insurance as a component of their benefits package. Sixty percent of Americans obtain health insurance from their employer. Employer-sponsored health-coverage plans are able to provide employees with a variety of options, including vision and dental coverage. In addition, employer-sponsored health-coverage plans are able to provide their employees with short-term and long-term disability, as well as a modest life-insurance policy. These programs may be HMO based, PPO based, or both; thus, employees have the option to choose an HMO or PPO.

Individual-Purchased Insurance

Individuals may purchase insurance for themselves or to cover members of their families instead of relying on coverage offered by an employer. Previously, **individual plans** offered coverage that was less than what is typically seen with group insurance plans. However, as a result of the Affordable Care Act, these plans now include benefits that are more robust.

Home Care Benefits

Insurance may elect to cover **home care services** so that individuals can remain in their home environment as opposed to being placed in a nursing home. Home care agencies can offer a variety of services in the home, especially help with activities of daily living such as bathing, dressing, grooming, and meal preparation.

43

Many home care services are covered by insurance companies specializing in long-term care; however, recipients must understand if there are any limits for the number of services that can be received in a single day or over a number of years.

COBRA

Passed in 1986, the **Consolidated Omnibus Reconciliation Act** (COBRA) established a mandate that employers provide their employees with the opportunity to maintain their insurance coverage through the employer in instances in which coverage would typically be terminated. Examples of such loss of insurance would include terminations, layoffs, deaths, Medicare coverage, or other changes in employment status.

Duration of Coverage
The qualifying event defines the length of COBRA coverage.

- Coverage is allowed for up to eighteen months if there is a job termination or reduction in work hours.

- Coverage is granted for up to twenty-nine months for those individuals who are disabled at any time during the initial sixty days of COBRA coverage.

- Coverage is allowed for up to thirty-six months in instances of death, divorce, legal separation, acquisition of Medicare, a change in a child's dependent status, or other **qualifying events**.

COBRA continuation can be expensive and, therefore, recipients may eventually look for more affordable options. While most group health plans are required to abide by COBRA provisions, employers are exempt from COBRA if they employed fewer than twenty employees during the previous calendar year.

Employers must send a notice to their employee once a **triggering event** takes place. Those who fail to do their due diligence in communicating with the employee put their organization at risk for litigation and create liability for plans.

COBRA Beneficiary Qualifications
An employee's beneficiary may also qualify for COBRA benefits. The **beneficiary** is a covered employee, spouse, dependent, or child of the said covered employee.

COBRA Election Period
Qualified beneficiaries may elect to maintain healthcare coverage from the employer's group health plan through COBRA within sixty days after the date on which plan coverage terminates. If the beneficiary fails to elect COBRA coverage, they lose all rights to benefits. There is some flexibility in the selection of COBRA coverage for beneficiaries. Beneficiaries have the ability to choose COBRA coverage independently, and parents can elect COBRA coverage on the behalf of a minor/child.

Coverage
COBRA coverage is equal to the previous insurance plan that the beneficiary received. **COBRA coverage** may include:

- Prescriptions
- Physician visits

44

- Dental/vision services
- Inpatient and outpatient services

COBRA Payments
Employees or those beneficiaries who qualify for COBRA are required to pay a percentage of administrative costs and the premium.

Public Benefit Programs

Supplemental Security Income (SSI)
Supplemental Security Income (SSI) provides payment of benefits to those individuals and their family members who are living with a limited income and resources (e.g., home, car, land) at their disposal.

Eligible recipients for SSI fall into one or more of the following categories:

- Aged (sixty-five years of age or older)
- Blind
- Disabled

In addition to falling under these categories and being a US citizen who resides in one of the fifty states, potential recipients must demonstrate that they are of limited income or resources. Next, they must have lived in the United States for a minimum of thirty consecutive days.

Children are also eligible for SSI. To qualify, children under the age of eighteen must exhibit a condition (medical or behavioral) that may:

- Result in death
- Be defined as chronic
- Cause severe functional limitations

Social Security Disability Insurance (SSDI)
Supplemental Security Disability Insurance (SSDI) provides payment of benefits for individuals and their family members if they have worked for enough years and paid Social Security taxes. People who become disabled before the age of retirement can apply for SSDI.

During an individual's lifetime of working, they earn four work credits for each year worked. To meet eligibility requirements for SSDI, applicants must have a diagnosis that meets the Social Security Administration's definition of a disability. The disabled condition must fall into the category of:

- **Severe**: A condition that prevents one from performing work-related functions
- **Long term**: A condition that will last greater than twelve months
- **Total disability**: A condition that prevents one from being able to perform SGA, also known as **substantial gainful activity**

Applicants for SSDI will not be approved to receive SSDI until they are disabled for five months. Once approved, there is an opportunity for receipt of retro payment of disability beginning in the sixth month.

Those who have not worked long enough to receive SSDI can apply for SSI.

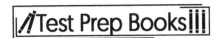

Medicare

Medicare was established in 1965 to provide healthcare coverage to adults over the age of sixty-five. Since then, the scope of Medicare has changed and now extends to those with disabilities who are younger than age sixty-five who also meet the Social Security Administration's criteria.

Medicare operates in four parts: Part A, Part B, Part C, and Part D.

Medicare Part A

Hospital Insurance

Medicare Part B

Supplementary Medical Insurance

Medicare Part C

Medicare Advantage Plan

Medicare Part D

Drug Insurance

Medicare Part A

Medicare Part A, sometimes referred to as Hospital Insurance, covers the hospital portion of healthcare, paying for acute care and skilled-nursing facility (SNF) care.

Medicare Part B

Medicare Part B, also known as Supplementary Medical Insurance, is an optional and additional coverage that pays for physician services, outpatient services, and ancillary charges such as durable medical equipment, preventive services, and some medications. Those who are covered by Part B have premiums deducted from their Social Security income check.

Medicare Part C

Established as a result of the Balanced Budget Act (BBA) of 1997, **Medicare Part C** was created to serve as the Medicare managed care option. Formerly known as **Medicare + Choice Plans** and now known as **Medicare Advantage Plans**, Medicare Part C allows recipients of Medicare to maintain their benefits; however, the managed care organization is chosen and paid by the federal government to administer the Medicare benefits. The MCO may opt to provide coverage for additional services.

Special needs plans deliver managed care services to individuals with special needs such as the chronically ill with conditions such as diabetes, congestive heart failure, or end-stage renal disease. Thus, they specialize in providing managed care that can support complex populations in a cost-effective manner using industry-recognized best practices.

Prescription Drug Plans

Prescription Drug Plans have standards that are dictated by Medicare, although managed by providing companies. While PDPs can provide more than the minimum required package, they can require a higher premium payment for increased coverage. PDPs earn revenue through their facilitation of delivery of prescription medications based on a cost that is less than income.

Medicare Part D provides coverage for those drugs that qualify under the Medicaid program, but this does not include those medications that are available under Part B.

Dual-eligible and low-income Medicare recipients can enroll in PDPs specifically designed for this population where Medicare pays the premium. They do not have to pay a deductible under this program. For those who qualify as indigent, Medicare provides a low-income subsidy that pays costs associated with cost-sharing and premiums.

Medicaid

Title XIX of the Social Security Act of 1965 established the system known as **Medicaid**. Families and individuals who require medical assistance but have limited resources to pay for those services may qualify for Medicaid. Medicaid is co-funded by both the state and federal governments to support the delivery of proper medical care to eligible individuals. State legislatures have the option to re-evaluate and update Medicaid eligibility and services offered during the year. The state government may also adjust reimbursement rates to accommodate trends in healthcare.

States must comply with Medicaid coverage expectations for certain groups to receive federal funds. While states may choose to deliver state-only programs, these are not funded by the federal government. The following mandatory Medicaid categorically needy groups are eligible for government funds:

- Pregnant women with a family income below 133 percent of the federal poverty level (FPL)
- SSI recipients (in most states)
- Those receiving adoption or foster care under Title IV of the Security Act
- Those who qualify for the AFDC or Aid to Families with Dependent Children program
- Children below the age of six whose household income is below 133 percent of the FPL

State programs must offer adequate medical support and services to their categorically needy populations, and those services include:

- Physician services
- Prenatal care
- Outpatient services
- Inpatient services
- Nursing facility services
- Laboratory services
- X-ray services
- Vaccines for children
- Rural health clinics
- Home health
- Skilled-nursing services

States may also elect to extend Medicaid coverage to other populations. These populations may have characteristics that are similar to the mandatory Medicaid recipient groups, but states have greater flexibility to define eligibility criteria for these other populations.

With the implementation of the Affordable Care Act of 2010, states can now choose to extend Medicaid coverage to all low-income Americans under the age of sixty-five. Currently, all but 12 states have extended their program to include this group.

While the federal government provides an overarching set of guidelines, states are responsible for administering their Medicaid programs and defining eligibility standards. The states establish payment rates and are responsible for determining the scope and type of services they wish to make available to recipients, as well as the amount and duration of those services.

Some states can also apply to participate in CMS waiver programs to provide Medicaid services that fall outside of the traditional set of services provided under state Medicaid plans.

Medically Needy

States can establish **Medically Needy** programs to provide access to care for people who earn too much income to qualify for Medicaid. These individuals may become eligible for Medicaid by having expenses that exceed their income and the state's medically needy income level, also known as a **spend down** amount. Once the individual meets this criteria, they can have costs for services covered by the Medicaid program.

Employer-based Health and Wellness Programs

Employer-based health and wellness programs have been around for some time with the goal of creating a culture of wellness. The effects of that culture of wellness usually include less absenteeism and lowering the cost of employer-provided health coverage. Many employees enjoy the rewards of the programs, which can include gift cards, contributions toward insurance, and discounts at fitness clubs, amongst other promotions. Programs can either be participatory, where participants earn rewards for participating in activities such as completing a health assessment, or health-contingent, where rewards are impacted by health factors such as being tobacco-free or enrolling in a health coaching program. The Affordable Care Act, the Americans with Disabilities Act, and the Genetic Information Nondiscrimination Act have regulations aimed at protecting patients with health conditions from having their benefits limited due to those conditions. These regulations should prevent employers from requiring employees to take medical exams or mandating them to provide their health information and may also state that employers cannot require participation in these programs or deny employees coverage access based on participation.

Reimbursement and Payment Methodologies

Case managers may be required to facilitate payments for their organization, as well as monitor for accuracy in billing by a servicing provider. There are several different types of reimbursement and payment methodologies that may be used.

Bundled

In the case of **bundled** payments, healthcare providers and facilities (separately or jointly) may receive a single payment to provide treatment for a condition. Providers assume greater financial risk with this particular payment model. Providers cannot predict what complications may or may not arise as a result of one's diagnosis, but if the actual cost of services proves to be less than the bundled amount there is an opportunity to retain the difference.

In today's landscape of healthcare, the bundled-payment model is used retrospectively. Providers receive payment from the payer once care is complete. Bundled payments may reduce costs while improving care coordination and quality for patients.

Case Rate

Case rates, sometimes referred to as global rates, are pre-negotiated rates put into place for a particular procedure. Case rates ideally include all of the anticipated services that would be required to deliver the treatment.

Prospective Payment System (PPS)

Medicare uses the **Prospective Payment System** (PPS) method of reimbursement. For the purpose of approximating the cost of the services provided, the PPS pays out to healthcare providers a preset amount based on the patient's DRG. The reimbursement is specific to each patient and the amount paid out will cover a predetermined time frame; it may cover a short time spent in the hospital, or even a long-term hospital stay (over 25 days), depending on what procedures are needed. Healthcare providers are then able to develop the most cost-effective plans to utilize the reimbursement given, helping promote shorter, more efficient diagnostics and treatments.

CMS uses a separate PPS for reimbursement for different healthcare services ranging from inpatient hospitals to psychiatric facilities to long-term care facilities. Inpatient hospitals use a PPS based on DRG. This reimbursement is determined by classifying patients into groups that need similar treatments for which costs are within a close range. The average number of resources needed for each patient in this group will be used to determine the set amount of the reimbursement. While long-term care facilities have their own system of DRG classification based on each discharge, psychiatric facilities use a DRG-structured PPS but with adjustments based on the facility's location.

Value-Based Purchasing (VBP)

The **Value-Based Purchasing** (VBP) program is an initiative utilized by CMS to persuade acute-care hospitals to provide quality-based care to Medicare beneficiaries through the use of incentive-based payments. This process involves close monitoring of how well hospitals follow best clinical practices. Hospitals also receive an evaluation for how well they can improve the patients' hospital stay experience.

CMS monitors hospital performance by using a set of measures and dimensions, which are grouped into specific quality-driven domains.

Measuring Hospital Total Performance

CMS evaluates the hospital's **total-performance** score, which compares achievement and improvement scores for each of the hospital's Value-Based Purchasing measures. The Achievement Points awarded to a hospital are directly tied to the comparison of an individual hospital's rates during a performance period with that of all hospitals' rates from a specified baseline period.

Improvement Points are granted based on a comparison of an individual hospital's ratings to its ratings during the baseline period.

Consistency Points are granted through a comparison of the hospital's HCAHPS base score and the hospital's HCAHPS consistency score.

Financial Risk Models

Under traditional payment models, providers were paid for services performed. After the ACA came into play, more alternative payment models were introduced. Under these alternative payment models, providers become financially responsible for the care given. In upside risk (sometimes called one-sided risk), providers receive a share of the savings when they save money by providing more efficient care

but are not penalized if they do not meet the benchmark. With downside risk (also known as two-sided risk), providers can receive a share of savings but can also lose revenue if the healthcare they provide doesn't financially meet the benchmark. Most ACOs who use alternative payment models prefer to only use the upside risk model. To hold more ACOs financially accountable, CMS has made Tracks for ACOs participating. Many of the tracks now require a three-year contract which includes a downside risk period after only an upside risk initially. The shift to allow more providers to use downside risk models is necessary for ACOs to be successful in saving money in overall care. More work must be done in building out post-acute care and preventive care to make alternative models and their financial risk models more appealing to providers.

Roles and Functions of Case Managers in Various Care/Practice Settings

Case management may take place in any setting throughout the care continuum. Case managers may work in a wide variety of settings, including hospitals, disease-management organizations, MCOs, ACOs, prisons, hospice organizations, independent case-management services, and corporations, to name a few.

Acute-Care Settings

Case managers who use the case-management process in an acute-care setting are required to support the hospital in providing care that is adequate and cost-effective.

Therefore, the goal of a case manager in an **acute-care setting** might include:

- Monitoring for a change in the level of care such that it is a lesser but appropriate level of care
- Monitoring for a reduction in the length of stay based on industry or organization guidelines for care
- Ensuring the delivery of those services that are medically necessary

Managed Care Settings

Managed care case managers, who are sometimes referred to as internal and/or external case managers working for a payer-based system, look to support the MCO's mission and goals, which may include but are not limited to a reduction of:

- The number of inpatient admissions
- The duration or length of hospital stays
- Delays in discharge to home with adequate home care services

Government Settings

Case managers may operate in **government settings,** including government-operated healthcare facilities and Health and Human Services. Due to their background and experiences, case managers may also support activities such as research and administrative tasks. Case managers may also work in settings in which they assist with grant writing, program development and implementation.

Home Health Care

Case managers who work in the **Home Health Care setting** are responsible for ensuring the safety of the environment for the patient. A comprehensive assessment is performed by a case manager to evaluate the patient's functional needs and the patient's ability to transfer from a hospital setting to a home environment. Comprehensive assessments can also assist in determining whether or not the patient or

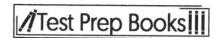

caregiver can provide adequate care. Much of the home care facilitated by case managers encompasses education and health progression.

Case managers who work for home healthcare agencies are provider-based case managers. **Provider-based** case managers work within organizations and facilities such as IPAs, rehabilitation centers, hospitals, and behavioral-healthcare locations.

For long-term illnesses, case managers may be required to assist families with enlisting attendant care or respite-care services where applicable and available.

Community-based case managers are those case managers who work with nonprofit agencies as well as local state departments. Their core population consists of those communities that are low income or Medicaid and Medicare recipients.

Roles and Functions of Other Healthcare Providers in Various Care/Practice Settings

Providers from **various settings** may be used throughout the continuum of care and to support case-management activities. Interdisciplinary teams are made up of many different types of providers, ensuring that the patient is getting the care needed in every area of life and functioning. It is important for the case manager to understand the role and function of each provider in order to most effectively coordinate the care the patient receives.

Many of these providers will be medical practitioners, such as doctors, nurse practitioners, nurses, nurse midwives, speech or physical therapists, and various specialists. General medical practitioners, such as doctors and nurse practitioners, will oversee the patient's medical care. A patient is likely to have a primary-care physician, who has the job of managing the patient's general health and referring them to other specialists. Depending on the patient's condition, they may also have other specialists involved, like oncologists, dieticians, chiropractors, surgeons, or cardiologists. Even professionals such as dentists or pharmacists may play a crucial role in the process of treatment. Some of the primary responsibilities fulfilled by these medical practitioners are diagnosis of the disease, prescription of medicines, surgeries and other treatments, and monitoring of the patient's overall health status.

Psychologists, psychiatrists, social workers, and therapists may also be involved in care to address the mental-health needs of the patient. Psychologists can conduct psychological evaluations or behavioral-health assessments to provide a more complete understanding of the patient's overall well-being. Therapists can provide counseling that a patient may need in order to deal with issues of anxiety, depression, or other mental illness that may occur as a result of experiencing acute or chronic illness. Psychiatrists typically prescribe mental-health medications for the patient. When a case manager is coordinating treatment for a patient, both the mental health and physical health must be fully understood and treated, as they can have a great impact on each other.

Along with medical practitioners and mental-health providers, the patient may have others involved in treatment, whether through community resources or informal providers, such as family or caregivers. This might include support groups that may be led by peers, home health aides, or organizations providing disease-specific financial aid or education. While these providers may not have a direct role in guiding medical care, they are certainly significant when it comes to the client's social, financial, and emotional well-being, which can all impact health.

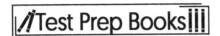
While every patient is different and will require a unique combination of providers, one of the tasks of the case manager is to evaluate whether a patient is receiving the necessary treatment, through the most appropriate providers. It is also important to remember that at the center of the decision-making team is the patient, and they should never be overlooked when treatment options and plans are being discussed among the professionals.

Transitions of Care/Transitional Care

The **transition of care** involves the movement of patients within and between various settings and providers. This change in the level of care is driven by a change in the patient's condition and medical or behavioral-health needs.

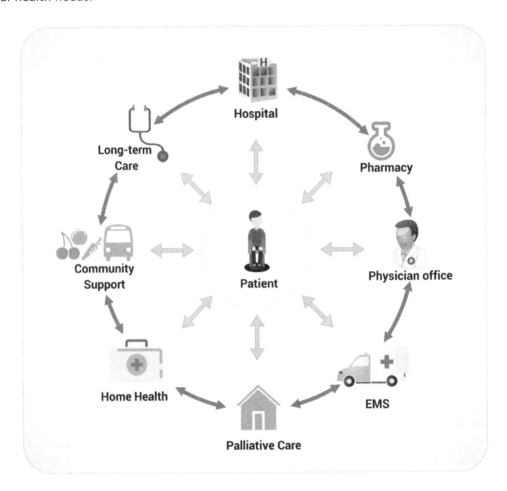

Successful transitions require effective care coordination and logistical planning to reduce the risk of health complications that could lead to readmissions, adverse events, an increase in healthcare costs, or a greater length of stay.

Open communication between highly trained practitioners and healthcare professionals and the patient/caregiver must take place to reduce the risk of an adverse health outcome for the patient. Good communication requires a comprehensive plan of care and collaboration between healthcare providers, who should all be made aware of the patient's goals, preferences, and clinical status. A successful transition plan includes scheduling and keeping follow-up appointments, home visits, and effective medication management, which includes ongoing medication reconciliation.

The purpose of the **National Transitions of Care Coalition** (NTOCC) is to address the problems associated with transitions of care.

The NTOCC recommends the following:

- Payment systems that align incentives
- Implementation of performance measures to encourage or/improve transitions of care
- Increased utilization of case-management services
- Utilization of pharmacists during the transition of care process as it relates to medication reconciliation

Utilization Management Principles and Guidelines

Utilization-management (UM) functions act as a predecessor to case management in many organizations. In fact, it often operates as a separate entity, determining the medical necessity for hospital admissions and procedures. It also determines the appropriateness of the assigned level of care.

UM clinicians act as stewards of insurance companies and other payers' dollars, using organization-specific criteria such as critical pathways and clinical guidelines, and industry-recognized criteria like McKesson InterQual or Milliman, to review the medical necessity of hospital care. UM clinicians can identify that the level of care is inappropriate based on the patient's clinical presentation. However, UM clinicians and medical directors must also use their clinical expertise and judgment to allow for medically necessary treatment even when, clinically, a patient's presentation does not fully align to the criteria sets.

UM clinicians work closely with case managers to not only gain a full picture of the patient but also to allow for continuity of care during the discharge-planning process.

Unlike case management, utilization management is more episodic in nature, and centers on the hospitalization and length of stay of a patient for an illness. Case management spans the continuum of care, following the patient throughout the various healthcare settings and back into their home environment.

Organizations who facilitate the utilization review process may apply for accreditation via the **Utilization Review Accreditation Commission** (URAC). URAC establishes standards and guidelines by which UM entities can evaluate themselves. These measures include the use of evidence-based guidelines, the level of review requirements for reviewers, and policies that address financial incentives given to providers.

Collaborative/Comprehensive/Integrated/Holistic Case Management Services

As healthcare continues to change, the role of the case manager continues to change. The shift to integrated and holistic case management is at the forefront of that change. The integrated case management process begins with the case manager developing a genuine relationship with a patient and considering together with the patient their goals, concerns, and needs. Integrated and holistic case management processes are especially important for patients who are medically complex. Using this process involves using appropriate assessment tools from the start and once a relationship is

53

established. A commonly used tool for assessment is the ICM-CAG (Integrated Case Management Complexity Assessment Grid).

This assessment tool assists the case manager to use a color-coded system to determine the levels of risks that the patient is facing, so that together the patient and case manager can address the immediate risks. This type of collaborative and integrated approach is especially important for patients that face behavioral and mental health struggles in addition to medical issues. Chronic conditions, such as heart disease or hypertension, become more difficult to manage when combined with mental illness, which can lead to poor outcomes. Case managers who use an integrated process help coordinate many types of services for an individual patient and tend to see better outcomes.

Caseload Considerations

In order to ensure that each case receives suitable and efficient attention, it is essential that all cases are assigned according to acuity. **Caseload calculations** allow for what equates to an appropriate volume of clients for case managers, while demonstrating the case managers' ability to provide quality case management services. The periodic tabulation of the caseload of any specific case manager is integral to combat inconsistencies within and among organizations. According to the **Caseload Concept Paper** published by the Case Management Society of America (CMSA) and the National Association of Social Workers (NASW) in 2008, the average caseload for case managers was in a range of 2 to 365. This study led to the creation of the **Case Load Capacity Calculator** by the CMSA and NASW in collaboration with Consulting Management Innovators. The free calculator enables teams to calculate comparative caseload capacities within case management departments for the domain the case manager is supporting; disseminates industry-based rules and weights (e.g., time allocation for various activities, complexity of the case, environmental factors/settings); and allows for caseload customization by creating a baseline for how cases are distributed.

The **Caseload Matrix** is a diagram, also known as a schematic chart, that is divided into four categories. Provided by the CMSA and the NASW Concept Paper, the matrix interprets those facets known to have an impact on the size and complexity of a caseload. Each of the four categories has elements that define the complex nature of a caseload and caseload size. Based on these four variables, case assignment is more efficient and equitable. Below are the caseload matrix categories. They provide an overview of how each category is defined and which elements align with each of these categories.

Any change in a factor of this chart has a direct impact on other categories and any associated elements. Case managers who follow their patients throughout the continuum of healthcare must monitor their

caseloads closely for changes that affect acuity. Utilizing the matrix will alert the case manager to changes in acuity and adjust case assignment in an effort to be proactive instead of being reactive.

Initial Elements Affecting Caseload:

- Business environment
- Technology
- Case management program complexity
- Market segment
- Regulatory and legal requirements

Comprehensive Needs Assessment Affecting Caseload:

- Presence and severity of clinical factors
- Psychosocial factors
- Primary caregiver status
- Support systems
- Environment

Case Management Interventions:

- Plans of care
- Interdisciplinary activities
- Establishing and executing goals

Outcomes:

- Intermediate and long-term outcomes
- Adherence
- Cost savings
- Enhanced health status

Alternative Care Sites

Non-Traditional Sites of Care

As the role of case management continues to evolve, non-traditional sites of care continue to emerge. Case managers find themselves working more in long-term care: provider's offices, insurance companies, surgery centers, mobile medical units, and shelters. Being able to work from these non-traditional sites of care means that instead of a case manager's job ending when a patient leaves the hospital, it is just beginning. With most non-traditional sites, the goal becomes keeping patients at their maximum level of health and decreasing hospitalizations. As the emphasis on population health increases, due in part to the goals of Healthy People 2020, case managers are likely to find their roles in these non-traditional sites of care more valuable than ever.

Telehealth

Technology is improving access to healthcare for many patients. Today, telehealth (also referred to as telemedicine) refers to patient care that happens without being in-person. Telehealth is especially useful for non-emergent, chronic illnesses. Telehealth is emerging as a way to optimize revenue for providers and increase patient satisfaction. Many patients prefer not to drive to a location and wait to access healthcare. Telehealth growth happened much quicker than expected in many types of healthcare, including case management, due to COVID-19. Telehealth is considered useful at expanding access to healthcare while keeping patients safe. At times, a patient will seek telehealth and be told that they need to seek in-person care because they cannot be safely treated via telehealth.

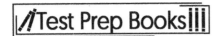

Virtual Care

Virtual care is a broader term than telehealth and describes the many different types of healthcare services that can be done virtually, including telehealth. Virtual care may refer to anything from electronic vital sign monitoring to responding via messenger to a patient's question. Virtual care includes reviewing the EHR, using wearable technology, and even using healthcare apps. Revenue can be optimized using virtual care, especially in alternative payment models, where keeping patients healthy and out of hospitals leads to more sharing in financial savings by ACOs. Case managers may find themselves using virtual care to engage with patients at high risk for not adhering to treatment plans. Discovering reasons for their non-adherence may help case managers direct patients to other forms of virtual care that keep patients at optimal levels of health. As more ACOs with alternative payment models enter the system, case managers' roles will likely change. With much of the case manager's job just beginning when the patient is discharged from the hospital and as they use all these virtual care resources to keep the patient adhering to their plan of care, they will keep the patient out of the hospital and thereby maximize financial sharing.

Psychosocial Concepts and Support Systems

Abuse and Neglect

Abuse takes many forms and is considered the inflicting of harm on another person so as to cause distress or pain. It is typically carried out by a person who is older, more powerful, or in a position of authority over the person toward whom the abuse is directed. Abuse commonly happens within families and may be perpetrated by a partner, parent, sibling, or someone else in a relationship of trust with the victim. Populations most at risk of abuse are children, the elderly, and those with physical or mental disabilities.

Physical abuse is the easiest to define and refers to bodily harm and includes everything from hitting to unnecessary confinements. **Emotional** or **psychological abuse** is harder to define and more subtly carried out, but the effects are just as damaging as physical abuse. It involves the manipulation of an individual through guilt and shame, or by alternatively withholding and extending kindness. This type of abuse may include **verbal abuse**, which relies on insults, criticisms, shouting, humiliation, and threats. **Sexual abuse** is forced sexual contact or exposure and can include the forced observation of sex acts. Finally, an elderly or disabled person is particularly vulnerable to **financial abuse**, through the misuse, theft, or unwarranted control of their money.

It is important to recognize some of the common symptoms of abuse, as many victims will either be too afraid to report the situation or may feel a conflicted sense of loyalty to the perpetrator. A common indicator of physical abuse is unexplained (or poorly explained) bruises or abrasions and a need for frequent medical treatment/trips to the hospital. A victim of abuse may become more withdrawn, sad, angry, distracted, anxious, or aggressive. Additionally, victims of abuse may present with psychological behavioral manifestations such as bedwetting/enuresis, tearfulness, vomiting, impulsivity, acting out, bullying, and self-injurious behaviors (i.e., cutting). Signs of financial abuse may present as a sudden or gradual change in a person's financial situation and independence, evidenced by difficulty paying bills, an increased need to borrow money, and over-extending on loans or credit cards.

Perpetrators of abuse are more likely to be those with a history of alcohol or substance abuse, or mental health issues. Another risk factor of abuse would be caregivers who become easily frustrated with the many needs of those in their care. Observation of caregivers is helpful for noting any concerning interactions with those dependent on them, i.e., if a person begins to display anxious or fearful behaviors in the presence of their caregiver.

While abuse is an active form of harm, **neglect** is a failure to provide care or protection. Neglect can be withholding food, money, education, protection, medical care, transportation, or any other necessities of life. The symptoms of neglect will often show themselves in a person's disheveled appearance, weight loss due to lack of food, untreated illnesses, or missed doctor visits. Neglect on the part of a caregiver may be deliberate, or it may unintentionally occur in a situation where the caregiver is overwhelmed or stressed.

It is imperative that abusive situations observed by mandated reporters be communicated to the necessary authorities, whether child protective services or adult protective services. In addition, addressing the needs of the caregiver can prevent ongoing abuse and neglect. This includes education related to the needs of their dependents, anger and stress management, and effective methods of self-care. Counseling to address depression or anxiety may also be helpful.

57

Behavioral Change Theories and Stages

There are many different theories related to behavioral change and the stages that an individual goes through in order to achieve lasting change. The Transtheoretical Model has been successful in helping people lose weight, quit smoking, and improve their nutrition and exercise habits. While the theories of Lewin and Kotter are primarily used to achieve change in an organizational setting, they can also be applied to the individual seeking behavioral change.

Stages of Change Model (Transtheoretical Model)

The **Transtheoretical Model** is unique in that it focuses on the thinking process a person goes through even before the active process of change begins. The first stage of this model is **precontemplation**. At this stage, a person is not prepared to make any change; in fact, they have not started thinking about it and may be oblivious to any need for change. In the next stage, **contemplation**, a person is still not ready to make change, but they are beginning to think about it, and intend to make changes in the foreseeable future. During the **preparation** stage, they are prepared to make changes in the immediate future and begin to actively get ready to make changes, by creating plans and setting goals.

The stage of **action** is when a person makes clear and decisive changes in their life. But these changes must be sustained during the **maintenance** stage, when they become enduring habits and continue for a significant period of time. Finally, once the person has overcome both unwanted behaviors and the temptation to return to them, the stage of **termination** has been reached. **Self-efficacy**, a person's view of their own ability to accomplish something, is an important concept in the termination stage as people should now have full confidence in their ability to continue with the new behaviors.

Lewin's Change Management Model

Lewin's model of change has three distinct stages, which are called unfreeze, change, refreeze. Just as an ice cube can be melted, remolded and refrozen, this model theorizes that the same process works with people seeking change. The first stage, **unfreeze**, involves looking at a situation and recognizing the need for change. It is helping people challenge their current attitudes, habits, or behaviors, and making a persuasive case for why change is needed. During the next stage of **change**, new methods are sought, examined, and accepted. Finally, during the **refreeze** stage, these new habits and behaviors are solidified.

Kotter's 8 Step Change Model

In **Kotter's theory**, the first step is to **create urgency**: to make use of a crisis situation in order to emphasize how urgently change is needed. The next step is to **form a coalition**, that is a team of professionals and family members who will work together to support the person making a change. After that, it is important to **create a vision and strategy for change**, with goals and objectives, and then **communicate the vision** to all those who are involved in the process. The next step is to identify and **remove obstacles** that might stand in the way of a person achieving the goals they set. The sixth stage in Kotter's model is to **create short-term wins** by recognizing and encouraging the small behavioral changes that are achieved. Once these small steps have been acknowledged, it is easy to **build on the change**, turning the small changes into bigger, long-lasting changes. The eighth and final step is to **anchor the change**, making the changes a permanent part of life.

The most effective means of facilitating change may be to use a combination of these theories and stages of change, depending on the needs of the individual.

Behavioral Health Concepts and Symptoms

Behavioral health includes a variety of behaviors that contribute to the health of the body, mind, and emotions. A behavioral health disorder usually refers to mental illness and substance use, but other behavior-related health issues can also be included, such as smoking or obesity. Behavioral health disorders can hinder the successful treatment of medical illnesses if they are not recognized and treated. Therefore, integrated treatment of both medical and mental health conditions is the best model of care.

Substance abuse, or substance use disorder, is the persistent overuse or misuse of a substance, such as drugs or alcohol, in spite of the negative effects that it has in the person's life. Substance abuse often classifies as an **addiction**, in which the person is psychologically and physically dependent on the substance and is unable to decrease or stop taking it. Addiction includes a **tolerance** to the substance, which means that the individual has to have an ever-increasing amount in order to get the same effects, and the presence of **withdrawal** symptoms if the person stops taking the substance. Withdrawal symptoms can be physical, such as headaches and shaking, and emotional, such as anxiety and irritability. Under certain circumstances the withdrawal symptoms can be dangerous, so detox should happen within the context of proper medical supervision. Substance abuse and addiction are incredibly destructive and inevitably lead to health complications, family difficulties, and legal issues.

There are many observable signs of substance abuse, such as red eyes or dilated pupils, agitated movements, slurred speech, confusion, inability to focus, changes in sleep or appetite, or increased anxiety or aggression. A person who struggles with an addiction is usually trying to hide this condition from those close to them; this may result in lying or secretive behaviors that can indicate to family members or others that something is wrong. If several of these symptoms are observed in a client, it is important to explore the possibility of substance use through careful and nonjudgmental questions.

The case manager can then connect the client to appropriate treatment services and provide support throughout the process of recovery. The first step may be detox and inpatient treatment, followed by outpatient care. Individual psychotherapy can also be helpful and cognitive behavioral therapy has proved the most effective form of therapy. Joining Alcoholics Anonymous or Narcotics Anonymous can also assist a person in remaining clean and sober. It is important to make sure that a client also involves family members and friends in the process of overcoming an addiction, as they can help to ensure that the environment the person lives in is conducive to recovery.

Often when a person struggles with substance abuse or addiction, they may also have a mental illness, such as depression, bipolar disorder, or anxiety. Either the mental illness or the substance use disorder may have existed first and can contribute to the development of the other; some mental health issues are substance induced. This condition of co-occurring disorders is referred to as a **dual diagnosis** and can make treatment particularly difficult, as each disorder has its own treatment needs. While treatment for both conditions can happen simultaneously, it will be difficult to adequately address the mental health issue until a person has stopped taking drugs or drinking, so this would be the most immediate treatment need.

Client Activation and Readiness to Change

Client activation, similar to the more commonly used term "patient activation," refers to how involved clients are in their own treatment and how capable they are of participating in meeting their own health and mental health needs. Client/patient activation encompasses the skills, knowledge, and motivation

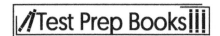

people have to manage their own health or mental health. Clients with higher levels of activation are likely to have better treatment outcomes, so both evaluation and improvement of activation levels are important. Activation can include a client's initiating or maintaining healthy habits, pursuing available resources, or engaging in education to gain applicable knowledge. Client activation has little to do with the specific diagnosis or needs but has more to do with the client's perspective and involvement, no matter what the problem may be. Some clients with low activation may be completely unaware of their need to participate in their own treatment, while others may have the desire but lack the skills or knowledge.

Those with high levels of activation are better able to advocate for themselves with doctors, therapists, case managers, and other service providers. They also have more success in establishing and maintaining healthy, positive habits at home that will contribute to an improvement in their overall well-being. Highly activated clients will be better at following treatment advice and better at maintaining good health and mental health even when not in treatment. High activation levels are correlated with better treatment outcomes and lower overall treatment costs. Those with low activation levels, on the other hand, lack either the skills or the confidence to be involved in their own health treatment and will play a minimal role.

Because client activation levels are changeable—not fixed—service providers should do all they can to increase a client's activation level. A client can go from being completely uninvolved to taking an active role in treatment and care. There are several methods for increasing client activation. One important strategy is to assist the client in developing new knowledge and skills. This could include training in decision-making and problem solving. Even teaching a client how to ask questions related to their own needs and treatment is significant, as well as providing education around their specific needs.

In addition to providing specific skills and knowledge, clients need help growing in confidence. Encouraging them to take initiative in their services and collaborating with them, instead of making decisions for them, are important means of achieving this. Another helpful strategy is to tailor support to the client's activation level. For example, clients with lower activation levels may need to take smaller steps and work on smaller challenges. Those who already have high activation levels may be able to handle bigger challenges. Those with lower levels of activation are more in need of resources to help them in increasing their levels of activation, but they are less likely to make use of such resources. Rather than providing services that low-activated clients will not participate in, it makes more sense to meet them on their level.

Client Empowerment

Client empowerment is built on the premise that a client's strengths should play an important role in the treatment. While social work and case management have historically focused on needs or problems, the strengths-based perspective focuses on the client's positive characteristics, such as their skills, knowledge, values, and other internal resources. **Empowerment** means allowing and helping the client to take control of their own treatment, and effectively utilizing strengths and skills instead of being overwhelmed by problems or deficits. Rather than focusing on what is broken or what is not working in a client's life, empowerment focuses on what is good, hopeful, and strong. Thus, instead of feeling powerless and unable to change anything in their life, a client feels motivated and inspired to make the necessary changes.

With the goal of empowering clients, case managers and social workers should not focus on client weaknesses or dictate to a client how to act. Rather, the goal is to support clients in setting and

60

achieving their own goals, through collaboration with the case manager. Clients should be encouraged to take charge of their lives, their mental and physical health, and their future. It is the client who takes the directive role, not the case manager. The client's **self-determination**, or the freedom to choose what is best for him or her, should be recognized and encouraged. The client's beliefs and value system should be validated and honored in the decisions that are made. It is not the job of the case manager to decide what is best for the client, but rather to allow them to choose the best option for themselves.

Instead of viewing the client as a barrier to change and goal setting, the client should be viewed as the most important resource and a collaborator in the process. Empowerment communicates that it is the client who has the power to change. Often a person will fulfill the expectations someone else has set for them. For example, when it is communicated to a client that they are powerless and helpless, they will often act accordingly. On the other hand, if it is communicated that they have the strength within themselves to change, they are more likely to be empowered to make those changes. Empowerment leads to independence and helps clients gain skills they can use even when they may not have a case manager alongside them.

Client Engagement

Client engagement, the initial stage of treatment, refers to the client choosing to participate in services and actively becoming involved in treatment. There are many things that contribute to effective client engagement, but it primarily depends on a successfully established therapeutic relationship with the clinician, social worker, or case manager.

At the outset, clients may be unsure about treatment, anxious about the change process, and hesitant about establishing a relationship of trust with the case manager. The first step in client engagement is to **establish rapport**, helping the client feel comfortable and relaxed in the new relationship. Without establishing rapport, the next stages of treatment will be much more difficult. Building rapport is done through **active listening**, in which the case manager reflects what the client is saying back to them so that they feel heard. It also means using appropriate body language and nonverbal communication, such as eye contact and leaning toward the person. Other important aspects of building rapport are **empathy** and genuine care. Empathy means identifying with the feelings of the client, even if the case manager has not experienced their exact situation. A client must feel accepted and validated, no matter what information they disclose; this is what Carl Rogers called **unconditional positive regard**. All of these things will contribute to establishing rapport, the first step in building a trusting relationship between client and case manager.

Maintaining confidentiality within this relationship is also crucial to establishing trust. **Confidentiality** is the assurance that whatever the client says will not be disclosed without their permission. At the same time, it is important that the limits of confidentiality are explained to the client, and the case manager's ethical obligations of disclosure are clarified. Another ethical issue relates to self-disclosure. While limited forms of self-disclosure on the part of the case manager may be helpful, it must be done with great caution and wisdom. Inappropriate self-disclosure by a case manager or clinician can be harmful to the relationship, as it takes attention away from the client and creates confusion about the boundaries of the professional relationship.

The next steps in client engagement are to begin the assessment and evaluation, identify appropriate services, and set goals. Asking good questions is imperative during this stage, but all questions should be asked in a nonjudgmental way, ensuring that clients feel comfortable revealing personal information about themselves. When the needs of the client are fully understood and appropriate services

identified, they will feel confidence in the skill and knowledge of the case manager. This will contribute to successful client engagement in services. Setting goals for treatment should be a joint effort between the client and case manager, and the client's empowerment and self-determination should be the guiding forces during the process.

There may be some significant barriers to engagement, especially if the client is involuntarily involved in services or has had a history of negative experience with other providers. Under such circumstances, it may take more time and effort to establish a supportive, positive, helping relationship with the client. In these cases, it is even more important to be diligent and patient in building rapport and trust.

Client Self-Care Management

Client self-care management is the practical outworking of the principles of client activation and client empowerment. For clients who have long-term physical or mental illnesses, it is important for them to be very involved in managing their own care. This includes both decision-making related to treatment and engaging in health-promoting behaviors on a day-to-day basis. For physical and mental illness, proper exercise and nutrition can significantly contribute to the management of symptoms and must be maintained daily by clients. Other management challenges can include taking medications consistently, scheduling and attending doctor appointments, and handling changing emotions.

The role of the case manager is to support the client in self-care management. Similar to client activation, promoting client self-care management involves education, confidence building, and skill development. This must include a focus on **self-directed care**, which is informed and controlled by the wishes, priorities, and values of the client. In other words, if there is a need for lifestyle change, the client should be the one to decide what the change will be and how it can best be carried out. It is more likely that these changes will endure if a client has been the one to decide on the appropriate strategies. Another significant aspect of self-care management is **self-advocacy**, in which clients learn to ask questions and advocate for their own perceived needs. Self-advocacy is important when working with many different service providers, such as doctors, case managers, therapists, and other clinicians. Self-advocacy can also involve identifying and accessing community resources.

Informed decision-making is also a critical element of client self-care management. Instead of dismissing the client as uninformed, the best method for the case manager is to help the client grow in understanding their own needs so that they can make decisions in an informed way. Clients should have all treatment options explained fully, as well as the ramifications of each. When it comes time for decisions related to health care, case managers should engage in **shared decision-making** in collaboration with the client. Finally, to ensure informed and effective self-care management, clients will need **health education**, particularly as it relates to their own physical, emotional, and psychological health.

The more that clients are able to manage their symptoms and health needs at home, the less emergency and professional care they will need. Although professional help can be sought when symptoms are exacerbated or crisis situations arise, daily self-managed care will minimize these more extreme problems and help the client to enjoy better overall health and stability.

Community Resources

There is a wide range of **community resources** available, making it confusing for some clients to navigate the system and identify what would be most helpful for them. Therefore, a case manager plays

a critical role in helping the client to find and utilize the community resources that would be most beneficial. When seeking resources, it is useful to look at the different domains of life—physical, psychological, emotional, spiritual, and educational—and then compile a collection of resources that may be useful for the client in each of these domains.

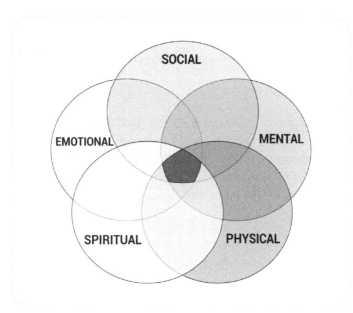

Physical needs can include food, shelter, clothing, or medical care, and there are many government programs available for these needs, such as free health care, affordable housing, and food stamps. For the elderly or disabled, their greatest need may be related to the accessibility of physical resources. In that case, the delivery of meals through Meals on Wheels or transportation services may be the most appropriate recommendation. Another help would be prescription assistance programs offered by some pharmaceutical companies, which provide medications for free or at reduced cost for low-income patients. Other resources for the elderly can be accessed through the Administration on Aging and other local departments for elder care.

Ensuring the provision of adequate **emotional** and **psychological services** would first involve making sure the client is receiving emotional support from family and friends or getting involved in support groups with others who have similar struggles. For the elderly, there may be community centers with programs to help seniors connect with each other and stay active. When it comes to finding the right psychological resources, both therapeutic and psychiatric, there are many options, so the client must be involved in the process of deciding what type and format of therapy would be best.

An often-overlooked area of whole-person care is the **spiritual needs** of the client. In addition to providing spiritual support, religious organizations are often nonprofits that can assist the client in physical or emotional ways as well. Fraternal organizations may provide similar benefits to a person, offering emotional, social, and spiritual components.

Educational resources should not be disregarded, especially in the case of someone who has **mental health** needs. Whether formal training or informal learning through the library or online, there are many resources for gaining knowledge in almost any area. As discussed, education related to the individual's specific health needs is a crucial element of self-management care, client activation, and empowerment.

Calling United Way's helpline at 211, checking the U.S. government website, or conducting an internet search are easy and effective means of identifying the relevant community resources in the client's locality. Collaborating with other service providers can also make use of those who already know the client and can also prevent overlap in the provision of services. Finally, and perhaps most important, help the client to find resources through the people and organizations with whom they are already connected, as this will help their **social needs**. Not only does this encourage self-determination and empowerment by helping the client see how many resources they already have in their life, but many clients will be most comfortable with places and people they already know.

Conflict Resolution Strategies

Conflict occurs whenever there is a disagreement between two or more people or groups of people. **Conflict resolution** is the effort to find a peaceful way of solving the conflict, one that will be acceptable to all parties. In the case management context, conflict can occur when there is a disagreement around provision of services or the direction of treatment. This conflict could be between service providers and the client or between the client and family members.

There are a few things for the case manager to keep in mind when engaged in a conflict or attempting to resolve conflict among others. First, treat everyone involved with respect and empathy. Second, listen well. Actively listen to people on both sides of the conflict; in other words, collect all the facts before making a judgment. Next, focus on the problem and refrain from attacking other people and relying on emotions. Finally, make sure to keep the needs of the client as the highest priority. Once the case manager has put these principles into practice, it will lay a better foundation for exploring all possible options.

Five common types or styles of conflict resolution have been identified on the **Thomas-Kilmann Instrument (TKI)**, some being more effective than others:

1. The first is called **collaboration** and it consists of all parties working together to find a solution that satisfies everyone. This should be the end goal in resolving all important issues that cannot be compromised, especially related to the health and safety of the client. Even though this is the best-case scenario, conflict is not always resolved this easily, nor is there always enough time to devote to this process.

2. **Compromise**, or negotiation, involves everyone compromising—or giving something up—in order to also win something. Everyone wins and everyone loses. Nobody gets exactly what they want, but at least everyone gets something that they wanted. This may be the best outcome that can be expected in high conflict situations, and it may be acceptable in conflicts of little significance.

3. The third type is **accommodation**. In this case, only one of the parties achieves what they want, while the other person gives up or gives in. While this is beneficial for the person who gets what they want and can sometimes be worthwhile for the purpose of maintaining relational harmony, it will likely cause ongoing tension and conflict in the future.

4. **Competition** is a negative way to deal with conflict. This is when people take a firm stand against each other and whoever proves stronger or more powerful gets their way. In this strategy, there is little compromise or cooperation. It is important to try to find a solution by working with other people, rather than actively working against them.

5. **Avoidance** is another unhelpful way to deal with conflict, unless the issue is small or insignificant. Without bringing the issue into the open and discussing it, the problem may possibly resolve itself. More likely, the conflict will remain under the surface and will continue to grow until it becomes more difficult to deal with.

Crisis Intervention Strategies

A **crisis** can occur whenever a client is in physical danger or has an extreme emotional need that goes unmet. For example, suicidal threats or ideation qualify as a crisis situation. When a crisis arises, the very first concern is always safety. It is important to get the client into a safe situation, protected from themselves or others. After safety is established, it is then possible to assess the level of need and what should happen next in order to best assist the client.

Another important strategy is **de-escalation**. When there is a crisis, extreme emotions are usually involved. If possible, a client should be guided through relaxation techniques to help calm them down. Oftentimes, a calm and neutral party who can facilitate a conversation or listen to the client empathetically, but without feeding the emotion, will automatically de-escalate the situation. Confrontation or matching the client's emotions will escalate the situation. Allowing the client to communicate the situation fully may help them to become less emotional and more focused on the facts. At this point, the client may be able to focus on the next steps and specific tasks that need to be done. If possible, help the client to regain emotional control so that extreme options, such as restraints, are unnecessary.

In cases where a client is suicidal, it is important to establish if there is a suicide plan or means of committing suicide in place. These two things will determine the severity of suicidal ideation and how at-risk the client is. If it is determined that a client is at imminent risk of suicide, they should be admitted to the hospital or a mental health facility for their own protection.

Creating **crisis plans** ahead of time, in collaboration with clients, may assist them in preventing crisis situations or more quickly regaining control when the crisis arises. If clients have been part of the planning process, they may feel empowered, even when their emotions are overwhelming them. Part of the plan should be to identify the potential triggers or warning signs and have immediate steps that can be taken to avoid a crisis. This could be engaging in relaxation strategies or calling a supportive friend, family member, or clinician.

Client Support System Dynamics

When providing services for a client, it is important to maintain a family systems perspective. In meeting the needs of someone with a significant illness, the dynamics of the family, both positive and negative, must be taken into consideration. For example, consider the role that the client has, or has had, in the family, as well as how that role may change with the progression of the illness. Every family has a system, with its own rules, expectations, and accepted ways of doing things. Family members include partners or spouses, siblings, children, or other extended family members.

Families can have a very positive effect on a client and can be the means of their best support. Adaptive and healthy families will share responsibility for financial, emotional, and physical support on a daily basis, and a family member may even play the role of caregiver. During crisis situations the healthy family will adapt and adjust, being able to meet the needs of the patient while continuing to function in a healthy way. Family members can be a huge asset to treatment, and whenever possible and

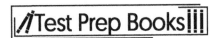

appropriate, they can collaborate with the treatment plans. On the other hand, families can sometimes also prove to be a hindrance to treatment or have a detrimental effect on the client. In these cases, it is important to respect the needs and wishes of the client as relates to family involvement.

There are a few questions to ask when assessing the dynamics of a family. How do the family members communicate with each other? How does the family view and treat the patient receiving treatment? Are they domineering, enabling, or empowering? What expectations do family members have of each other? How do family members manage emotions during a crisis? How does the family deal with conflict? Are family members making decisions on behalf of the client because of physical or mental limitations? If so, are they honoring the wishes of the client? As information is gained related to these questions, it will be easier to understand what aspects of the family may contribute to, or stand in the way of, successful treatment. It is critically important to make sure that the family is contributing in positive ways to treatment. If there is mistreatment or abuse on the part of family members, this must be dealt with and reported, when necessary. Even if the family is positively collaborating with the client in accessing services, it is important for the case manager to protect the confidentiality and self-determination of the client.

As with the individual, it is important to focus on the strengths of the family and promote empowerment within the family. If needed, a case manager can provide communication skills training, conflict resolution, or a referral for family counseling. In addition, it is important to educate the family about the illness and symptoms of the patient, especially if one or more family members are serving as caregivers. This will give them better skills in supporting and helping the client. For those who are involved in caring for the patient, they may need psychosocial support and stress management.

Health Coaching

Health coaching, or wellness coaching, supports people in assessing personal health risks and developing positive health behaviors that lead to overall well-being. The field of health coaching is relatively new and is still growing and evolving in many ways. Coaching is done through education, collaborative goal setting, and emotional support. People from many different professional fields are now involved in health coaching, including nurses, social workers, therapists, and medical assistants. For those with chronic or mental health illnesses, this type of coaching can make all the difference in their quality of life. Coaching encompasses the idea of coming alongside a patient and helping them establish and move toward their own goals, choosing to make decisions that are healthy for them. It is about teaching them how to care for themselves.

As with the provision of all services, the first step in health coaching is to **engage** the client or patient in services by establishing a positive and comfortable relationship. After building rapport with the client, a coach can move on to assessing the client's readiness for change by using **motivational interviewing**. Instead of focusing on specific symptoms or behaviors, motivational interviewing focuses on underlying contributors to change, such as intrinsic motivation, self-efficacy, and belief in the ability to change. The purpose is to find what internally motivates the client and what barriers may be causing indecision and ambivalence about change. There are many things that may be causing the client to feel conflicted, and it is the job of the coach to explore all aspects with the client and help them remove any obstacles to change.

The next step in coaching is **goal-setting**. Setting goals is a collaborative process with the client. It is important to set an overall vision that reflects the client's long-term goal for health and wellness. Then it will be easier to set large goals, and for each of those to set smaller, measurable objectives. In this way,

clients will take small, manageable steps at first, but always be moving toward the overall vision of health that has been established. When it comes to nutritional and health changes, it is often nearly impossible to make huge changes all at once, and most clients will have more success if they can first gain confidence by meeting smaller goals.

Finally, a health coach provides **ongoing coaching** and encouragement in the healthy lifestyle changes that have been made. This can include evaluation of the progress made by the client on goals and updating or adjusting goals as needed. At this stage, the coach may play a less involved but still supportive role in the client's life.

New initiatives in health coaching are now looking at group coaching as well as peer coaching. Both of these provide the benefit of connection and encouragement from others who have similar struggles and may be more cost effective. More research needs to be done into the effectiveness of these new models.

Health Literacy

Health literacy refers to a patient's ability to read and understand medical and nutritional terms. This includes words related to illnesses, parts of the body, medicines, and medical forms. If it is observed that a patient has difficulty reading or completing health forms, or relies on others to access medications, this may be a sign of limited literacy. Some simple, non-threatening questions can be asked about whether a patient picks up medications or fills out forms independently. If the answer is no, a health literacy assessment can be used to confirm a patient's level of literacy. Obviously, if a patient is unable to follow directions or understand the treatment being recommended by the doctor, this could be a hindrance to effective medical care.

There are now many options for measurement tools to assess levels of health literacy. Two of the most validated and tested tools are the **Test of Functional Health Literacy in Adults** (TOFHLA) and the **Rapid Estimate of Adult Literacy in Medicine** (REALM). TOFHLA has some short-answer comprehension questions and some numerical-calculation questions, and utilizes real materials, such as medicine labels and medical forms. It provides each patient with a categorical score of inadequate, marginal, or adequate. TOFHLA also has an abbreviated form and has been translated into Spanish and other languages. REALM focuses primarily on word recognition and reading grade level, not on comprehension. A patient is given a list of words and asked to read the ones that are familiar. Whichever words are skipped or mispronounced are not scored. REALM also has a shortened version, the REALM-R, which takes only two minutes to administer. As of yet, the REALM has not been successfully translated into other languages.

The **Newest Vital Sign** (NVS), which also is available in Spanish, is a straightforward test that uses a sample nutritional label from an ice cream carton and the test administrator asks a few simple questions about it to assess the patient's level of literacy. A score of 4-6 indicates adequate literacy; a score of less than 4 could indicate limited literacy.

The **eHealth Literacy Scale** (eHEALS) assesses a person's ability to access and understand electronic or internet related health resources and services. This is an important measure as e-health, the use of digital records and resources in medical care, continues to grow in popularity. Some other measurements are the **Short Assessment of Health Literacy** (SAHL), in both Spanish and English, and the **Health Literacy Skills Instrument** (HLSI), a computer-based assessment.

Because the different health assessment tools are slightly different in focus, though there is high correlation between them, it may be helpful to administer more than one assessment tool in order to attain the best understanding of the patient's literacy level. REALM and NVS are quick and easy and may be a good starting place. TOFHLA is more extensive and time consuming, and so would be appropriate in situations where limited literacy is suspected. In these cases, a more in-depth assessment would help to direct health education.

Interpersonal Communication

Interpersonal communication is the process by which people exchange ideas, meanings, and feelings with each other. It happens between two or more people and most usually refers to face-to-face communication through words and nonverbal cues. Phone calls, emails and now text messages are also important means of communication. It is very important for case managers to have strong interpersonal communication skills; this type of communication is the main focus of the job, and happens not only with the client, but with other service providers and family members as well.

Effective interpersonal communication can build strong relationships and is integral to establishing rapport, empowering the client, and resolving conflict, among other things. Skillful communication begins with active listening. One aspect of good listening is to use open-ended questions, which can also elicit more extensive information from the client. Good communication also involves nonverbal expression, including body position and facial expressions.

Along with active listening and helpful nonverbal cues, the actual content of the message needs to be clear. This means contextualizing what is being said for the specific client or situation and choosing the words that will most clearly deliver the message. Education level and cultural background are just two things that should be considered when choosing what to say and how to say it. The best way to determine if the information is being understood and accepted is to observe the reaction and attention of the listener. For example, if a client nonverbally expresses anger or confusion about what is being said, it may be appropriate to stop and ask the client to share their feelings.

Being aware of barriers to communication can prevent a breakdown in the delivery of the message. Disruptive noise, for example, can distort or hide the message that is being communicated. This can include external sounds from the environment, or the way the person is communicating, through difficult words or in an inappropriate way. The barriers may also be on the part of the listener, if they are distracted or too emotionally upset to accept what is being said. Or there may be cultural or language barriers. In these cases, whatever is causing the distraction should first be addressed and the attention of the listener regained.

Effective interpersonal communication within a group can be more complex, as there are many people who have different ideas to share and different ways of communicating. A group can have a positive influence, as it takes the ideas and strengths of many people and puts them together to create a stronger whole. On the other hand, group dynamics can also suppress the voice of the individual. In groups, it is even more important to make sure that people are being listened to, that respect is shown for all opinions, and that each person is given the time and confidence to share their thoughts. Each group needs positive rules and expectations that are stated clearly, and harmful communication should not be tolerated.

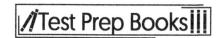

Interview Tools and Techniques

The main goal of interviewing a client is to gather the necessary information for a collaborative treatment plan. Proper interviewing can also serve to establish rapport and assist the client in developing an empowered view of themselves and the situation. While interviewing clients, it is helpful to also keep in mind the principles of good interpersonal communication, as these all apply during the interview process.

The first thing to consider when holding an initial interview with a client is the environment. The interview should be in a place, and at a time, that is conducive to the needs of the client. For example, if a client struggles with agoraphobia, the best place to meet may be in their home rather than in an office. Prior to the interview, the client should be informed of what to expect in order to decrease any anxiety that they may be experiencing. During the interview, very personal and potentially difficult information will be gathered from the client, so it is imperative that the client feels comfortable sharing this private information. Providing options of places and times to meet for the interview will immediately give the client some control and empowerment in the treatment process.

Another key to successful interviewing is asking the necessary questions in such a way that the client feels comfortable and relaxed in the relationship. This helps to establish rapport, which is the foundation of positive treatment and care. The case manager should clearly introduce themselves and be as honest as possible without compromising on professionalism. Building rapport can also involve finding common ground, communicating genuine care for the client, and using humor or non-threatening questions to help break the ice.

There are two types of questions that can be used when interviewing: **close-ended** and **open-ended** questions. Both are important, depending on what kind of information is being gathered. When gathering simple demographic information, the case manager may want to use close-ended questions to get straightforward answers (such as the age of the client). Using only close-ended questions will not provide the client with an opportunity to share other information that is important to them. Their struggles, fears, concerns, and needs will better be explored and understood by asking open-ended questions. Clients may not be able to easily say everything they want to, or even know exactly what they want to say. In this case, good questions can help them in the process of expressing their own thoughts and feelings. Using clarifying questions can also ensure that the case manager really understands what the client is communicating. One example of this could be, "Would you explain what you mean by _____?"

Asking questions is not the only aspect of interviewing. Interviewing also involves active listening and empathetic responding. While a client is answering questions and telling their story, the case manager should still be fully engaged. This happens through non-verbal responses and eye contact, as well as reflecting what the client says back to them. An effective way of doing this is to say, "What I hear you saying is _____ - is that correct?" The first interview will either make a positive or negative impression on the client and will influence their decision to engage in treatment.

The final step in the interview is to collaborate and agree on follow-up steps. Whether this is to decide on goals for care or when a follow-up interview can take place, the decisions need to be made with the client.

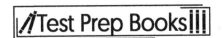
Multicultural, Spiritual, and Religious Factors That May Affect the Client's Health Status

Multiculturalism is an integral aspect of culture in the United States, which comprises people from many countries and cultures, often speaking different languages. When it comes to case management, each client will come from a different cultural and religious background. This can lead to many challenges, such as language barriers, or more subtle but complex differences. Both the client and the case manager will have their own cultural and religious biases and beliefs that will influence the way they look at treatment.

One aspect of multiculturalism is that cultures can be individualistic or collectivist, which will play a part in how the client views health and healthcare. In **individualistic** societies, decisions are made by the individual and things like privacy and independence are valued. On the other hand, in a **collectivist** society, decisions related to health may be a community responsibility, and the assumption will be that the whole family will be involved in a client's treatment. This may not only involve the family but also the spiritual or religious community. While upholding ethical guidelines around confidentiality and privacy, a case manager must also respect the culture that the client comes from and involve the community as much or as little as the client desires.

There are many things that are affected by spiritual, religious, and cultural beliefs. First, it is beneficial to describe the difference between spirituality and religion. **Spirituality** is a client's belief in the operation of a higher self and/or higher components of the universe. A spiritual client may not profess a certain religion but may engage in practices such as yoga or meditation. On the other hand, **religion** is a profession of belief in a God(s) or divine being and a belief in a higher order that controls the universe. Religious clients often identify by the title of the doctrine they subscribed to.

Consequently, it is important for the case manager to be aware of differing practices such as cupping, candling, acupuncture, refusal to accept blood transfusions, and dietary restrictions that could be confused with abuse or neglect when compared against traditional Western American culture. Traditional medicines of the client's culture or medical practices of that culture may be preferred over what doctors recommend. Moreover, there are gender roles that may affect the nature of the relationship with the client and the services provided. For example, there may be a gender preference with a doctor, or the client may opt out of medical care altogether when in the presence of an opposite-sex provider. Different cultures also have different views of doctors: some are held in such high esteem that they will never be questioned, even if a client is confused or in disagreement. In addition, the client's view of death and what happens after death may play a large role in decisions that are made and will be particularly significant in palliative and hospice care.

While many doctors and case managers may avoid discussing spiritual beliefs with clients, it is one of the many aspects of whole-person care that affects a client's health and cannot be ignored. The spiritual and religious beliefs of clients should not be minimized or overlooked, even when they are viewed by physicians as prohibiting or interfering with treatment. If these beliefs are important to the client, they should be acknowledged by the case manager even as education and information continues to be provided regarding the objectionable treatment. Case managers must affirm the spiritually-guided health care decisions made by the client whenever possible.

A client's spirituality, just like their cultural background, will affect all aspects of health care including views of illness and treatment. Clients may have various ideas about the causes of illness. There may also be differing ideas about the best methods of treatment, or some treatments may conflict with the

client's religious beliefs. For example, a diet suggested by a doctor may contain items that are contrary to what a client eats according to their religion. Spiritual beliefs about life and death will also play a role in decisions made by the client related to end-of-life care. As clients face the end of their lives, spirituality may become even more important to them as they reflect on the meaning of life.

In general, spirituality has been shown to have a positive impact on illness. Clients with strong spirituality may experience increased health benefits such as decreased stress and greater longevity. Moreover, spirituality tends to provide greater peace and joy even in the midst of challenging circumstances because it can bring meaning to suffering. The spiritual community that a client is a part of can also prove to be a strong social, emotional, and even financial support for the client.

Being culturally competent is a necessity for every case manager. **Cultural competency** refers to the ability to understand, accept, and respect a client's culture and religion, while recognizing one's own cultural and religious biases. Case managers cannot assume that every client will share the same cultural and ideological beliefs but must view every single client as different and coming from a unique cultural background. One obvious aspect of cultural competence is to ensure that there are no language or communication barriers, and if needed, that a translator or another case manager is available. It is also important for the case manager to understand, recognize, and support the client's specific cultural and religious beliefs. This is done by asking questions and learning everything possible about their culture. Diversity should not be feared or avoided but embraced and affirmed by the case manager. Educate and inform the client about treatment options while acknowledging and respecting their beliefs.

Psychological and Neuropsychological Assessments

While case managers are able to conduct informal psychological assessments, it may be appropriate to refer a client for a formal psychological evaluation if there are relevant concerns. Psychological and neuropsychological assessments are conducted by psychologists or neuropsychologists. **Psychological assessments** should be done once a medical exam has been completed in order to rule out medical causes of the symptoms. The psychological evaluation is less comprehensive than a neuropsychological assessment, providing basic personality information, cognitive functioning, and psychological diagnoses. A **neuropsychological assessment** is a more in-depth evaluation of how one's brain operates. Specifically, it addresses a subject's cognitive, motor, behavioral, and linguistic functioning. Neuropsychological testing may be done when there is suspicion of a disorder linked to cognitive or neurological impairment.

Psychological evaluations are provided for a variety of reasons, i.e., employment testing, school/social difficulties in children, or people facing trials. Psychological assessments look at intellectual functionality, personality, and behaviors. There are four primary components of psychological assessment. The first component is a norm-referenced test that provides a scale of measurement to assess differences in a person's knowledge, skill, or personality. The next two components are interviews and observations, which can either be formal or informal. The final component is an informal assessment, which may be used to supplement the norm-referenced test, but with decreased scientific validity.

One tool commonly used in psychological evaluations for personality assessment is the **Minnesota Multiphasic Personality Inventory** (MMPI). There are 567 true-false questions on the test, and the results provide the client with a score on 10 scales, including hypomania and paranoia. It is an objective test that can be scored by a computer and is useful for psychiatric diagnosis. Some other personality tools sometimes used in a psychological evaluation are the **Rorschach Inkblot Test** and the **Thematic**

Apperception Test (TAT), both of which utilize ambiguous images and ask the client to interpret them. These more subjective tools are based on a psychoanalytic perspective and are meant to expose a person's underlying fears, concerns, or unconscious feelings. The most popular intelligence tests are the **Wechsler Adult Intelligence Scale** (WAIS), or **Wechsler Intelligence Scale for Children** (WISC). In addition to the administration of these formal assessment tools, there is an extensive clinical interview with the client and possible interviews with others who know the client.

A neuropsychological evaluation contains many of the same components as a psychological evaluation, but in addition the neuropsychologist may test other aspects of neurology, such as memory, language, and executive functioning. Neuropsychology is intended to target things like dementia or brain injuries. When it is suspected that there is a more physiological (instead of emotional or psychological) reason for behaviors, then a neuropsychological assessment will be recommended.

The psychological assessment report is a summary of the findings from all the different assessment tools and methods. It points to themes, strengths, and needs of the client. It also provides a psychological diagnosis, according to the *Diagnostic and Statistical Manual of Mental Disorders, Fifth Edition (DSM-5)*. Previously there was a multi-axial approach to diagnosis, but the newest edition of the DSM has eliminated this aspect. The first three axes are now combined into one, providing the primary diagnosis or diagnoses. Separate notes are added to indicate any significant psychosocial or environmental factors, but these are no longer separate axes.

Psychosocial Aspects of Chronic Illness and Disability

For people struggling with a chronic illness or disability, there are many factors other than physical ones that will affect their overall functioning and well-being. A client should never be viewed as one-dimensional but should always be supported and helped from a biopsychosocial approach. Those diagnosed with a chronic illness, or those having dealt with it for a long time, may struggle with depression and feelings of hopelessness. There may also be other mental or emotional concerns such as stress, grief, anxiety, or loneliness. Some of the symptoms of mental illness may at first be confused with the symptoms of a physical illness, but it is important to distinguish between the two. Age, personality, socioeconomic status, and education level, along with many other factors, may contribute to a person's ability to adjust and cope with the new diagnosis. Conditions such as depression will directly influence a person's health and physical state, and there is a worse prognosis for those who are also struggling with mental illness in addition to a physical one.

The impact of the illness or disability will not be confined to the client alone; it will also influence the community and social structure within which the individual functions. A person who has a chronic diagnosis will play a different role in the family than previously and may need more support than they are able to provide to others. It is important to consider the adjustments a family may have to make in such situations and the different struggles they will also have to undergo in getting used to a new reality. This adjustment will be particularly profound within the immediate family and be very difficult for partners, parents, or children of the client.

While a client is receiving medical treatment for an illness, a case worker must provide whole-person care, making sure that emotional, social, and psychological needs are simultaneously being addressed. The family may also need education around the illness, and family counseling may be useful in helping everyone adjust to the changes. Identifying and connecting the client to other social supports and resources may also keep them from feeling alone and will give them others who have experienced the same things to talk to and receive encouragement from. A few other strategies to empower a client to

successfully cope with a chronic illness are stress management techniques, education about the best treatments for the disease, and individual therapy. The client may also benefit from practical coaching on how to accomplish daily tasks with the limitations of the disability or illness. Antidepressants or other mental health medications may be helpful if they do not interfere with the treatment for the physical illness.

Resources for the Uninsured and Underinsured

A factor that may add to the already overwhelming and stressful nature of illness is the financial burden that faces those who are not adequately covered by insurance. While some people may have no insurance, others might have partial or inadequate insurance that covers doctor visits but not medicines or co-pays. The role of the case manager is to help the client advocate for themselves with doctors and care providers and explore options for various types of medical assistance. A case manager should also be aware of specific state and community resources that are available.

The first step is to see if an uninsured client is qualified to apply for insurance. A case manager can assist clients with the process of applying for insurance, as this can be a daunting process for many people. Insurance options can be explored through the **Health Insurance Marketplace**, run by the federal government at www.healthcare.gov, where various insurance options are presented for people in all different situations and with different levels of income. For most insurance programs a person has to apply during the open enrollment period, which is from November-January each year.

However, some insurance programs can be applied for at any point, such as **Medicaid**, for low-income families, and **Children's Health Insurance Program** (CHIP), for children in families whose income disqualifies them from getting Medicaid. **Medicare** is also available for those over 65 or with certain disabilities and can be used in conjunction with Medicaid when needed. If a client does not qualify for any of these options, private insurance may prove to be the best route for the client.

For the underinsured, there may still be higher medical costs than they can afford, often related to prescription costs, co-pays, or maxed out benefits. There are several options for getting assistance with prescription medication. Those on Medicare may qualify for additional help with prescription drug coverage through Extra Help, a program that covers the gap in coverage. There are also **patient assistance programs**, run by pharmaceutical companies, that provide affordable medications for low-income patients. Patients should ask their doctors and pharmacists for information about applying for these patient assistance programs. There are also medication assistance programs offered by individual states, some connected with Medicare and others independent of it.

Finally, there are many programs offered through nonprofit companies that connect people to free or affordable medications, disease-specific resources, or assistance with co-payments. For example, **Partnership for Prescription Assistance** connects patients to resources for the specific drug needed or to free and low-cost health clinics in the patient's area. **Patient Advocate Foundation** connects patients to a whole range of different medical-related services, including help with co-pays, and is specifically intended to assist the underinsured. Case managers should spend some time with clients exploring all the possible options for assistance with medication costs.

Supportive Care Programs

Support programs can provide important assistance to people who suffer from many different forms of illness. There are countless organizations and programs that can provide emotional, social, and financial

73

support to clients. While some clients may have full schedules and strong support systems, additional support should at least be considered for each client. Some clients may need more help and support than the case manager and other service providers can give. Support programs should be utilized in addition to comprehensive medical care, not in place of it.

Support groups are meetings of people who have similar struggles and can share their experiences and stories with each other. They may be formal or informal, online or in person, structured or unstructured. Sometimes these groups are led by a trained therapist or clinician while other times they are peer led. Whatever the specific form they take, support groups can prevent the feelings of isolation and hopelessness that people can feel when facing a long-term illness. Popular examples of support groups are Alcoholics Anonymous and Narcotics Anonymous. There are also support groups for almost any other population or issue (i.e., parents who have lost a child, cancer, and depression). Support groups may be intended for the person diagnosed with the illness or for the caregivers and family members who also face unique needs and challenges.

There are also **disease-specific organizations** that provide help and support to those who struggle with a particular illness. For example, the **American Cancer Society**, in addition to support groups, also offers advocacy and education and provides practical and financial support for those with cancer. Multiple sclerosis, arthritis, heart disease, and brain injuries are just a few other examples of diseases that have whole organizations devoted to providing support to the individuals who suffer from these diseases.

Another unique form of support that may be very important for some clients is **pastoral counseling**. Qualified pastoral counselors are trained in both mental health issues and religious/spiritual issues. These counselors are uniquely able to integrate spiritual and psychological aspects of treatment and care. Many clients are concerned about their spiritual needs as well as physical and emotional needs, and pastoral counseling should be considered in these cases. Pastoral counseling may be especially important when someone is facing a terminal illness or dealing with end-of-life issues. Some pastoral counselors are certified by the American Association of Pastoral Counselors (AAPC), and this may be a good way of finding a counselor if the client is not part of a local religious congregation.

Bereavement counseling can help families or individuals cope and move forward after experiencing a loss. Whether this is losing someone to death or losing one's independence and health, bereavement counseling can help someone grieve and adjust to a loss in a healthy way. Other types of services will often end as soon as a person dies, but for the family members the process has only just begun as they begin to adjust to life without their loved one. Though grief is a natural and normal process, each person experiences it differently, so bereavement counseling should be tailored to meet the needs of the individual. Bereavement counseling may be accessed through hospice facilities or the hospital.

Wellness and Illness Prevention Programs, Concepts, and Strategies

There are many important principles for preventing illness and increasing overall health. **Wellness-focused programs** are cost effective and can contribute to a better quality of life for the patient, even those with a serious illness. The maintenance of healthy habits not only helps prevent illness but can also slow the progression of a disease. Good health depends not only on getting good medical treatment for a specific sickness, but also maintaining a healthy lifestyle and daily habits. Addressing a particular illness without emphasizing a more holistic view of health will have fewer long-term benefits.

Several basic steps should be emphasized in wellness and illness prevention programs. These are changes that everyone, with or without major illnesses, should consider implementing in their lives. The

first step is eliminating unhealthy practices such as smoking, drug use, and excessive drinking. Not only do these exacerbate and cause illnesses, but they can also affect a person's mental health and relationships, which also contribute to a person's well-being. Better nutrition and exercise are also key components of wellness programs. Poor dietary habits can lead to things like heart disease and obesity, which are not only harmful but can also complicate other health issues. Daily exercise is important for everyone and can increase energy, decrease stress, prevent obesity, and contribute to better mental health.

Another important way to maintain the best health possible is to attend doctor visits regularly and consistently, and follow through with all recommended treatments, immunizations, and dietary restrictions. This includes scheduling appointments for early detection methods such as mammograms and cancer screenings. According to a person's family history of illness, there may be a greater risk for specific diseases. Doctors will be able to identify the risk factors and provide patients with particular prevention methods for these diseases.

Case managers should begin with education when encouraging their clients to begin and maintain healthy habits. Motivational interviewing should be used in helping clients to take charge of their own health and to identify any of the barriers there may be to change. It may also be appropriate to refer the client for nutritional counseling, health coaching, or addiction recovery programs. **Health coaching**, done by the case manager or someone else, may help clients find the encouragement they need to make healthy changes that will increase both the quality and length of their lives. Each client is unique, and the case manager has to be creative in utilizing different methods that will be efficient, depending on the client's level of self-determination, empowerment, and activation. For example, some clients will be self-motivated while others may need the help of a support group or weight loss program.

Social Determinants of Health

Health begins long before a patient enters a hospital and includes many factors, including social determinants of health (SDoH). Healthy People 2020 identified social determinants of health as one of the focuses of their new prevention agenda with the goal of creating environments that promote good health for everyone. Healthcare-specific social determinants of health include access to healthcare, access to primary care, and health literacy, but research has shown that economic stability, education, social context, and neighborhood environment are also social determinants that directly impact health. For example, evidence shows that patients that reside in high-poverty neighborhoods are around 25 percent more likely to have hospital readmissions.

Case managers can begin by understanding the population they serve--what are the major contributing social determinants of health (SDoH) in the specific community? By analyzing the relationships between the population that the case manager serves and the healthcare community, the case manager can begin to optimize the relationship. Case managers can explore programs in their area that address SDoH to refer patients to. Case managers in hospital settings can use an assessment to help discover the patient's SDoH that may be affecting health and discover gaps in care caused by SDoH. Case managers can bridge the gap by coordinating community resources and organizations and providing follow-up communication to make sure that SDoH improvements have been made.

Gender Health

Healthy People, as one of their 2020 goals, aims to improve the health, safety, and wellbeing of the LGBT community. Sexual orientation is defined as a person's attraction to another person and the

affiliations that result from these attractions. Gender identity is defined as a person's sense of themselves and gender expression is the way people present their gender to others.

LGBT patients say that sexual orientation is often a factor that causes delays in healthcare, so case managers can direct patients to LGBT-friendly providers through online resources such as the Gay and Lesbian Medical Association. Healthcare providers who would like to become more educated about LGBT needs can access online resources such as the National LGBT Health Education Center. Case managers should be aware of the following factors that many people in the LGBT community face: increased risk of disease transmission, decreased lifespans, increased mental health issues with higher rates of suicide, and increased rates of drug and alcohol abuse. Case managers can help meet the needs of LGBT patients by being aware of social programs and community resources that are targeted to the LGBT community.

Quality Outcomes Evaluation and Measurements

Accreditation Standards and Requirements

Many organizations look to attain an industry-recognized stamp of approval that demonstrates their ability to deliver and facilitate quality health care. There are a variety of accrediting bodies within the healthcare arena that provide validation of this ability by certifying healthcare establishments using core standards and performance measures.

Cost-Benefit Analysis

Organizations face the challenge of having to demonstrate the ability to provide quality case management services. In addition, they also must demonstrate the ability to reduce the cost of care while executing these quality case management services at the same time. **Cost-benefit analysis** enables an organization to demonstrate the value of case management activities and services. It can be difficult to prove the worth of case management services and activities due to the spending required to support and operate a case management program. There are a variety of tasks that case managers can document to demonstrate cost savings as well as case status.

Below is an example of the cost savings formula.

$$\text{Cost Savings} = \text{Potential Costs} - (\text{Actual Cost} + \text{Cost of Case Management})$$

Quarterly reports should outline fees, service costs, and resources while also providing plan of care updates for those cases that remain active. Case management reports must demonstrate a movement of the patient along the continuum of care, including those interventions by the case manager that contribute to a reduction in unnecessary spending. Specific examples include hospital admission reductions, a decrease in the number of hospital days, transitions to lower levels of care, reductions in the number of emergency room visits, a decrease in medical or behavioral exacerbations, and fewer case rate negotiations. At the same time, an increase in less costly home care and outpatient services must be documented.

Case managers must create a report that tells a story in a succinct manner. Reports must present a clear picture of the patient's medical or behavioral history, treatment plan, duration of case management services, case management interventions, and outcomes. Finally, the cost-benefit analysis should provide a comparison of the costs associated with case management intervention versus the costs of managing the case without intervention.

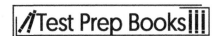

Data Interpretation and Reporting

Case managers play a significant role in collecting data that provides an analysis of the progress of a patient in case management and provides the ability for both case managers and organizations to interpret the trends, progress, and performance measures of a case. Data and reporting assists organizations in identifying trends and establishing benchmarks for their programs.

The application or information technology system used to collect data may vary among organizations. Many software companies allow groups to customize systems to support their business needs and goals. Case managers must have a clear understanding of how to navigate these systems and document ongoing case management activities and metrics.

Business and metrics analysts leverage case management systems, and in some instances, utilization management systems, to measure utilization trends, financial costs, case management delivery, and those benchmarks for which the organization is working toward achieving. Organizations establish benchmarks internally to monitor the overall effectiveness of case management within the organization, and they also use the data to compare their performance to that of other agencies. To perform such a task, case managers must be uniform in their documentation of data and consistent with the collection of that data. Failure to follow a standardized process increases the risk for missed data or poor documentation practices. Organizations must ensure that their case managers understand the importance of accurate and consistent documentation practices.

Some states mandate that Medicaid managed care organizations provide accurate data for certain populations, such as those with special healthcare needs, demonstrating specific case management activities and measurable outcomes.

Health Care Analytics

Healthcare analytics have a significant impact on the measurement and evaluation of outcomes. Without the right tools, resources, case manager knowledge, skills, and ability, however, healthcare analytics can prove worthless in examining and measuring data and outcomes.

Health Risk Assessment

Health risk assessments (HRAs) are screening tools widely used by case management and disease management professionals to gather information about a patient's health history and current health status. These tools should be created using a team of healthcare professionals, including a physician who can provide input. HRAs enable clinicians to better understand an individual's current quality of life and care, as well as recently prescribed treatment regimens. Also, they provide some insight into the patient's current perception of their health status.

Next, HRAs provide a preliminary overview of the patient's healthcare utilization. There are occasions in which the patient's previous healthcare experience may not be readily available by way of historical documentation, and HRAs may help to uncover what are otherwise undocumented experiences, particularly for those individuals who may be more transient than others. HRAs are in use by most case management and disease management departments and are often a primary means for identifying clients who might benefit most from case and disease management services.

Health risk assessment tools vary by organization, and the method in which the data are collected and stored may also differ. The same may be true internally for the case management and disease

78

management departments within an organization for various populations and groups. The reason for this deviation between teams is a result of the need to attain, monitor, and measure different pieces of information. Some of these differences are driven by internal policies, best practices, state or federal requirements, accreditation requirements, or quality measures. There are several forms that are well known in the industry of case management and are either a component of an internal assessment or used independently to help gather information.

One example of a health risk assessment is the **Mini-Mental State Examination** (MMSE), which provides an assessment of cognitive impairment. Also known as the 30-point Folstein test, the MMSE is useful for individuals with dementia or identifying memory loss. It is not used for diagnosis but can be useful in screening for possible cognitive deficits.

Another example of a health risk assessment is the **SF-36**, which provides a measurement of the overall health status of the client and is most beneficial under a disease management model. While every organization is not using this form, there are a number of questions and characteristics that are in use by various entities. This form presents the patient's perception of their current health status and becomes an oral record of sorts that is based purely on the patient's self-report of their health history, pain, perceived limitations, mental health, social support, and environment and safety.

Health risk assessment tools can be an asset in the predictive modeling process. The HRA can support the data revealed by the model itself and can further support stratification of clients into a risk category or domain. In addition, they may reveal elements not otherwise available in a predictive model score, such as comorbid conditions that are not yet visual in the detail of claims or pharmacy data. Overall, health risk assessments should be easy to navigate and must be a component of a regular schedule.

Predictive Modeling

Predictive modeling is a tool that many organizations use to identify individuals within their population who have a diagnosis that may pose the greatest risk for preventable costs. Predictive modeling tools take claims data coupled with high-cost diagnoses to produce a score that identifies how stable an individual's condition is or is not. This results in a "risk score" that explains the likelihood that the same individual will experience a future hospitalization if there is not an episode of case management intervention and support. These tools stratify individuals within a population based on their risk over a period of time (e.g., six to twelve months).

The likelihood of hospitalization model is commonly used by managed care organizations to identify those individuals who are the best candidates for case management services over time. There are employers who also use predictive modeling data via high risk assessments to anticipate costs. This model, however, is only as good as the data available to provide an accurate picture of the patient. While it typically leverages twelve months of data to determine and handicap the model, it does mimic real-world experiences. It works best for chronic conditions including but not limited to: diabetes, congestive heart failure, chronic obstructive pulmonary disease, asthma, renal failure, and pneumonia.

Organizations target those diagnoses or conditions that are known to result in higher costs and have high readmission rates. Predictive modeling enables case management departments to establish critical interventions, implement performance measures, and develop individualized strategies to support the facilitation of specific services, in an effort to greatly reduce the risk of an unanticipated or catastrophic health event.

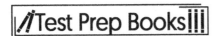

Predictive modeling is a proven asset to case management departments. It allows case managers to focus on those populations that will benefit most from case management intervention strategies, including outreach and education, and provides the opportunity to effectively develop a plan of care that is both collaborative and comprehensive.

Adjusted Clinical Group

Adjusted Clinical Groups System (ACG), a creation of researchers at Johns Hopkins University School of Hygiene and Public Health in Baltimore, Maryland, was developed more than twenty years ago out of a necessity to better understand the profile of a patient's morbidity and the overall presentation of some populations, allowing for the measurement of performance and quality for the purposes of capitation payment.

ACGs, formerly known as Ambulatory Care Groups, measure health status by grouping diagnoses into clinical groups using the patient's age, sex, and diagnosis over twelve months.

The ACG system has a role in assigning individuals a particular ACG value, which is in direct correlation to their anticipated or actual utilization of services.

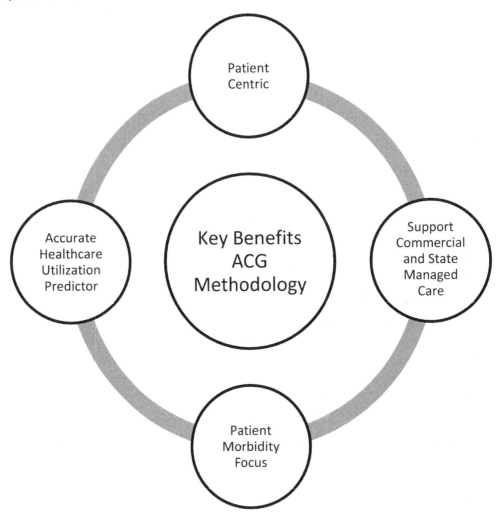

The benefits associated with adjusted clinical groups are patient centric and affect the patient and the organization. This is a model that fits the description of being patient focused, which is a key ingredient of any program seeking a way to evaluate the quality of care metrics. **Patient-centric models** tend to focus primarily on the patient as an individual, including characteristics such as their current state of health, treatment plan, and ongoing monitoring throughout the continuum of care. The focus is not only on a patient's procedures but delves deeper into a patient's morbidity.

Unlike some models that focus mainly on those populations that are complex and at risk for catastrophic outcomes, the ACG system provides for the ability to monitor both healthy populations and physically challenged persons, and it can support both commercial and Medicaid managed care programs. This system can better predict the likelihood of inpatient admissions/readmissions and emergency department visits; it can also better identify which individuals will be high cost-utilizers when compared with other models.

Use of the ACG has a direct impact on the improvement of both healthcare resource allocation and the disease profile of the population. Users of ACG should be aware of the following: There are diagnoses data (medical services and physician claims) that may need to be excluded; users must have access to the research registry and identify an index date of interest; and ACG utilizes the International Classification of Disease ICD-9/ICD-10 codes.

Over the past twenty years, the ACG system has undergone an evolution, using predictive modeling strategies, incorporating pharmacy measurements, and deploying care management applications as a component of its system. One such development has included the use of predictive modeling as part of ACGs. These models monitor future costs, potential hospitalizations, and the greater risk for increased pharmacy utilization.

Expert clinicians and the ACG system categorize ICD-9 and ICD-10 codes into one of thirty-two groups or clusters known as **Aggregated Diagnosis Groups™** (ADGs®). Patients may not be assigned any ADGs, or they may have as many as thirty-two ADGs. ADGs are assigned based on the patient's health condition. Therefore, those individuals with more than one health condition are likely to have more than one ADG. Different diseases or conditions define a single ADG. Individuals are given a unique ACG based on their ADGs. The expectation is that those who fall within the same ACG will have the same healthcare utilization experience. Both ACG and ADGs were created to better understand healthcare utilization. ADG criteria consists primarily of the severity of the illness; etiology of the illness; diagnostic certainty; specialty care interventions for the illness; and persistence of the diagnosis.

Severity of Illness	Etiology	Diagnostic Certainty
Specialty Care Interventions	Persistence of Diagnosis	

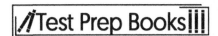

The system defines ADGs as "major" or "minor." The ACG system assigns each of the medical diagnosis codes, except a few, to a patient. Several clinical and expected utilization criteria form the foundation of the ADGs. The variables include: duration of the condition; severity of the condition; diagnostic certainty (disease based on diagnostic evaluation rather than documented disease focusing on treatment services); the etiology of the condition (injury, infection); and specialty care involvement (e.g., obstetric, surgical, medical, hematology).

Program Evaluation Methods

Periodically, programs must undergo some form of evaluation to determine the effectiveness of function, delivery, and overall quality of the services provided to clients. Owners of those programs must decide if the program is addressing the needs of their customers and what opportunities exist for overall improvement. Methods used to evaluate a program include the deployment of quality management and improvement programs. There are entire departments within a company that have the role of systematically analyzing, monitoring, and suggesting ways to improve performance that will lead to the best possible outcomes for populations. Outcomes measurement provides the opportunity to examine and evaluate current practices and generate change for positive patient results. Surveys can serve as an evaluating tool that may provide insight into how well a program is operating and can present an opportunity for improvement.

Quality and Performance Improvement Concepts

Case management programs utilize a **performance improvement process** to understand better what components of their program work well and which components of their programs require modification to support the achievement of the best possible outcomes for the patient. The primary focus of **continuous quality improvement** (CQI) programs is to improve the overall quality of healthcare delivery and identify and remove potential barriers, while continuing to maintain an emphasis on both outcomes and processes of care. Enhancement of the quality of care is completed through the implementation of a specific process. Initially, the problem is clearly identified. Second, a **Corrective Action Plan** (CAP) is employed. Next, thorough observation and close monitoring of the CAP occurs, followed by a review and evaluation of outcomes. Finally, reinforcement of the required changes in processes is expected.

Case management CQI practices have been formulated to improve healthcare access and facilitation; professional case management execution and support of the client within the healthcare delivery team; client outcomes; promotion of clients' safety; and the overall improvement of customer satisfaction. **Quality improvement** examines three specific measures of improvement, including structure (physical structure and buildings), process (systems functionality), and outcome (the result). Program administrators and health providers deploy the practice of root cause analysis to identify those factors that directly contribute to mediocre performance and have a causal effect on outcomes, or those things that may lead to an adverse event.

An assortment of models may be used to measure quality improvement, and two of the most commonly seen models are Six Sigma and the PDSA Model. Both models supply a foundational framework to organizations in need of a clear strategy to measure quality improvement activities. **Six Sigma** has a primary goal of implementing a measurement-based strategy that concentrates on process improvement. It had its beginnings with Motorola during the 1980s. Six Sigma is a business strategy that boasts the ability to save millions, if not billions, of dollars. Though it began with Motorola, Six Sigma has a strong reputation in several sectors including health care. Six Sigma may use one of two sub-methodologies to achieve this improvement. The **DMAIC** (define, measure, analyze, improve, control)

82

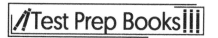

process is best for those existing processes that fall below specification and require an incremental improvement.

The **DMADV** (define, measure, analyze, design, verify) process assists with the development of new processes or for those processes that require more than just an incremental improvement.

D Define → M Measure → A Analyze → D Design → V Verify

Six Sigma boasts numerous advantages. Primarily, the results will include improved patient outcomes stemming from a renewed customer-focused approach; problem resolution; the reduction or removal of defects; cost savings and subsequent revenue increases; and a more proactive work environment. Implementing the Six Sigma strategies also brings some disadvantages. First, it is known to create a bit of bureaucracy and foster a climate that can feel limiting. Executing Six Sigma strategies can also lead to process backlogs and limit the ability to be innovative. Nevertheless, Six Sigma is useful in healthcare and enables medical professionals to identify variances and process gaps easily in those instances where inconsistencies in performance are difficult to see.

The **PDSA model** is self-described as being a "Model for Improvement." It fast-tracks improvement within the healthcare setting and operates as a supplement to existing quality improvement models that are already in place. The model is divided into two parts: Fundamental Questions and Four Stages.

The model challenges its users to ask themselves three fundamental questions before starting. What are we trying to accomplish? Answering this question yields clear and measurable goals, which are a component in establishing what one is looking to accomplish. The answer to this question should include those issues that affect the team, leadership, and client. This effort may entail identifying industry standards, metrics, and best practices as a component of the answer. How will we know that a change is an improvement? The team will need to clearly describe how a change will indicate an improvement. This will require ongoing measurement of outcomes and show real, sustainable improvement over time. It will be necessary to collect data in order to determine if a change will truly lead to an improvement and whether or not it will be measurable. What changes can we make that will result in improvement? More than likely, the number of changes will be small in number to result in improvement, but the work to get there will require various stakeholders to achieve success.

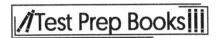
The PDSA model involves four stages in which a process improvement plan is initiated to execute a change.

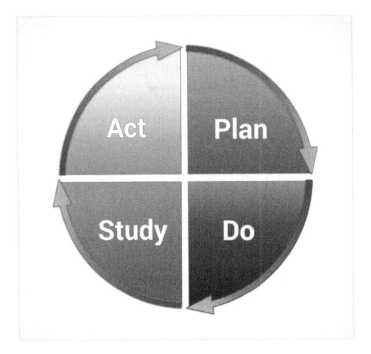

The implementation of the PDSA model involves four components:

- The **Plan phase** focuses on establishing objectives, making predictions, and creating a plan for data collection.

- The **Do phase** requires the execution of the plan (who, what, when, where) and documentation of the data.

- In the **Study phase**, the findings are analyzed and evaluated.

- The final **Act phase** involves refining the change based on the findings and planning for that change.

PDSA requires commitment and long-term planning for optimal success. This model works for pilot programs because it allows for small-scale testing before large-scale implementations. Whether choosing Six Sigma or PDSA, either model can support the facilitation of a strategy and enable organizations to demonstrate their quality improvement activities.

Quality Indicators and Applications

Quality indicators exist to enable the measurement of quality and cost of care. Organizations establish key metrics to support the process of both examining and evaluating the results of healthcare delivery by not only providers but by their internal teams, including those in the role of case manager.

Health Plan Employer Data and Information Set (HEDIS) provides insight into the ongoing effort to prevent illness. It also enables health plans to compare best practices based on overall performance. The **National Committee for Quality Assurance** (NCQA) utilizes HEDIS scores to measure the

performance of managed care organizations. Certified auditors have a responsibility to validate HEDIS results, following the process instituted by NCQA.

A component of HEDIS is the CAHPS® 5.0 survey. The **CAHPS® 5.0 survey** examines the satisfaction that members do or do not have with the following areas: claims processing, customer service, and access to care.

Benchmarking is another method that allows for the analysis of healthcare delivery, trends, and best practices. **Benchmarks** are useful in that they permit the comparison of apples to apples. This is especially true when audits are internal to an organization. In addition, benchmarking also allows the comparison of results with state, regional, or national organizations that are similar in structure. For example, the average length of stay or number of bed days may be a metric that is monitored and even tied to the performance of an organization.

Industry benchmarks in managed care organizations include: acute-care admissions per thousand; acute-care bed days per thousand; skilled nursing bed days per thousand; home care admissions per thousand; and home care visits per thousand. The benchmarking exercise can also help to identify processes that have an opportunity for improvement. The exercise supports monitoring of consistency in practice while also enabling compliance with quality standards. Patients, caregivers, providers, payers, and a variety of other participants in the patient's care should be a part of evaluating their experience with the case management. Their feedback is critical in the evaluation of the overall effectiveness of a program. Also, case managers are often the face of the business, and this means that there must be a measurement of performance.

Sources of Quality Indicators

Quality indicators come from a variety of sources that are discussed in this guide, including the Centers for Medicare and Medicaid Services (CMS); the Utilization Review Accreditation Commission (URAC); the National Committee for Quality Assurance (NCQA); the National Quality Forum (NQF); and the Agency for Healthcare Research and Quality (AHRQ). **Quality indicators** are used to establish a set of standards that may be used to evaluate and measure the quality of care.

Centers for Medicare and Medicaid Services

The CMS requires providers (e.g., professionals and hospitals) to submit **clinical quality measures** (CQMs) to demonstrate their ability to provide care that is safe, effective, efficient, timely, and patient-centered. CMS updates CQMs or clinical quality measures each year. CQMs provide a method of evaluation to measure and monitor the quality of care that healthcare providers and hospitals deliver. Key measurements include: cost effectiveness; safety; health outcomes; clinical processes; coordination of care and patient engagement; and adherence. Providers utilize certified Electronic Health Record (EHR) technology to submit their CQM data. EHR technology allows providers to share data about their patients while also gaining a full perspective on those trends and outcomes associated with the patient and the quality of care.

Outcome and Assessment Information Set (OASIS)

Healthcare services provided at patients' residences are conducted by home health agencies. Home health agency PPS reimbursement amounts are determined by Home Health Resource Groups (HHRGs). They are based on a comprehensive assessment system called the Outcome and Assessment Information Set (OASIS), which assigns a score to each patient for classification into an HHRG to determine reimbursement amounts. The score depends on dozens of different factors related to the

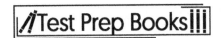

type of services needed for each patient. OASIS's data is collected by home health agency staff from each patient as they go through the processes of admission, transfer, discharge, 60-day follow-up, and change of condition notations. This data would determine a patient's HHRG by comparing them to others with similar treatments. A patient's HHRG will be used to calculate their reimbursement through the PPS.

OASIS was created to develop a standard for determining reimbursements needed for home health care services. The results come from patients' data relating to their demographics, social conditions, home setting, health, diagnostic codes, ability to function, psychological state, psychosocial state, amount of emergency or hospital care needed, as well as other various factors relating to the condition of the individual. All Medicare or Medicaid patients over the age of eighteen are required to go through the OASIS assessment in order to determine their reimbursement amount, and consequently develop a treatment plan.

To receive the maximum amount of reimbursement, healthcare agencies have to do the assessment as accurately as possible. This will include maintaining consistent records that can be updated frequently and keeping complete and accurate information by OASIS's standards.

Utilization Review Accreditation Commission
URAC, formerly known as the Utilization Review Accreditation Commission, serves as a nonprofit accrediting body for healthcare organizations, enabling them to facilitate quality care. Various stakeholders are used to develop core measures and standards. URAC accreditation is an industry-recognized validation that demonstrates an excellence in quality and care coordination.

URAC's performance measures provide the opportunity for awareness as it relates to reviewing healthcare quality and opportunities for quality improvement. URAC selects performance measures that will provide value to various stakeholders, including consumers and purchasers. These measures are also compared with other reported measures from other entities, such as AHRQ National Measures Clearing House and NQF.

Measures must demonstrate relevance, feasibility, and appropriateness. The review process includes a close examination by URAC Measures Advisory Group and URAC Health Standards Committees, as well as other advisory committees. These committee positions are filled by clinicians, providers, consumers, and experts who specialize in these metrics. Those measures are subject to public comment. The process concludes with a final review and adoption by the URAC board of directors.

Measures are divided into the categories of mandatory measures and exploratory measures.

Mandatory Measures
- Required for accreditation
- URAC Annual Report is a requirement

Exploratory Measures
- This might need a little bit of explanation. How are the two connected?
- Unclear as it relates to how to measure the concept
- Organizational reporting is optional

URAC incorporates various performance measures into its accreditation programs. The measures include: Disease Management; Health Plan with Health Insurance Exchange; Health Plan; Specialty Pharmacy; Mail-Service Pharmacy; Drug Therapy Management; Case Management; and Comprehensive Wellness. Organizations with URAC accreditation have a requirement to gather data that tie to the measures and report them each year to URAC by a specific date.

URAC operates a case management accreditation program with a primary focus on enabling health plans to build a program that is actively capable of managing transitions effectively, ultimately supporting the goal of reducing the risk for inpatient admissions as well as having a positive impact on health outcomes. Any organization such as an accountable care organization, hospital, managed care organization, long-term care organization, or behavioral health organization, just to name a few, may apply for URAC accreditation.

Organizations that receive the URAC accreditation can meet the performance measures and standards as set forth by this accrediting body. Case management entities now have the option of pursuing the designation for Transitions of Care. Measures included in the case management area of the URAC accreditation consists of the following domains: medical readmissions; disability and workers' compensation: percentage of those medically released to return to work; timeliness of response to complaints; consumer satisfaction; and a three-item care transition measure.

National Committee for Quality Assurance

NCQA uses HEDIS to accredit and monitor the quality of healthcare delivery activities. HEDIS consists of approximately eighty-one measures, and more than ninety percent of health plans in America use it to gauge the performance of organizations that are associated with care and service. HEDIS measures can improve health plans by identifying opportunities for improvement. HEDIS measures concentrate on health issues that affect Americans, including breast cancer screenings, comprehensive diabetes care, asthma medication use, and beta-blocker treatment following a heart attack.

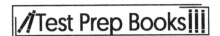

Certified auditors assess the validity of HEDIS results using a NCQA-designed method. HEDIS measures form the basis of health plan report cards. The report card that is available to consumers provides ratings for: access and service; qualified providers; staying healthy; getting better; and living with illness. Organizations submit HEDIS measures via the HEDIS Data Submission System which includes the Healthcare Organization Questionnaire (HOQ) and the Interactive Data Submission System (IDSS).

NCQA works to utilize evidence-based research to improve the quality of healthcare. Accreditation through NCQA enables organizations to demonstrate that they are qualified to provide a higher standard of care and services. Also, as a result of this accreditation, organizations prove that they adhere to regulatory requirements, thus allowing them to stand out from those establishments that are not accredited. NCQA collaborates with state and government entities to create healthcare policies and are always seeking the best way to provide quality care. NCQA is the gold standard of accrediting bodies for various entities including: health plans; provider organizations; health plans' contracting organizations; stand-alone vendors; managed behavioral health organizations; and community care teams.

Health plans seek accreditation from NCQA for different programs, including health plan-specific accreditation, disease management, case management, wellness and health promotion programs, and case management for long-term services and support programs. Health plans may seek NCQA accreditation to support their efforts in not only receiving market advantage but also request-for-proposal requirements.

NCQA provides a report that ranks and reports on various health insurance companies and helps to communicate how well a managed care organization is doing in the prevention of illness. Consumers can use HEDIS to compare the performance of one health plan with another. NCQA utilizes a standard set of performance measures that defines key dimensions of care for individuals with the following conditions: asthma, diabetes, chronic obstructive pulmonary disease, heart failure, and ischemic vascular disease. Also, NCQA reviews influenza and pneumococcal vaccinations along with tobacco use as components of their performance measures framework.

Organizations may have multiple programs that receive accreditation, and they are responsible for the development and operations of these programs. Those who are unable to demonstrate the ability to meet NCQA standards will be denied. Disease management organizations who can meet some or all of the standards may receive accreditation within one of three levels.

The three levels of disease management accreditation are: Accredited, Accredited with Performance Reporting, and Provisional Accreditation. **Accredited** is the highest level of accreditation and tells the industry that an organization either meets or exceeds NCQA standards. Next, **accredited with performance reporting** is the level of accreditation for a disease management organization in which an organization is required to provide reporting of their disease management measures. While the organization did meet or exceed NCQA standards, NCQA still expects to see a report. Finally, **provisional accreditation** alerts the industry that a disease management team does not meet all of the NCQA guidelines or standards.

88

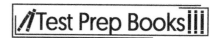

However, provisional accreditation teams do have an opportunity to act within the next twelve months to attain a higher accreditation status.

Case management accreditation requires an organization to demonstrate its ability to guarantee the safe transition of its members between various levels of care and settings. Organizations must show their capacity to not only effectively provide case management services but also to adequately coordinate care. Case management programs receive accreditation based on how their performance compares to NCQA Guidelines and Standards and may dictate the term for which they are accredited. Those organizations who fail to meet NCQA requirements during the Accreditation Survey are denied NCQA status. Agencies may be accredited for a three-year period or receive accreditation for a two-year period. A three-year accreditation is the highest level of accreditation, demonstrates a high level of performance, and is a testimony to the degree of services available.

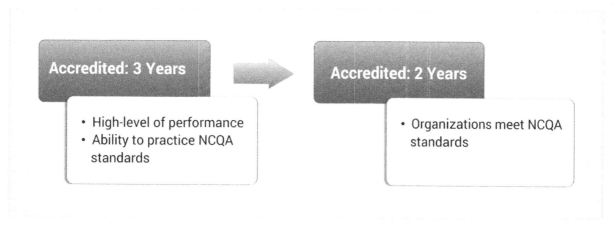

Programs that manage long-term services and supports such as health plans, independent living centers, and case management organizations, are eligible to seek NCQA accreditation for their program. Organizations that demonstrate an ability to manage transitions between levels of care or long-term services and supports (LTSS) settings, the ability to perform quality individualized assessments, and the capacity to handle critical incidents may be eligible for NCQA accreditation. As more and more managed care organizations contract to service this population, NCQA accreditation becomes that much more attractive, as it serves as a testimony to the quality of services that are available to this population and how well the organization is able to facilitate and manage those services.

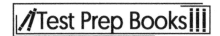
National Quality Forum

The **National Quality Forum** (NQF) mission entails the maintenance of a portfolio of performance measures. These performance measures have the endorsement from the NQF, which allows for the measurement and quantification of healthcare processes, outcomes, patient perceptions, and organizational structures and/or systems that have a direct impact on the ability to deliver high-quality care.

NQF endorses performance measures, best practices, frameworks, and reporting guidelines utilizing a Consensus Development Process (CDP). This process enables NQF to cautiously weigh the needs and interests of various stakeholder groups that represent the healthcare arena.

NQF Quality Measures

Examples of a few Composite NQF quality measures include:

- Comprehensive Diabetes Care: Hemoglobin A1c (HbA1c) Testing
- Comprehensive Diabetes Care: Hemoglobin A1c (HbA1c) Poor Control
- Comprehensive Diabetes Care: Hemoglobin A1c (HbA1c) Eye Exam Performed

Examples of Outcomes NQF quality measures include:

- Acute Stroke Mortality Rate (IQI 17)
- Asthma in Younger Adults Admission Rate
- Bacterial Pneumonia Admission Rate (PQI 11)

Examples of Structure NQF quality measures include:

- Adoption of Medication e-Prescribing
- Cultural Competency Implementation Measure
- Ability to Use Health Information Technology to Perform Care Management at the Point of Care

Examples of Process NQF quality measures include:

- Adherence to Chronic Medications
- Adherence to Statins
- Advance Care Plan
- Age-Related Macular Degeneration (AMD): Counseling on Antioxidant Supplement

NQF allows for public reporting on multiple facets of the healthcare delivery system. The NQF standards are considered to be the "gold standard" in measuring the quality of healthcare.

Hospitals, healthcare systems, and government agencies, including the Centers for Medicare and Medicaid Services, can use performance measures upon endorsement by the NQF for public reporting and quality improvement. In those instances, where a performance metric is not yet in place, a "practice" may serve as a method of providing the necessary structure to evaluate the creation, expansion, and modification of a new or existing program. A practice provides organizations with a pathway for improved outcomes.

NQF uses a set of performance-based standards that multiple groups, including states, the federal government, and private sectors, recognize and utilize in the evaluation of the quality of performance and overall contribution to improving care.

NQF comprises members that represent coalitions, physicians, nurses, hospitals, ancillary agencies, and quality improvement organizations, as well as private and public entities. NQF has a board of directors that has four committees responsible for facilitating NQF activities. Those committees include: The Leadership Network; National Priorities Partnership; Health IT Advisory Committee; and Consensus Standards Approval Committee.

Each committee or group has a distinct role for the work that they perform, and leverages chosen experts to execute tasks that enable standards to be put into place.

The Leadership Network	National Priorities Partnership	Health IT Advisory Committee	Consensus Standards Approval Committee
• Guides program convening • Directs education • Guides recognition programs	• 48 organizations • Healthcare influence	• Guides work around the health IT portfolio • Advisory role for health IT project	• Review of consensus standards • Leverage healthcare quality improvement and performance measures knowledge

NQF utilizes eight member councils to support the tasks of improving the quality of healthcare and building accord. The eight councils include the Consumer Council; the Health Plan Council; the Health Professionals Council; the Provider Organizations Council; the Public/Community Health Agency Council; the Purchasers Council; the Quality Measurement, Research, and Improvement Council; and the Supplier and Industry Council.

Joint Commission Standards and National Patient Safety Goals

Many healthcare organizations utilize **Joint Commission Standards** as a foundation for accreditation. Standards for various aspects of care and patient management are available from the Joint Commission. CCM may use the Joint Commission Standards to monitor for organizational compliance, performance, and outcomes management. The **National Patient Safety Goals** (or NPSGs) were created by the Joint Commission in an effort to provide a method to enhance patient safety for various settings and levels of care. These settings include, but are not limited to, the following: ambulatory health care, behavioral health, home care, hospitals, long-term care, laboratories, and nursing care centers.

Agency for Healthcare Research and Quality

AHRQ provides the opportunity for healthcare improvement by sharing research information that improves the accessibility, effectiveness, efficiency, and quality of health care that consumers receive. For professionals, AHRQ provides access to research data, statistics, and evidence-based best clinical practices that can have a significant impact on those decisions made by clinical professionals. Clinical guidelines can greatly support clinical professionals in their decision-making activities. They serve as a significant tool to reinforce clinical decisions and are sometimes easily accessible to both the patient and the physician.

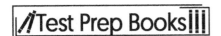

The **National Guideline Clearinghouse™** (NGC) provides healthcare professionals access to a wide variety of clinical practice guidelines. These guidelines are public and readily accessible by both professionals and clients. Therefore, patients also have the ability to access this information and interpret the best potential treatment options and possible risks associated with their condition and treatment. The guidelines are written in a patient-friendly way, making them easy to read and understand. This area of AHRQ provides specific patient-centered outcomes that outline the most effective medical treatments for a particular condition based on current research.

The **United States Preventive Services Task Force** (USPSTF) is composed of national experts who function independently to provide evidence-based recommendations regarding those preventive services that improve the health of Americans, including healthcare screenings, preventative medications, and primary care settings. USPSTF utilizes the expertise of sixteen volunteer members who operate within various fields of primary and preventative care including: behavioral health, nursing, internal and family medicine, obstetrics, and gynecology. AHRQ has a pivotal role in supporting research initiatives in the realm of patient safety and quality improvement. This research provides insight into patient safety threats and the overall impact of medical errors. Research in this area by AHRQ includes medical liability reform, patient safety, and tools to improve performance and patient safety.

AHRQ participates in efforts to reduce **healthcare-associated infections** also known as **HAIs**. With one in twenty-five patients suffering from HAIs, AHRQ supports research initiatives that are designed to identify those methods that organizations can utilize to decrease the risk. As a result of the HAI program, new tools and resources, such as toolkits and checklists, are made available for use by organizations to aid in the task of preventing HAIs and improving patient safety in a variety of settings, including nursing homes, long-term care facilities, and acute care facilities such as hospitals and physician offices.

Core measures enable reporting of quality measures that best align with the improvement of patient outcomes. **Core measures** provide a critical pathway of evidence-based treatments that decrease the risk for complications commonly seen in certain conditions including but not limited to the following: perinatal care, stroke, asthma in children, substance use, and heart failure. CMS publishes groups of core measures and CQMs, also known as clinical quality measures.

The **Health Information Technology for Economic and Clinical Health** (HITECH) Act, which was signed into law by President Obama in 2009 as a component of the American Recovery and Reinvest Act of 2009, was drafted to support and expedite the adoption of EHR-provided incentives to those providers who adopted the implementation and use of EHR systems through 2015. The HITECH Act increases the accessibility and exchange of **Protected Health Information** (PHI) and supports the electronic exchange of health information using EHR and EMR (Electronic Medical Record) information. Under this act, patients or their appointed designees can gain access to their PHI or medical charts in an electronic format, which enables patients to see their complete medical history and provides an enhanced method for information sharing among providers.

Providers and organizations must report security breaches related to electronic PHI (ePHI) as soon as it occurs per established requirements or they will face civil and/or criminal penalties. Also, the HITECH Act calls for physicians and hospitals that have meaningful use attestation to perform a HIPAA (Health Insurance Portability and Accountability Act) security risk assessment. There are three stages of

meaningful use. To move between stages, providers must demonstrate the ability to function within each of the stages for two years before they can proceed to the next one.

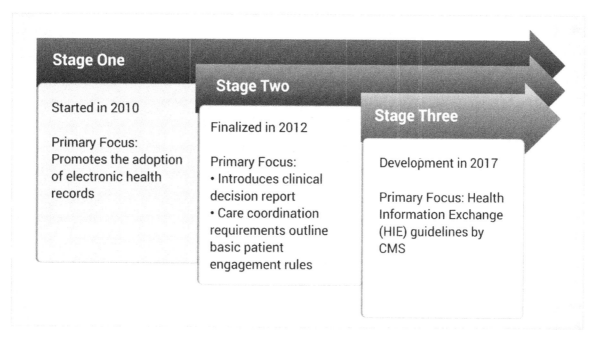

Due to a lack of budget or progress, some organizations have elected to opt out of stage two and stage three. While HIPAA and the HITECH Act are standalone laws, they do have requirements that directly impact the other.

The Agency for Healthcare Research and Quality (AHRQ) uses Quality Indicators (QIs) to measure the quality of healthcare and assist in the identification of quality concerns as well as identify areas of opportunity for additional research and study. AHRQ Quality Indicators are classified into four categories: Prevention QIs; Inpatient QIs; Patient Safety QIs; and Pediatric QIs.

Prevention Quality Indicators

Prevention Quality Indicators (PQIs) are population-driven with some adjustments that are tied to age and gender. PQIs can flag issues that need additional investigation. They are an inexpensive screening mechanism for opportunities to improve care. PQIs highlight access to care challenges and carefully examine community healthcare systems and available outpatient services that can assist in the prevention of inpatient admissions. They form the foundation for evaluating community-based programs that are in place and determining where gaps exist. PQIs also serve as a component of comparative public reporting, trending, and pay-for-performance initiatives.

Examples of PQIs include but are not limited to the following:

- PQI 01 Diabetes Short-term Complications Admission Rate
- PQI 07 Hypertension Admission Rate
- PQI 08 Heart Failure Admission Rate
- PQI 11 Bacterial Pneumonia Admission Rate
- PQI 12 Urinary Tract Infection Admission Rate

Inpatient Quality Indicators

Inpatient Quality Indicators (IQIs) assess the quality of inpatient care. This assessment is done using the data that is a component of a hospital discharge abstract or subset. Indicators that accompany this data include mortality, utilization, and volume.

Examples of IQIs include but are not limited to the following:

- IQI 16 Heart Failure Mortality Rate
- IQI 17 Acute Stroke Mortality Rate
- IQI 19 Hip Fracture Mortality Rate
- IQI 21 Cesarean Delivery Rate, Uncomplicated
- IQI 23 Laparoscopic Cholecystectomy Rate

Inpatient Quality Indicators allow hospitals to identify and target areas for study and investigation. They are representative of the quality of care that is available in a hospital and risks for excessive surgeries, high mortality, and volumes of procedures.

Patient Safety Indicators

Patient Safety Indicators (PSIs) provide information for events such as surgeries, procedures, and childbirth. They allow for an assessment of adverse events incidence and hospital complications. Administrative data commonly found in the discharge record provides this information. The goal of retrieving this information is to enhance the overall safety of patient care delivery.

Patient Safety Indicators provide opportunities for the following:

- Comparative public reporting
- Trending
- Pay-for-performance initiatives
- Identification of avoidable complications

Examples of Patient Safety Indicators include but are not limited to the following:

- PSI 03 Pressure Ulcer Rate
- PSI 13 Post-operative Sepsis Rate
- PSI 14 Post-operative Wound Dehiscence Rate
- PSI 26 Transfusion Reaction Rate
- PSI 27 Perioperative Hemorrhage or Hematoma Rate

Pediatric Quality Indicators

Pediatric Quality Indicators (PDIs) concentrate on potentially preventable complications and errors that affect the pediatric population. **Neonatal Quality Indicators** are also an element of the Pediatric Quality Indicators. The indicators provide a screening of problems that might have otherwise been prevented and also give insight into opportunities for risk adjustment where applicable. Area-level indicators that identify conditions that are preventable with outpatient care, as well as potential safety risks or issues that might take place during the hospital stay, are also examined.

Aspects of care that are measured by CQMs vary. Common areas of the measurement process include: health outcomes, clinical processes, patient safety, use of healthcare resources, timeliness of care coordination, frequency and quality of patient engagements, population and public health, and general

adherence to clinical guidelines. Organizations must submit CQMs to receive incentives associated with the Medicare and Medicaid Electronic Health Record Incentive Program.

National Quality Strategy

The Affordable Care Act required that HHS create a strategy to improve healthcare delivery, so the Agency for Healthcare Research and Quality created the National Quality Strategy (NQS) in 2011. The National Quality Strategy begins with the "Triple Aim" developed by IHI, which seeks to deliver affordable care, increase patient satisfaction, and create healthier communities. To help reach these three aims, the AHRQ further included six priorities which later became six domains. The Six NQS Domains are: Patient Safety; Patient/Family Engagement; Care Coordination and Communication; Effective Clinical Processes, Prevention, and Treatment Practices; Promoting Public Health; and making Quality Care Affordable. CMS aligned with AHRQ to release the CMS Quality Strategy, which uses the same triple aim and six goals to describe their quality strategy.

Types of Quality Indicators

There are multiple types of quality indicators that organizations, hospitals, and professional providers may measure, including clinical, client, financial, productivity, and utilization indicators. Much of the quality indicator data is gathered through various data sources already in place.

Clinical Indicators

Case management programs may leverage a variety of clinical indicators, but they are mainly driven by the type of program in place and the population it is serving. **Clinical indicators** enable case management programs to evaluate the efficiency in which assessments, plans of care, and appropriate treatment protocol are being executed.

While accrediting bodies such as NCQA and URAC may drive certain metrics that are being tracked and managed, case management programs may then use those pre-established metrics to validate those indicators that are monitored and documented closely. This study guide has already highlighted a few examples in which a condition drives the metric. Conditions that have key indicators assigned to them include but are not limited to the following: diabetes, congestive heart failure, stroke, renal failure, HIV, acute myocardial infarction, pneumonia, and hypertension.

Financial Indicators

Financial and utilization indicators are similar if not the same. How organizations choose to use the data are what categorizes the indicator. **Financial indicators** are closely related to cost effectiveness and cost savings. Common metrics consist of a close look at average length of stay, outlier rates, readmission, emergency room diversion, and outpatient services, such as home care. Organizations may also elect to monitor case management costs and the level of skill required to support a case management model. For example, the cost to hire a registered nurse or social worker to facilitate services differs from the cost of hiring a non-licensed employee to facilitate administrative duties, such as entering service requests into a system.

Productivity Indicators

Organizations often track productivity to demonstrate need of services, validate staffing models, and establish client acuity. Data collection of **productivity indicators** for case managers may concentrate heavily on time, tasks, and activities. Each time a case manager completes an activity or task, they enter that information into a case management software that calculates their productivity. For example, an

 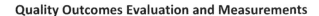
organization may leverage software that calculates the number of times a case manager executes a single task every day with the amount of time it takes to complete that task. The total number of hours is divided into the total hours worked to demonstrate the amount of productivity.

Organizations can collect this information to validate if case managers are as productive as they should be for a case given the acuity of a client, and the data enables leaders to extract reports that allows them to visualize the overall productivity of not only the case manager but departments as well.

Utilization Indicators

Utilization indicators are tracked to not only evaluate the effectiveness of case and disease management programs but general trends and behaviors of the population that is being served. Utilization indicators that are measured to evaluate the overall effectiveness of a program for clients may include an evaluation of multiple elements that include: data that provides month-to-date and year-to-date encounters information by product line for both ambulatory and inpatient services; average length of stay, which provides a comparison of benchmark length of stay detail to that of a facility; emergency department visits; readmissions within 30 days; daily census reporting, which provides an overview of budgeted inpatient days per 1000 to current inpatient days per 1000 with a seven- and thirty-day trend; acute care utilization (e.g., hospitalizations); outpatient services utilization (e.g., home care); and time to access (e.g., potential delays in care). Other indicators under review could include an evaluation of how departments utilize their case management staffing models to support client and provider needs.

Client Experience Indicators

The collection of **client experience indicator** data is pulled from data that is the result of information provided by the client. Data collection may come from surveys or may also be the result of random case reviews. Common dimensions or indicators of the customer's experience are frequently concerning service and providers. While there are a number of subsets that also tie into these two areas such as access, efficiency (timeliness), and engagement by the business owners of various events, most surveys or evaluations will focus on these two items. They examine things such as treatment, communication with professionals, and responsiveness, as well as trustworthiness and cultural sensitivity. Each of these indicators has a significant impact on the client experience and are taken seriously by accrediting bodies.

Evidence-Based Care Guidelines Related to Case Management

Case managers are constantly being tasked with making sure patients are being given high-quality care in a cost-effective way, and to do so efficiently, evidence-based care guidelines should be used. Evidence-based guidelines for common illnesses can help point case managers and teams to where a patient should transition to next, and what resources could be most effective for the patient. Case managers should stay up-to-date on case studies that impact their area of work and use scientific evidence to back up practice. For example, if a new study shows decreased readmission rates when home health and telehealth are used for two weeks post discharge, the case manager must bring this information to their hospital and advocate for this to be the new discharge plan. Avoiding reimbursement penalties for readmission rates may offset the cost of these additional services.

Rehabilitation Concepts and Strategies

Certified case managers (CCMs) will invariably work with individuals requiring rehabilitative care in some form. Whether disabled due to a chronic or acute illness, all patients will benefit from CCM intervention and the formulation of an effective plan of care. One of the primary roles of the case manager is to act as an expert, maintaining a full awareness of the needs of the client as well as the appropriate providers necessary to intervene. Acting as the collaborator, the clinician must form an interdisciplinary team of social workers, psychologists, physicians, physical and occupational therapists, and other ancillary staff to begin the plan for inpatient care and discharge. Through ongoing interaction, the CCM must continually collaborate with the client and interdisciplinary team members to develop a focused approach to manage the case.

When working in an inpatient unit, cases are primarily provided to the CCM through inpatient census reports. Without census reports, CCMs must hope to be alerted to new admissions by walking each unit or maintaining a perch in the emergency room. Alternatively, the clinician reviews the daily census periodically throughout the day as admissions occur, providing CCMs with up-to-the-minute information.

Checking with the charge nurse on each unit and checking the census report daily is helpful, but these techniques will not yield a full list of patients within the diagnosis-related groups (DRGs) that would likely benefit from CCM intervention. The primary DRGs typically referred to the CCM for rehabilitative intervention include but are not limited to: industrial accident victims, amputees, individuals with workplace injuries, burn victims, and those who have sustained a traumatic brain injury (TBI). Based on the census report, the CCM can decide which patients within these groups may need intervention and assistance with discharge planning. Typically, the CCM is responsible for ensuring the patient's appropriate level of care, proving consistent support, and guiding decisions about whether to utilize and exhaust all available financial resources prior to discharge.

Most clients recovering from a workplace injury do plan to return to work, and most can do so within a short period of time. Little, if any, CCM involvement is required for clients with mild injuries or injuries outside of basic coordination of medical benefits to ensure coverage. However, clients who are unable to return to work as expected may face a longer road to recovery. The case manager will typically devote the majority of their time to preparing care plans and following up with clients affected by severe chronic illness and calamitous injuries.

For all of the aforementioned cases, the CCMs must be familiar with the myriad needs of these individuals. The necessary knowledge often includes available assistive devices, functional capacity assessments, ongoing needs post injury, acute versus chronic rehabilitation concepts, occupational rehab delivery systems, vocational considerations related to chronic illness, and permanent disability issues. Through supportive counseling, motivational interviewing, and a largely solution-focused approach, the client can slowly reach their goals. Overall, familiarity with the application of these concepts will be integral in the completion of a working care plan.

Adaptive Technologies

For individuals with pervasive or temporary injuries, it can be difficult to navigate daily life independently. The injury may also impact the client's ability to perform their occupational duties. In an effort to help clients return to a life that mirrors their previous level of functioning as closely as possible,

97

assistive devices are often implemented. **Assistive devices** are utilized for short- or long-term use. Common types improve functional impairment (mobility and self-care aids) or augment sensory impairment (visual, auditory, speech devices). The primary objective is always to steer the patient toward the types of devices that engender self-confidence and increase self-reliance.

Depending on the type and severity of the patient's injury, several assistive devices may be required. The CCM must act as the collaborator and join forces with the patient and associated providers to determine: the type, severity, and impact of the injury; the type(s) of devices needed; and the estimated duration of the injury, which will be directly proportional to the overall costs incurred. For best practice, the CCM must also be knowledgeable of the safety, reliability, and pricing of the apparatus once it is deemed necessary. Acting again as an expert, the CCM must prepare to present the client with the available options. Collecting a list of similar items allows for comparable recommendations, freeing the patient to choose the most efficient and cost-effective devices whenever possible.

Once the list is compiled, the next step is to gauge the member's perceived versus actual needs related to assistive devices, as well as gain an understanding of the environment in which the desired items will be used. A basic understanding of the home and work environments, along with a basic blueprint of the floor plan(s) is helpful. Appropriate questions include: Does the client live in a ranch-style, split-level, or multi-level home? Is there an elevator in the workplace? How far is the client's bedroom from the main entry of the home? Are there any steps to navigate to enter the home and workplace? Does the workplace have wheelchair access or an elevator? How will toileting needs be addressed?

Numerous questions must be asked and answered in order to prepare the best plan for ongoing rehabilitative therapy and return to work. For example, individuals with acute disabilities don't necessarily have similar requirements. An individual who has a broken leg would likely need less recovery time and fewer assistive devices, and have a shorter expected recovery time, than an individual who has broken both legs. Although mobility is affected in both scenarios, the first individual would have an increased probability of performing basic self-care tasks than would someone with two broken legs. Handling crutches, although cumbersome, allows for the patient to navigate their home environment, while two broken legs would result in a bed-bound status, increasing the need for more assistive devices (toileting aids, transfer devices, dressing aids, wheelchair, etc.).

The most effective approach when working with these patients is to periodically assess their perceived needs and confirm that they are being met. As the patient recovers, their needs change and the prudent clinician must remain flexible and prepared to adjust the plan of care accordingly.

An individualized plan may reveal even more pertinent information. The same patient with one broken leg may be single, live alone, and have no social support, requiring additional help such as a folding cane chair. The clinician may need to locate a local service to assist with house cleaning, grocery shopping, and other basic tasks that require more mobility than the member is capable of. Moreover, if that same individual lives in a multi-level home, with narrow halls or carpeting, and is also already physically frail, they may require a less imaginative care plan. Although having two broken legs denotes the need for extensive support, that individual may live with many caring and available family members, indicating less actual need for basic house cleaning and errands. If this same person lives in close quarters, has a shared bedroom, and is physically strong, their care plan would constitute fewer devices and more planning in other areas.

If possible, the case manager should consider the option of encouraging the client to attend support groups for individuals with similar prostheses. Perhaps that individual may also benefit from the clinician

providing instruction to the caregiver regarding the needs of the patient. It is crucial, however, not to guide the client toward any specific decision. Self-determination is paramount in cases such as these, and the client must be allowed to decide if wearing a prosthetic device is an option to consider.

Injuries of a more serious and/or permanent nature will require equally permanent activity and daily living aids. The patient may need hearing aids, text telephone devices (TTD), teletypewriters (TTY), transfer devices (hydraulic lifts, modified or electric stair lifts), or augmentative and alternative communication devices (AAC). The injuries sustained may require the actual purchase of the items, rather than simply renting them.

An orthosis is an item used to correct, support, or improve declining muscle or limb function in a way that restores that function. Specifically, orthoses like braces must be purchased because they require customized design. A prosthesis actually replaces a missing limb or body part for both cosmetic and functional reasons. These two types of assistive devices must be produced by those specifically trained and certified to design, properly fit, and align them for each individual patient. The clinician will need to investigate the training of the prosthetist, the costs of the items, the available insurance coverage, and applicable state and federal assistance programs. A more comprehensive evaluation will likely be necessary in order to procure these items, as they typically require a prescription and assessment and/or evaluation by a licensed health care professional in the specific area of injury.

Functional Capacity Evaluation

Once the nature of the injury, required devices, and client needs are determined, an individualized assessment of the patient is also imperative. A typical **functional capacity assessment** includes an evaluation of an individual's ability to perform basic and job-specific tasks. An interdisciplinary team consisting of physicians, physical therapists (PTs), occupational therapists (OTs), and psychologists collaborate to interview, assess, and diagnose the patient in relation to their ability to perform the duties associated with their current job description and associated activities. The CCM's responsibility is to help locate the appropriate providers, facilitate the necessary appointments, and support the member through the assessment process. With the use of the necessary assistive devices, the member's functional threshold is established. Any deficits in functioning are addressed and, if required for a return to work, added to a PT or OT plan of care.

One of the objectives of the functional assessment is to answer several questions in relation to the injury: Can you do your job? Can you do your job in your current work environment? How well can you do your job in your current work environment? Are the assistive devices truly necessary? Are you able to manipulate the assistive devices, or are they too cumbersome?

The answers to the aforementioned questions help to build a simulation of the type of work environment, average daily tasks, and associated time frames. Baseline performance levels and endurance of treatment are obtained to be compared with the final assessment. Although maximum effort from the patient is expected, the assessment is not meant to be punitive or severe. The PT or OT will typically plan the activities to build upon themselves, progressing in difficulty as the client's mobility and/or range of motion improves. Barriers to the achievement of the most favorable outcome are identified, and strategies to intervene and correct the problems are developed. Once completed, the inventories will guide further intervention and assist the care team in recommending the individual for a return to work.

The clinician must also assess the client's needs as the client perceives them. Do the devices provide aid or support their ability to accomplish the tasks of daily living? Does the patient feel they can perform the necessary tasks with only the devices provided? Has the client considered an alternate occupation if a return to work is not obtained? How supportive is the client's home environment? What, if any, emotional or psychological deficits need to be met? How best can the CCM support the client in working through those concerns? Is the client willing or able to seek out other sources of emotional support through this process?

The answers to these questions are also crucial, as the treatment plan can be adjusted. If the client's needs have changed during the assessment process, those needs can be addressed and added to the plan of care. Whenever necessary, the clinician should involve the family and caregivers in the discussion, so that their concerns can also be addressed. Upon the final report's completion, the case manager then guides the member's return to work, with any assistive devices, prostheses, or orthotics deemed necessary for the member to perform at an optimal level of functioning.

Rehabilitation assessment tools are presented in the following table.

Functional Domains	Tools
Activities of Daily Living (ADL)	Barthel Index (Mahoney and Barthel 1965) FIM™ Instrument (Uniform Data System for Medical Rehabilitation 1997) Katz Index (Katz, et al., 1963) LIFEware℠ System (Baker, et al., 1997)
Ambulation/Locomotion	Dynamic Gait Index (DGI) (Jonsdottir and Cattaneo 2007) Functional Ambulation Profile (FAP) (Nelson 1974) Gait Abnormality Rating Scale (GARS) (Wolfson, et al., 1990) Physical Performance Battery (Guralnik, et al., 1994) Six Minute Walk (Butland, et al., 1982) Timed Up & Go (Podsiadlo and Richardson 1991) Walking Speed (Graham, et al., 2008)
Balance	Berg Balance Scale (Berg, et al., 1989) Balance Self-Perceptions Test (Shumway-Cook, et al., 1997) Functional Reach Test (Duncan, et al., 1990)
Cognitive Functioning	Mini-Mental-State Exam (MMSE) (Folstein, et al., 1975)
Depression	Beck Depression Inventory (BDI) (Beck, et al., 1988) Center for Epidemiologic Studies Depression Scale (CES-D) (Radloff 1977)
Executive Functioning	Stroop Test (Stroop 1935) Trails A & B Tests (Reitan 1955)
Instrumental Activities of Daily Living (IADL)	Everyday Problems Test (EPT) (Willis, et al., 1992) Lawton Index (Lawton and Brody 1969) LIFEware℠ System (Baker, et al., 1997) Pfeffer Index (Pfeffer, et al., 1982)
Memory	Wechsler Memory Scale (Tulsky and Ledbetter 2000)
Pain	McGill Pain Questionnaire (Melzack 1975) Visual Analog Scale (Revill, et al., 1976)
Well-Being/Health-Related Quality of Life (HRQOL)	36-Item Short-Form Health Survey (SF-36®) (Ware and Sherbourne 1992)

Sickness Impact Profile (SIP) (Bergner, et al., 1981)

Rehabilitation Post Hospitalization or Acute Health Condition

Once the functional assessment has been completed with the necessary assistive devices, the next step is to formulate the care plan. At all times, the team must consider how the client will manage their lives in their home and work environments. The interdisciplinary team will determine which type of therapy is best suited to achieve optimal functioning. Equally important is the type of injury. Whether the injury requires occupational therapy or physical therapy, all injuries require a rehabilitation regimen. Generally, workplace injuries are characterized as minor/mild, moderate, severe/calamitous, or fatal.

The majority of minor/mild occupational injuries include cuts and bruises and may require only a brief urgent-care visit. Rehabilitative therapy, if necessary, can typically begin within days and is more likely to be short term. These patients are usually able to return to work quickly with little interruption of, or adjustments to, their workflow and environment. The utilization of assistive devices is often minimal and temporary. Also included in the mild category are repetitive injuries. The most familiar repetitive injury is carpal tunnel syndrome. Largely related to typists, hairdressers, and others who predominantly use their hands in repetitive motions, these patients can move swiftly into the moderate category if they continue to work in the same occupation. The CCM will work with all of these members to determine how quickly they can return to work and utilize their paid time off (PTO) to offset any time away from work (TAFW) as needed. These cases typically require less intervention.

When a workplace injury is moderate, requiring an ambulance transport and/or emergency room visit, more extensive planning and follow up are required. Moderate injuries can include but are not limited to slip and falls, sprains, strains, back injuries, and broken bones. Although these types of injuries will require immediate medical attention, once stabilized, these patients usually are able to return to work within a short, specified amount of time.

The case manager can advocate for the member to receive Family Medical Leave (FMLA) if necessary, and supplemental pay for TAFW. Other state and federal legislation such as the Consolidated Omnibus Budget Reconciliation Act (COBRA) may be applicable in cases like these. The application of the rules of COBRA would provide the client with continued medical benefits should they be unable to return to work.

For rehabilitative purposes, these patients will usually be given a list of restrictions and exercises to complete while recovering briefly at home. The essential work tasks to complete are the general focus of these interventions. The patient will meet with the physical therapist, occupational therapist, and/or physician to retrieve a "return to work" memorandum once cleared.

As the fatal injury requires no rehabilitative efforts, the next most significant area of concern for the CCM is the enormous classification of serious/catastrophic injury. For severe/calamitous occupational injuries, the member will not only need immediate medical attention, but a hospital admission for observation and additional treatment. The CCM's responsibility is to work in partnership with the patient, family members, and interdisciplinary team at the hospital in order to formulate the best short-term and long-term plan of care. A short list of these types of injuries includes: closed/open head injuries, machine-related crushing accidents, inclement-weather exposure, chemical-related accidents/spills, and electrocutions. Once the client's overall level of functioning is gauged, this will guide the CCM, patient, family members, and inpatient team to determine the most appropriate level of post-discharge care.

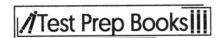

Unfortunately for patients requiring rehabilitative services after their initial medical hospitalization, the road to recovery is long and arduous. Workplace injuries and acute-illness management are treated similarly. An innumerable number of diagnostic tests and periodic functional assessments will occur during their inpatient stay in rehab. The CCM will work together with the inpatient team to periodically assess the patient's progress and adjust the care plan as needed. All aspects of daily living will be assessed regarding the patient's ability to perform self-care tasks and the degree to which that individual is prepared to return to the community. Emotional, physical, sensory, and processing deficits are also targeted.

These patients will receive a specialized discharge plan intended to complement their current level of independence. The majority of their rehabilitative discharge plan of care will act as scaffolding, remaining in place until the individual has been returned to an optimal level of functioning. For example, an individual who experienced a traumatic brain injury (TBI) as a result of a fall or industrial accident would likely be cared for initially in a regular hospital until cleared by their physician to undergo the intensive therapies of a rehabilitation center or hospital. Once the physical injuries have healed, the next task is to focus on the emotional, physical, and sensory aspects of the injury. Many of these patients experience substantial memory loss, poor coordination or spatial recognition, inability to process language or ideas, and difficulty verbalizing feelings or ideas.

For example, an individual with a frontal-lobe injury will likely experience difficulties with aggression or promiscuity. Damage in this area often results in a failure to inhibit emotions. If asked to make a sandwich, the individual may become overwhelmed with the details of the task, responding with frustration. Whereas someone without a TBI may become frustrated, they would likely possess the ability to inhibit a reflexive aggressive outburst. An individual with a cerebellar brain injury may be unable to hold the tools necessary to even complete the task.

Depending on the types of skills that need to be relearned, the CCM must continually support the patient and the family, providing assurance of the care plan while also delivering a realistic evaluation of the member's progress. Recovery for these patients can be slow, frustrating, and confusing. Periodic discussions regarding the client's motivation to continue are often required. These patients tend to require extensive services and ongoing rehabilitation either on an outpatient basis or with subsequent transfer to their home setting, an assisted-living facility, a subacute rehabilitative facility, or long-term skilled nursing care. Each treatment milieu builds from its predecessor, slowly integrating the member back into society.

Vocational and Rehabilitation Service Delivery Systems

For the vast majority of more serious cases, the patient will likely continue to receive extensive evaluation once discharged from the hospital. It is incumbent upon the CCM to ensure that this care continues uninterrupted; for this to occur, payment of the required services must be obtained. Individuals receiving rehabilitative services are engaged in a "system" consisting of a group of health care providers, the actual care setting, and the services themselves. This system implies that the community as a whole must be integrated into the care plan. All aspects of the patient's life must be reviewed in regard to the new disability. Care coordination with the correct entities is vital at this stage. Care can be delivered on a fee-for-service basis, through tele-health, managed care, or self-directed care.

In a **fee-for-service system**, providers are paid based on the specific services they provide. Each instance is paid separately, with reimbursement commensurate with the federally acceptable guidelines. This

type of care is considered to be the most traditional and is utilized most often. It is performed in-person and occurs at some point throughout the life of every case. For example, providers are generally reimbursed for diagnostic tests, office visits, consultations, and specific procedures.

Tele-health is quickly becoming one of the most popular modalities with both health professionals and patients. The use of technology in the provision of health care is both convenient and cost effective. Patient-provider interactions are conducted over the telephone or through the computer. Members self-report symptoms, concerns, and reactions to medications or services.

Managed health care delivery involves an organization enlisted to monitor the costs and utilization of care. The managed-care organization (MCO) serves as the gatekeeper, with a predetermined allotment for services per member, otherwise known as capitation. Through applying capitation, MCOs preserve resources and prevent misuse or abuse of those resources.

These systems of delivery have two important functions. First, at the federal level, certain services are categorized as mandatory. These types of services represent basic care needs, are nonnegotiable, and include inpatient and outpatient hospitalization, in-home services, and family planning. Second, there is an allowance for the states to determine which non-compulsory services will be covered. Some of the features of the latter include podiatric care, optometry, and chiropractic care. Unfortunately, physical and occupational therapies are also on the list of optional services. The CCM must work in collaboration with the member's medical insurer and health care providers to coordinate payment for services. Whenever possible, the clinician must act as an advocate on behalf of the client to maintain the continuity of care.

Vocational Aspects of Disability(ies) and Illness

The **Americans with Disabilities Act** (ADA) expressly forbids discrimination by employers toward the hiring, firing, or unequal treatment of any individual with a qualifying disability. This prohibition includes accessibility to: education, transportation, employment, public places, and recreational activities. Any employer found to be in violation of the ADA can face a minimum fine in civil cases of $55,000 and a maximum of $150,000.

Formally, a **disability** is defined as a psychological or medical condition that reduces a person's functional capacity in at least one area of the body. When a client with a disability is returning to work, they will likely need accommodations in order to perform their job. To ensure the client's return to work, the CCM must compare the functional assessment to the formal job description of the client. It is crucial to utilize the functional assessment at this stage and ensure the employer does not alter expectations to prevent the client's return to work. If, upon comparison of the essential job functions and the functional assessment, the CCM is able to determine that the client does qualify as disabled, the next step is to arrange reasonable accommodations.

At times, even after completing physical and occupational therapies, the client is not yet ready to return to work, even if accommodations are provided. For example, a bus driver recovering from injuries related to a vehicular accident may have regained the use of their extremities after traditional treatment, but residual injuries may still remain. That same individual may continue to suffer from chronic back pain from sitting and driving for hours, or experience anxiety or post-traumatic stress disorder (PTSD), including flashbacks of the incident when driving or in a vehicle.

103

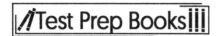

To ease an individual back into the physical demands of their job, ergonomics may be used. Ergonomics is the science of matching the physical requirements of a job to the physical abilities of the worker. Musculoskeletal injuries can occur if physical demands are greater than the employee's physical capabilities. Body mechanics refers to how the body moves during activities of daily living. Understanding and practicing the use of proper body mechanics is imperative to preventing injury. Ergonomic devices such as special seat pads, back braces, or pillows can be provided to ease physical demands and reduce the risk of injury. If these additions do not cause relief, more therapies may be required. In this instance, a work-hardening program is the next logical step.

Also referred to as "functional restoration" or "work conditioning," work-hardening programs were created as a bridge between where the medical treatment ends and where the client's work environment begins. The CCM must assemble a team from a variety of specialties: ergonomics, prosthetics, physical and occupational therapy, and psychology. With the team in place, it is also necessary to confirm that the employer agrees to allow the client to return to work. The CCM must confirm the client knows they will not be forced to return to work unprepared. Although the client may be emotionally ready to return to work, they may not be physically able to do so. The goal is to provide a simulated work environment and gradually reintroduce the client to specific tasks and activities directly associated with the position to which they will be returning.

In the above example, the member may be asked to sit with the use of the ergonomic assistive devices (such as a specially designed chair or chair pad) for minutes, then hours, gradually building up to the specified time expected to complete a shift. The psychologist on the team can then work directly with the member to address PTSD and/or anxiety through cognitive behavioral therapy, positive self-talk, or affirmations. Throughout the duration of the treatment, the team will be working toward the goal of helping the member reach the functional capability to return to work.

Rehabilitation Concepts

As case managers attempt to move their patients along the continuum of care, they should be familiar with rehabilitation concepts. A major role of case managers is to educate patients on their available benefits so that they will be able to receive services whenever they move to the next step along the continuum.

The case manager should have a working knowledge of what qualifies a patient for inpatient versus outpatient rehabilitation. For patients to qualify under CMS for inpatient medical rehabilitation facilities, patients must be able to actively participate in multiple therapies for a total of three hours per day, five days per week, with providers documenting the benefits they expect to see from this rehabilitation.

The case manager must evaluate the patient and know the most appropriate types of facilities available for referral. For example, many medical rehabilitation facilities require that patients not be ventilator dependent and that they do not frequently require urinary catheterization as part of their guidelines for admission. The case manager must work with the patient, the patient's family, the provider, and the rest of the disciplinary team to present rehabilitation options that the family can choose from.

Vocational rehabilitation is an individualized program for employment designed to help patients with a disability return to the labor force. Vocational rehab includes services such as counseling, training, job placement, assistive technology, and career exploration. Each state offers different services, and some include independent living programs, so case managers should be aware of services offered in their state to help make appropriate referrals.

Substance use rehabilitation may be needed for patients at many points along the continuum. Funding for substance use rehab is often a difficult hurdle to overcome and varies greatly state by state. If patients have health insurance, contacting the insurer for possible participating facilities may be useful. Case managers should be aware of local substance use rehabs. Some rehabs accept Medicare and Medicaid, and some facilities are willing to charge on a sliding scale for fees. The U.S. Department of Health and Human Services offers the SAMHSA website, which has a behavioral health treatment services locator. Case management services are needed for patients with substance use disorder because these patients often suffer further from lack of coordinated services and other health and social problems.

Job Analysis, Job Accommodation, and Job Modification

Rehabilitation Job Analysis

A job analysis is not a test one has to take, but instead is the practice of gathering information to define a person's job requirements and related job responsibilities, both essential and nonessential. This information is gathered from interviews with current workers, from observations of the work being done, and from assessing other position's descriptions within the company. A job analysis is used to assess the major requirements of the position, including the physical, mental, and behavioral demands of the position. Job analyses are also used to assess work scheduling, locations of the work being done, and equipment needed in order to perform the job successfully.

For patients in rehabilitation programs, the purpose of a job analysis is to determine the essential requirements of the job necessary to effectively perform the required tasks. It is important to keep in mind that the job requirements should be the main focus during this process. Individual patient's skills would be addresses further into the rehabilitation process.

A rehabilitation job analysis can be performed within one discipline or within an interdisciplinary rehabilitation team. The following are the most common disciplines that regularly perform these job analyses:

Physical Therapists
Occupational Therapists
Vocational Rehabilitation Specialists
Ergonomists

Job Modifications and Job Accommodation

It might be easy to assume the phrases, job modification and job accommodation, to be interchangeable. However, these terms focus on different aspects of an individual's needs and the requirements of a job.

A job modification involves changing the actual job description based on the individual's skills. This could look like reconstructing the job, eliminating certain job functions, dividing the responsibilities between additional workers, or even adapting the company policy.

Job accommodations focus on making the work more accessible. This could look like incorporating voice recognition technology or even incorporating an adjustable desk to accommodate a wheelchair bound worker. In order for a worker to receive accommodations in the workplace, there is a process they must go through:

105

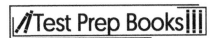

Requesting Accommodation: In order to start the accommodation process, the individual with the disability must voice their needs and request the accommodation(s).

Identify Functional Limitations: The next step is to identify the individual's functional limitations and determine where those cross with the required job duties. This way, the individual does not have to perform those duties without an appropriate accommodation.

Identify Potential Accommodations: Next, the accommodation options are discussed with the employee. Sometimes the necessary accommodation can be obvious, but other times it may require some creative thinking, investigation/research, or even outside assistance. Both employee and employer can also consult with the Job Accommodations Network (JAN) to get either more information or ideas for accommodations. JAN works to help individuals with disabilities highlight their employability and showcase their skills and value in the workplace.

The Americans with Disabilities Act (ADA) lists six categories for accommodations outside of adjustment to physical equipment and modifications:

1. Job Restructuring-Altering work procedures

2. Assistive Devices-Equipment or technology that assists the employee with completing their responsibilities

3. Training-Teach an employee the job responsibilities

4. Personal Assistant-Person to assist the employee with their job responsibilities

5. Building Modification-Adjustments to the physical environment that make it more accessible for the individual

6. Job Reassignment-Transferring a task to another employee either temporarily or permanently, or dividing the job between employees

Determining Reasonable Solutions: Employers are required by the ADA to provide the most reasonable accommodations for an individual with a disability unless providing the accommodation would result in undue hardship. Undue hardship can look like financial difficulty for the company, disrupting the workplace, or even fundamentally changing business operations.

Making the Accommodation: While the employee's preferences should-and most likely will be-taken into account, the employee will ultimately decide which accommodation(s) can be applied based on cost, feasibility, and overall effectiveness.

Monitoring Effectiveness: Once the accommodation(s) goes into effect, the employer and employee should monitor its effectiveness, making adjustments as needed. If the desired outcome is still not realistic or achieved, then the employer and employee should restart the process.

Life Care Planning

Life Care Plan

Life care planning is a way to ensure that a patient (with disabilities) is being taken care of and will be taken care of in the future. A life care plan (LCP) is a document based on comprehensive assessment,

data, and research which makes up a specific plan for the current and future needs of a person with a disability.

Many factors are considered for inclusion in an LCP. These include:

Evaluations
Therapies
Testing
Medical/adaptive equipment/technology
Aids
Medications, prescription and non-prescription
Home care
Transportation
Surgical needs
Any potential complications

A procedure must be followed in order to gather information for developing an LCP. This includes conducting an interview with the client and their family members, going over medical records and any supporting documents, any life videos, school documents, employment records, and any tax return information, consulting with treatment experts, and lastly, researching the costs and reasonable sources for any necessary treatments.

Life care planners consists of a variety of rehabilitation professionals including nurses, counselors, occupational therapists, physical therapists, social workers, physicians, and even psychologists. Some associations for LCPs include: the International Academy of Life Care Planners (IALCP), the American Association of Nurse Life Care Planners (AANLCP), and the American Academy of Physician Life Care Planners (AAPLCP).

Medical Cost Projection

A Medical Cost Projection (MCP) consists of funds that have been devoted to future medical expenses, regardless of Medicare coverage. The creation of an MCP can occur at any point during treatment, is assessed based on reviewing medical records and provider communication, and includes medical research to cover a portion of the care. Some qualities of an MCP include:

May be limited
Used in less severe types of injuries
May only be requested for one procedure
Is not a legal document; is an abbreviated document of some sort (letter, report, email, etc.)
Requires less time than an LCP to complete
Can be referred from attorneys or insurance adjusters
Used to prepare for a settlement or for testifying in court

Medicare Set Aside

A Medicare Set Aside (MSA) devotes a certain amount from a worker's (compensation) settlement to cover all future work-related medical costs, covered and reimbursed by Medicare. An MSA is put in place to protect Medicare during a worker's compensation settlement.

There are three essential elements for an MSA:

- **Medical Allocation**: This is the line-item listing of treatment and prescriptions covered by Medicare. This listing would include information on the frequency, dosage, costs and more.

- **Sum to Structure**: Funded as either a lump-sum or structured annuity

- **Administration**: When administering the MSA funds, it is recommended that settlement receives use

The National Medicare Secondary Payer (MSP) Network, previously known as the National Alliance of Medicare Set-Aside Professionals (NAMSAP), is a non-profit organization that exclusively addresses the challenges of the Medicare Secondary Payer Statute, legislation making Medicare the secondary payer for certain primary care plans.

Work Adjustment, Transitional Employment, and Work Hardening

Work adjustment, transitional employment, and work hardening are programs in place to help individuals with disabilities or work-related injuries be as effective as possible in their given role(s) without jeopardizing the individual's condition.

Work Adjustment

Work adjustment can be defined as using real or simulated work activity at a rehabilitation center to foster appropriate behaviors, attitudes, or characteristics. This may involve work adjustment training, a program for individuals whose disabilities might inhibit them competing for employment in the workforce. This would usually involve goal directed services to improve areas like attendance, stamina, dress, hygiene, and even interpersonal relationships. Services would continue until either all the goals have been met or until significant, noticeable progress has been made.

Transitional Employment

Transitional employment, or Transitional Work Duty (TWD), can be implemented when an employee has been injured and is unable to perform their normal job functions but are still able to work in a different capacity. An employer must conform the work to meet the individual's physician's restrictions. Additionally, only employees with impermanent injuries are eligible for TWD. Meaning, so long as an employee has temporary injuries, is still able to work, and plans to return to their normal duties, they will qualify for TWD.

Work Hardening

Work hardening can be defined as a rigidly structured, goal-oriented, and personalized intervention process providing the individual with a smooth transition between their injured stage to their safe, productive return to their previously normal work. The focus is to capitalize on a person's ability to safely work without increasing the chance for repeated injury. Like work adjustment, work hardening programs use real or simulated activities to help rehabilitate the worker's functions physically, behaviorally, and vocationally.

Ethical, Legal, and Practice Standards

For the certified case manager, it is vital to possess a working knowledge of the basics of employer, local, state, and federal requirements for the care and maintenance of individuals affected by workplace injuries. This knowledge, combined with evidence-based decision-making, is integral in formulating an appropriate care plan and ensuring coverage for that care. Certain state and federal legislations require very specific accommodations for persons with disabilities, and benefits can be immediate. Specifically, all CCMs must at least be acquainted with the concepts of evidence-based practices regarding treatment guidelines, ethical considerations, regulatory requirements, privacy/confidentiality issues, risk management, and the overall scope of their practice.

Case Recording and Documentation

It is imperative that the CCM maintain immaculate and accurate case records. **Records** contain the chronological life of the case and provide a detailed description of and justification for services recommended and rendered. This is necessary due to a possible audit of the records by the responsible employer or other interdisciplinary team members and possible litigation. For example, if an employer decided to dispute the stipulations in a previously agreed upon return to work, the clinician can refer to the case file to negotiate. Accurate record keeping can also guide the interventions of an alternate CCM if the primary clinician is unavailable. Any planned or unexpected absence would not derail the progression of the case. Throughout the life of every case, the CCM will communicate with various providers, family members, and clients. Whenever possible, the CCM can record the sessions, as well as take notes, in an effort to ensure that no information is lost.

All case files require specific information to be considered complete. First, **basic demographic information** such as the client's name, past medical history, current diagnoses, medications, and contact information are required. Next, the clinician must **document the plan of care**, including the discharge plan and contingency plan if the patient decompensates unexpectedly. Also important to include in the client's case file is a **basic needs analysis**. The needs analysis is an outcropping of the functional assessment but also includes the client's perceived needs and hopes regarding the outcome of their treatment. As previously mentioned, all patient and provider communication is essential, with coinciding dates and times if available. Finally, it is crucial that the **cost of treatment** with and without case management be included. This is an extension of informed consent. This stipulation allows the client to consider the financial and medical advantages and disadvantages of working with the CCM and allows the client to make their decision based on all available information.

The certified case manager can maintain case-file information in various ways, like paper documents, audio or visual recordings, or a specific document management system (DMS). This type of record keeping utilizes a computer program that operates as a filing system. Several different formats exist with the goal of streamlining documentation while gleaning significantly more information to track clients' progress and outcomes and to later evaluate interventions. Reports can be quickly generated, and specific functions allow for multiple clients to be tracked for program evaluation purposes or trends with regards to diagnosis-related groups. These reports can then impact future interventions based on the successes garnered through work with similar clients.

In addition to the information in each specific client's file, the CCM must clearly delineate the supervision and/or consultation received on each case. This type of documentation shows that the clinician was not making decisions in a vacuum but in collaboration with other experienced colleagues. It

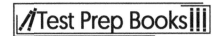

is also important to cite all evidence-based bodies of knowledge, periodicals, seminars, articles, and books utilized in the care of clients. Verifying that the interventions provided by the clinician are evidence based and current is both necessary and professional. Appropriate documentation of consultations helps to provide a clear and logical template of the plan of care should case files be audited.

Case managers frequently receive reports for the clients on their caseload. The majority of these reports include: a copy of the proposed plan of care, the client's progress with treatment, any actual barriers to achieving the necessary tasks to complete the plan of care, solutions to remove any deficits in functioning, and current cost analysis. These reports allow for the CCM to observe the client's progress over time, recognize any trends, and communicate effectively regarding the care plan with the patient and interdisciplinary team.

Ethics Related to Care Delivery

When providing consultation and case management, the CCM will inevitably encounter cases that present an ethical dilemma. Some of the most common dilemmas presented to the CCM include the client's refusal of services/treatment, experimental treatments and protocols, and end-of-life decisions. In these types of situations, the CCM must weigh the advantages and disadvantages of the proposed treatment in order to guide the patient to make an informed decision.

One of the preferred techniques to utilize when working with clients is motivational interviewing. This method is especially effective when working with clients who are struggling with ambivalence, or indifference, to beginning treatment. **Motivational interviewing** is a coaching technique that involves asking a series of open-ended and probing questions while summarizing the client's responses. As the client responds to the questions, they clarify their motivations and most desirable outcomes. The client's own words become the primary tool for building the plan of care. The CCM must also affirm the client's ability to verbalize their own goals. The main objective of this technique is to use the client's own words to help determine if the plan actually aligns with their verbalized goals.

Encountering the **refusal of treatment** by a client can be difficult to navigate. It is the task of the CCM to evoke not only the client's reason for declining treatment but to also determine what other options, if any, exist that would guide the client to a similar or more desirable outcome. For example, consider the dilemma of working with a patient that experienced a crushing injury that required a total left-knee replacement (TKR) who is also a Jehovah's Witness. For the majority of patients who undergo TKR, post-operative blood transfusions are warranted. It is widely known that Jehovah's Witnesses do not accept allogenic, or blood from a compatible donor, transfusions. Typically, the CCM would have the benefit of basic demographic information, including gender, marital status, and religious affiliations.

In this circumstance, the CCM would need to prepare an alternative intervention for the client, prior to the presentation. Enlisting the assistance of the orthopedic surgeon and hematologist, the CCM would be able to determine if autologous, or collection and reinfusion of the client's own blood components, would be an acceptable option. Once an alternative to the traditional option of allogenic blood transfusion is prepared, both can be presented to the client. In so doing, the clinical care team is not only providing full disclosure but also practicing with an open awareness of their client's religious convictions. Ultimately, it is the client who must decide the result; the CCM must honor that choice as long as there is no harm to come to the client as a result of that choice.

An additional ethical dilemma encountered by the CCM directly related to rehabilitative medicine is the decision of whether or not to utilize experimental treatments. Consider the same patient with a crushing knee injury. For this example, the individual is not a Jehovah's Witness and did agree to receive the transfusion. This client must weigh the decision of accepting a traditional prosthetic limb versus living life with a transplanted cadaver limb. The CCM in this situation must consider the client's autonomy, allowing the patient to determine which option to accept. Consideration of the client's hesitance to accept a cadaver limb is crucial. The CCM may suggest that the client attend support groups for amputees, consider being counseled on the available research involving the transplantation of the cadaver limb, or talking with their clergy for spiritual guidance.

For end-of-life versus palliative-care concerns, especially where no advance directives are present, the CCM must follow state statutes and consult the legal next of kin. When advance directives are present, the CCM must preserve the client's autonomy and honor their wishes.

Ethics Related to Professional Practice

Certified case managers are required by the dictates of their licensing board to provide compassionate, ethical, and professional care at all times. The **Case Management Society of America** (CMSA) formulated a specific plan to address ethical concerns routinely faced by CCMs.

The **five basic ethical principles** are shown in the following graphic.

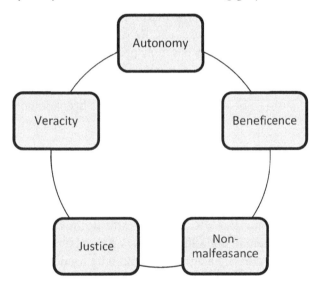

The generous application of these guiding principles is crucial to maintain a cohesive relationship between the CCM and the client. Although every human being has their own personal biases, morals, and values, the clinician must cast them aside, as much as possible, in order to provide clinically competent care. For the CCM, the roles of professional, advocate, communicator, and clinically competent collaborator come into focus.

Certified case managers must always conduct themselves in a professional manner. More importantly, it is vital that the CCM practices within the law. In order to do this, the clinician must obtain prior informed consent from the client or other responsible party. To be valid, the informed consent must contain a full explanation of the information needed to provide support, allow for the patient to specify a time frame for which the agreement is in effect, and evidence the signature of a third party to confirm

the patient was not in duress at the time the contract was signed. It is the responsibility of the CCM to periodically evaluate the client's comfort level with the services received and confirm that expectations for ongoing care are clearly outlined.

Once the initial plan of care is agreed upon, the first step is for the CCM to enlist the member to identify their most crucial needs. By encouraging the member to be **autonomous**, the clinician is placing the client in the position to develop the confidence necessary to trust themselves to articulate their needs effectively. The member may articulate emotional issues or concerns that require the intervention of a psychologist for ongoing psychotherapy and/or prescribed medications. This strategy also teaches the member how to develop an internal locus of control, leading to the establishment of a foundation of self-confidence on which to build. During this process, the stage of change that the member is grappling with becomes clear. Having moved beyond precontemplation, through contemplation and goal-setting in the preparation phase, the member is slowly steered into action. In this instance, the clinician is acting in the roles of both communicator and advocate, placing the client in the position to utilize their own voice in setting the goals for recovery.

Both **beneficence** and **nonmalfeasance** are closely related. It is not enough to provide empathetic and compassionate care. The CCM must also continually evaluate the plan of care so as not to inadvertently cause harm. The notion of **justice** combines the ideas behind beneficence and nonmalfeasance, along with practicing in an ethically sound manner. Fundamental to every relationship is the expectation of fair treatment. There are additional considerations for the CCM regarding ethical service delivery. The expectation of receiving appropriate care is bolstered by the trust that has developed from previous interactions with the clinician. Acting as a collaborator, the CCM is focused on guiding the client to work toward viable solutions and to act. Practicing **veracity** is simply providing solution-focused options that are grounded in reality and truth. This technique is more pronounced in the relationship between the client and the CCM as time passes. Further, because of the trust required by the client to allow another individual to guide their decisions, failure to be authentic can result in a breakdown in the patient-client relationship.

Health Care and Disability Related Legislation

An innumerable amount of state and federal mandates, policies, and regulations govern how patients are to receive rehabilitative services. Other legislation was adopted to monitor the administration of financial support. The CCM must actively navigate the applicable statutes for each client and manage the team's approach to exhausting all available benefits. The myriad number of disability and health care laws will not be discussed in full, but additional information can be found at https://www.disability.gov/health-related-laws/. Some of the most notable statutes regarding disability are discussed below.

Americans With Disabilities Act (ADA)

The **Americans with Disabilities Act** (ADA) is one of the most significant pieces of legislation relating to persons with disabilities is Section 504 of the Rehabilitation Act of 1973. This civil rights legislation prohibits discrimination against persons with disabilities in programs that receive federal funding and led to the creation of the Americans With Disabilities Act (ADA) of 1990. The ADA was enacted to enforce strict sanctions on those who discriminate against persons who have a documented history of a disability, are viewed as having a disability, or are diagnosed with a mental or physical condition that has resulted in functional impairment. The prudent clinician will utilize the ADA when securing appropriate accommodations for their patients.

Family Medical Leave Act of 1993 (FMLA)

The Family Medical Leave Act of 1993 (FMLA) was written to allow for individuals to take an unpaid leave of absence to care for ill family members for a maximum of twelve weeks per calendar year while pre-servicing their medical benefits at up to 102% of the cost of their original employer premium.

The Health Insurance Portability and Accountability Act of 1996 (HIPAA)

The **Health Insurance Portability and Accountability Act** of 1996 (HIPAA) was enacted to remedy a number of issues faced by American citizens seeking medical coverage. This law provides the following: **Title I** focuses on portable health benefits, meaning that individuals with pre-existing conditions cannot be fired or lose coverage when renewing benefits; **Title II** is meant to curtail fraud and abuse of power by insurance companies and imposes strict requirements that personal health information be protected and confidential; **Title III** created optional savings accounts designed to offset medical care costs and lowered the cost of annual premiums paid by consumers; **Title IV** authorizes the Office of Civil Rights to enforce all provisions of this law; and **Title V**, "Revenue offsets" deals with regulations on how employers can deduct company-owned life insurance premiums for income tax purposes.

Workforce Innovation and Opportunity Act of 2014 (WIOA)

The establishment of the **Workforce Innovation and Opportunity Act** WIOA improved upon the Workforce Investment Act of 1998 and resulted in provisions to increase vocational training and job placement for disabled individuals. The clinician's application of the rules within this legislation is crucial in securing a return to work for clients.

Employee Retirement Income Security Act of 1974 (ERISA)

The **Employee Retirement Income Security Act** (ERISA) is a federal law that seeks to ensure that insurance companies adhere to very strict turn-around times when processing disability claims. Although the initial intent was to standardize basic coverage for disabled persons, this act has expanded over time to serve as a platform for insurers to deny coverage, as long as that denial of benefits falls within the law. Clients usually have to file an appeal in writing to any denied claim for medical benefits within sixty days of receiving the notification in the mail. Any claims submitted after that time do not legally have to be honored. The CCM must be aware of this common tactic to initially deny disability claims then pursue an appeal and exhaust the appeals process.

COBRA

Clinicians must also be familiar with the **Consolidated Omnibus Budget Reconciliation Act** (COBRA) of 1986. This piece of legislation allows individuals to maintain their medical benefits in the event of unexpected loss of employment, whether voluntary or involuntary. The employer bears the responsibility of notifying the client of their eligibility for COBRA once employment is terminated. Notification generally occurs within two weeks after job loss. The enrollment period is sixty days and is a continuation of the employer's elected benefits packages, including dental, vision, and medical. The advantage to the client is that they can elect to maintain only the specific coverage that they need.

Specifically related to rehabilitation, this act allows for the employee, spouse, or dependent children to continue to receive medical coverage for a minimum of eighteen months and a maximum of thirty-six months. However, the premiums must be paid and can reach as much as 102% of the annual premium. Premature termination of this benefit can occur if the premiums are unpaid, the client becomes eligible for Medicare, the employer is unable to maintain the group plan, or the client acquires alternate employer-based coverage.

Mental Health Parity Act Rehabilitation Act of 1996

Mental Health Parity Act Rehabilitation Act of 1996 was established to prevent the discrimination against individuals with mental health problems. This is a federal law that strictly prohibits placing financial caps of mental health treatments unless those same limits also apply to medical benefit coverage.

Occupational Safety and Health Administration (OSHA)

OSHA began in 1970 as a way to enforce occupational safety concerns. OSHA works together with certain parts of the Americans with Disabilities Act to ensure that employees have rights, protection, and compensation.

Affordable Care Act

The **Patient Protection and Affordable Care Act** (PPACA), often referred to as **Obamacare**, ensures that all patients receive the necessary health care services at reasonable costs. Conceptualized by President Barack Obama, the PPACA was officially declared law on March 23, 2010. The law created an open marketplace in which patients are free to choose from a variety of different insurers, intended to exemplify capitalism at its best. The PPACA was not only developed to provide American citizens with appropriate health care, no matter their financial status, it was also created to aid small-business owners by providing an incentivized system. Individuals are able to secure basic medical benefits through their employer, directly through insurance companies, or in the health insurance marketplace. These marketplaces, or health care exchanges, create an opportunity for clients and their families to obtain the most affordable coverage with fewer opt-out clauses for insurers.

A specific website, or portal, was developed to allow easy access to compare the different plans. Once the individual enters their demographic and financial information into the system, they are presented with several appropriate and comparable coverage options. The PPACA was enacted to ensure certain benefits are treated as indispensable. They include but are not limited to: maternity and infant care; dental and vision care; hospitalizations; emergent and outpatient services; mental health; preventative care; and rehabilitative services. When the client chooses their preferred plan, they are allowed to access the associated hospitals, providers, and physicians that have agreed to provide care to the patients that have chosen that particular health care plan, also known as the "network."

Since its beginning, the PPACA has been challenged in court for its constitutionality. In 2012, the provision that stated citizens must have a minimum level of health insurance or pay a penalty was upheld in NFIB v. Sebelius. The 2017 Tax Cuts and Jobs Act changed the payment that the provision required for failure to maintain insurance to zero dollars. This led to a group of states, led by Texas, to again challenge the PPACA, in a case known as California vs. Texas. In December of 2019, The U.S Court of Appeals for the 5th circuit ruled that that provision was unconstitutional. The Supreme Court will now review the decision to decide whether reducing the amount of minimum coverage to zero makes this unconstitutional, and if so, whether that provision be removed from the rest of the PPACA. If the PPACA is removed, the consequences could include elimination of subsidies that makes insurance cost less, decreased eligibility for Medicaid, and removal of protections for patients that have preexisting conditions.

HITECH Act

The Health Information Technology for Economic and Clinical Health Act (HITECH), introduced in 2009, had the goal of promoting electronic health records. The act gave incentives to encourage providers to

make the change to electronic health records as well as increased penalties for those found violating HIPAA.

As previously mentioned, the CCM often utilizes electronic health records (EHR) to document care provided to patients. Other health care professionals also contribute to the client's medical record. Although the maintenance of a client's records must be secure and private, there are other considerations. Record keeping is not meant to simply show what was accomplished in any given case. The record keeping must also present the purpose of the initiation of the case and how the introduction of the CCM added value to that case.

The clinician is expected to show that their participation in the client's treatment closed the apparent gaps in care and that the CCM identified previously unknown or unattended gaps in care. The Meaningful Use Clause (a part of HITECH) created not only a clearinghouse of information that all providers can access but also required providers to verify that the use of the database results in improved outcomes for patients. HITECH also held businesses associated with healthcare that had access to medical records accountable to HIPAA standards. They became legally required to protect PHI and could now face civil or criminal penalty for failure to do so.

Widespread use of the EHR has resulted in a more efficient and cost-effective health care model. Practitioners can now present their value to the case. By showing that their interventions have both quantitative and qualitative value, they justify continuing to provide that care. Along with the inception of the EHR came changes in coding for patient treatment and penalties for the failure to adhere to basic standards of practice. Since the HITECH act, now at least 96% of acute care hospitals have implemented EHRs.

Legal and Regulatory Requirements Applicable to Case Management Practice

In this litigious society, the prudent case manager must be diligent in their provision of care. It is not enough to simply follow basic practice standards. The CCM must also provide a culturally sensitive and compassionate approach. Despite acting in good faith to maintain professionalism and provide excellent care, a certified case manager may face legal action. In a malpractice suit, it must be proven that the clinician was negligent in their actions and that negligence did cause harm to the client.

As previously discussed in the case-recording section, the CCM's best defense against malpractice is an accurate case file. It is vital to remember that the case file can serve as a legal document and is permissible as evidence in court proceedings. Since the majority of litigants do not seek legal recourse immediately, the CCM must not hope to rely upon their memory. As a licensed practitioner, the certified case manager should consider the following issues: lack of informed consent, breach of confidentiality, negligent referral, bad faith, and premature discharge. Unless it is documented thoroughly in the client's case record, an intervention strategy is not considered complete. Any pertinent information left out of the case file may be perceived as an actual gap in care and possible evidence of negligence.

Without informed consent, a client cannot agree to treatment. Even if a client has signed consent forms upon entry into the hospital, it is also vital that the CCM obtain separate consent for ongoing services post discharge. This is particularly important for working with clients who may not be capable of providing informed consent. For clients suffering from a TBI, the CCM must make note of the consequences of that injury, especially affected brain functions.

If the capacity to fully comprehend the advantages and disadvantages of their treatment is compromised, the patient's attorney, spouse or domestic partner, eldest child, or legal next of kin can be consulted. Unfortunately, this may then lead to the breach of confidentiality for that client. A breach of confidentiality occurs when a clinician provides protected health information that somehow causes harm to the client. If the client is unaware of the potential release of protected health information, even for the continuity of their care, the client may seek legal action. For this reason, it is crucial that the CCM completely disclose the scope of their practice and situations in which they will need to disclose the client's medical information.

For professional and practical purposes, the CCM must be aware of the fact that bad faith is characterized as "consciously doing wrong." Since the CCM is working in collaboration with the patient, insurer, and employer, all interests must be protected. The three components of bad faith include denial of benefits without proper explanation or cause, the clinician's awareness that the denial is erroneous, and improper administration of claims processing once the appeal is filed. If the CCM must issue a denial of benefits while acting in accordance with the dictates of the insurer, it is bad faith for the case manager to issue that denial without proper cause. The bad faith continues if the clinician does not attempt to provide the client with the necessary information to appeal the denial. If the client is able to provide evidence of improper behavior, the CCM may face civil or criminal charges, or experience a temporary or permanent loss of licensure.

Privacy and Confidentiality

Throughout their work with patients, CCMs must uphold the strictest level of confidentiality. As previously stated in the case recording section, the CCM must guard the client's medical records. Unfortunately, the case manager is not the only individual with access to the medical records. Administrative support staff, physicians and nurses, government agencies, and other members of the interdisciplinary team all require access. The Health Insurance Portability and Accountability Act (HIPAA) provides the CCM with the parameters to guard against unlawful or unnecessary use and release of medical information. Whether paper documents, prescriptions, diagnoses, treatment plans, or electronic records are in question, HIPAA regulations require that the prudent clinician exercise extreme caution regarding their release.

Compliance with an organization-wide privacy policy is of paramount importance. Each individual with the potential to come into contact with protected health information must be advised of the privacy policy. The clinician must act as the gatekeeper, providing the information about any particular client's case to those specifically entitled to the information.

The rule of thumb to maintain the secured control of access to medical records is to provide that information on a need-to-know basis. The need-to-know rule refers to individuals who must view the client's protected health information for the sole purpose of providing care. These individuals are to have access to the minimum amount of information necessary to perform the task at hand, nothing more. Only the minimum amount of information required to complete the tasks of caring for the patient should ever be released. Signed, dated, and witnessed informed-consent forms that outline the types of information that can be released must be a mandatory facet of any treatment plan.

Paper documents must be stored under lock and key with access only to the CCM and necessary staff. Destruction of paper documents must occur through the shredding of those documents, or professionals proficient in document destruction can be enlisted for larger organizations. For electronic files and reports, the clinician must be diligent to secure their desktop and the actual computer through

116

the use of computer screen locks, shortened time-out locks, or black-out screens whenever the computer is left unattended. Computer access must also be limited. The clinician should consider placing the computer behind locked doors, with passwords that are changed frequently, multiple firewalls, and careful screening of incoming emails and documents to guard against computer viruses.

Whenever possible, electronic transfers of medical information, including emails and faxes, must be sent securely. The most effective process is to verbally confirm that the fax number is correct and stored in a secure location away from those without a need to know. Again, limit information to the individuals who must have the information to perform their jobs.

Finally, any transmission of electronic medical records must contain a basic disclaimer advising the recipient on how to proceed if the documents were received in error, such as:

- This communication contains confidential information.

- If you have received this information in error, please notify the sender immediately by phone and return the original to the address listed on the form.

- Any distribution or reproduction of this transmission by anyone other than the intended party is strictly prohibited.

That verbiage, or something similar to it, should be added to all documents, emails, and other transmitted medical records. The role adopted by the clinician in this instance is as a gatekeeper, ensuring that only the correct individuals receive the necessary information.

Risk Management

Inherent in all types of work environments is some degree of occupational hazard. From retail to construction, to the medical or corporate realms, each cross section must develop a plan of action to prevent workplace injuries. **Risk management** is the process of identifying actual and potential hazards and developing cost-effective and efficient strategies to prevent their occurrence. A **sentinel event** can be described as an adverse incident that has led to, or has the potential to lead to, a catastrophic outcome requiring immediate intervention. The CCM is often utilized during a postmortem examination of a sentinel event or near miss, in order to help establish a comprehensive plan to prevent the incidence of future injuries. In this instance, the clinician is acting as a communicator, navigator, collaborator, and advocate.

Immediately after any workplace accident or near miss, it is necessary to complete an **incident report**. Within this report are the variables that contributed to the problem. Individuals involved are interviewed, the scene is examined, and management is notified. The CCM reviewing the incident report is generally looking for the following information: Who was involved? What happened? When did it happen? Where did it happen? Why did it happen? How did it happen?

Acting as the investigator, the clinician starts at the beginning. The "who" refers to the specific employees involved, who may also be seeking benefit coverage. The "what" refers to the incident itself. Describing what happened in as much detail as possible will help guide later concerns of how to implement proposed changes. When the incident occurred is equally important. If the incident occurred during peak business hours, after normal business hours, during approved overtime, or during inclement weather, the "when" plays a role in managing future risks. The "where" of the incident is the exact location of the occurrence. Did the event occur in the office, adjacent or nonessential work areas,

parking garage, elevator, etc.? The "why," however, is one of the most crucial aspects of this investigation. Why refers to whether or not proper procedures and policies were followed, which may directly impact liability in many workplace-injury cases.

Finally, the "how" is the most necessary question to answer. How the incident occurred refers to three main possibilities. Was the incident precipitated by: **human error**, such as operating the machinery while overtired or wearing improper clothing; **technical error**, such as malfunctioning or poorly maintained equipment; or **procedural error**, like failing to adhere to proper safety protocols? The answers to each of these questions will guide the CCM and the rest of the risk-management team to the next step in the process, which is the root-cause analysis.

During the **root-cause analysis**, the risk-management team will utilize the answers gleaned from the incident reports and interviews to determine the main cause of the sentinel event. Changing the focus from the problem to the solution, the CCM will act as the collaborator with the risk-management team to move into a dialogue regarding the gaps in procedures, policies, the workforce, and/or the environment that need to be addressed. The primary objective is to prevent future occurrences of a similar nature while preserving the factors that did not contribute to the problem. The best changes to implement are feasible, efficient, and cost effective. Once it is confirmed which changes will be made and the management team agrees with the proposal, the policies are changed as needed and the workforce is informed. Acting as the communicator, the CCM may be asked to contribute the memorandum prepared for company-wide distribution.

Depending on the type of event and related injuries, the risk management process can take hours, weeks, or months to be completed.

Self-Care and Well-Being as a Professional

The CCM is tasked with the responsibility to ensure that their patients receive timely, effective, and appropriate care at all times. The expectation is that the CCM enlists and exhausts all available resource services in an effort to guarantee the interventions provided are uninterrupted, detailed, and personalized for each patient they encounter. The CCM, acting as the single point of contact for the family and caregivers, must periodically support their needs for respite. For clients with profound disability, respite may be required more often for their caregivers. Patients are encouraged to consider their emotional needs as well. Conversely, the CCM must utilize those same skills to care for themselves.

It is crucial that the CCM creates an atmosphere of self-acceptance, empathy, and compassion when working with their patients. This cannot be accomplished if the CCM is overtired, functioning on little sleep, or neglects their own needs. In order to model these capabilities, the CCM must first possess them. Time away from work (TAFW) and preplanned time off (PPTO) are essential. Ideally, the best option is to remove oneself from the work environment completely. Eliminating access to voicemail, email, or patient's files will prevent any opportunity for distraction from the goal of relaxing. This further illustrates the importance of maintaining accurate records, so that alternate clinicians may follow up with the cases that require attention.

Repeated daily immersion in their caseloads and resolving the problems of patients affected by trauma can be emotionally draining. This prolonged interaction with clients in their weakest state can also be physically taxing and may lead to caregiver burnout. The old adage is true: You cannot drink from an empty cup. It is crucial that the CCM develop strategies to detect caregiver burnout early and address it

118

quickly. Simple, self-care activities like practicing proper nutrition, meditation, journaling, exercise, or spending time with family and friends can "recharge" the batteries.

Another crucial aspect of self-care can include psychotherapy, religious counseling, and/or support groups for mental health professionals. All of these environments respect the confidentiality of the client and normalize the feelings that the CCM may have that are typically associated with caregiver burnout. The majority of mental health professionals acknowledge the need to receive concurrent therapy themselves. It is inevitable that work with clients in various stages of recovery, with different reactions and emotional states, may trigger feelings in the clinician that need to be addressed. These groups also help to delineate the line between personal and professional responsibilities. The comradery of the group dynamic can serve as a forum to receive positive feedback as a practitioner, not consulting on individual cases. Each clinician may be encouraged to highlight times in their work with anonymous clients, providing insight to their colleagues. The group members can hold each other accountable for lapses in self-care while maintaining appropriate boundaries. Overall, any legal activity that creates a safe space to relax and release the tensions of the workday are acceptable.

Standards of Practice

The certified case manager plays numerous roles throughout the life of any case. **The Case Management Society of America** (CMSA) governs the scope of practice for the CCM. Whether acting as the collaborator, advocate, manager, communicator, professional, or navigator, the goal is always to achieve the best possible outcome for all parties involved. These guiding principles of practice empower the client to achieve the best possible outcomes. Although each role has a specific purpose, the CCM utilizes them interchangeably, often taking on several roles at once.

Acting as the collaborator and professional, the clinician works together with the client, their family, and appropriate health care providers to create and execute the plan of care. During the initial portion of any case, the CCM remains aware of the need to join forces with multiple providers to assess the plan of care periodically and adjust the treatment plan as needed.

Next, the CCM takes on the roles of advocate and expert. Following evidence-based standards of care, the clinician is able to guide the client toward traditional and nontraditional options regarding their treatment. Once an informed decision is made, the plan is followed. The adoption of the role as the expert moves the CCM to take the initiative to present the client with the typical results of each intervention.

When the clinician acts as the manager, their role is to merely supervise the situation, stepping up only as the situation requires them to do so. Empowering the client to self-determine the results of treatment whenever it is feasible engenders a sense of trust and rebuilds the client's confidence in themselves.

CCM Practice Test #1

1. "Adherence to care" is often confused with which other medical practice?
   a. Discharge plan
   b. Sustainability
   c. Compliance
   d. Prescription orders

2. Joan has been provided a detailed care plan after surgery. This plan has been reviewed with her by an interdisciplinary health care team. Joan considers herself highly educated and well versed in medical matters. At her first follow-up visit, she appears to be recovering well. She continues her outlined at-home care protocol but fails to attend her next follow-up visit, as she feels it is unnecessary. Soon after, she develops a fever, which is later discovered to be a difficult secondary infection at her surgical site. Which of the following best describes Joan?
   a. A nonadherent patient due to poor health literacy
   b. A noncompliant patient due to failure to continue prescribed medication
   c. A noncompliant patient due to financial limitations
   d. A nonadherent patient due to lack of follow-up activities relating to post-appointment visits

3. What is the most important skill set a health care case manager must possess?
   a. A working knowledge of various pharmaceuticals
   b. Communication skills
   c. Health care administration skills
   d. Familiarity with state social service agencies

4. Which of the following is a type of financial model presented to residents in continuing care retirement communities?
   a. Tax-advantaged model
   b. All-inclusive model
   c. Medicare
   d. IRA

5. Which type of care community allows senior citizens to remain mostly independent but receive care if and when it is needed?
   a. Assisted-living facilities
   b. Senior apartment centers
   c. Health-aide housing
   d. All-inclusive model

6. Unconditional positive regard is a part of which of the following concepts?
   a. Client empowerment
   b. End-of-life issues
   c. Crisis intervention
   d. Client engagement

7. Which of the following is a component of establishing rapport?
   a. Active listening and showing empathy
   b. Making sure the client is truthful and makes eye contact
   c. Focusing on what is good and hopeful in the client
   d. Effectively assessing and evaluating the client's problem

8. Informed decision-making is an element of which of the following concepts?
   a. Client engagement
   b. Substance abuse treatment
   c. Client self-care management
   d. Client empowerment

9. Which is the case manager's primary role in clients' use of community resources?
   a. Empowering clients to find their own resources without help
   b. Helping clients find and access appropriate resources
   c. Collaborating with families to assist clients with resources
   d. Not referring clients to resources in order to protect confidentiality

10. Which is the first step for case managers in the conflict resolution process?
    a. Use eye contact, nodding, and appropriate active listening skills.
    b. Be respectful and treat the client with empathy.
    c. Stay focused on the conflict and not the emotions.
    d. Gather the appropriate facts.

11. Which of the following is NOT considered to be one of the variables that form the foundation of the Aggregated Diagnosis Groups (ADGs)?
    a. Specialty care involvement
    b. Etiology of the condition
    c. Diagnostic certainty
    d. Genetic predisposition to the condition

12. Which tool is used to evaluate a program to provide insight into how well it is operating, along with identifying opportunities for improvement?
    a. Survey
    b. Observation
    c. Case study
    d. Suggestion box

13. Which statement BEST explains the Six Sigma model that is used to measure quality improvement?
    a. DMADV is used when an existing process needs improvement because it is not meeting standards.
    b. Many feel it has a limited effect in the healthcare industry due to the process backlogs that result.
    c. It results in a renewed customer approach, cost savings, and the reduction or removal of defects.
    d. DMAIC is used to develop a new process or when an existing process requires more than an incremental improvement.

14. The CCM is aware that appropriate rehabilitation after injury depends on effective transitional care. Which of the following is a primary element of the transitional care model?
   a. Documentation and quality monitoring
   b. Insurance appeals for coverage denials
   c. Assessment of dollar costs per client for CCM management
   d. Management of the acute-care census

15. The CCM is aware that the validity of the client's score on the depression scale assessment can be most affected by which of the following?
   a. The number of times the client has answered the questions
   b. Previous history of clinical depression or psychiatric disease
   c. The skill of the person administering the test
   d. The intended use of the results of the assessment

16. The CCM is evaluating a client with a communication deficit. Which of the following tools would provide the most reliable assessment of the client's deficit?
   a. Katz Index
   b. Pfeffer Index
   c. Stroop test
   d. Frenchay Aphasia Screening Test

17. The CCM understands that the Commission for Case Manager Certification has recently reviewed and reaffirmed the code of conduct for certified case managers. Which of the following statements is consistent with the revised code of conduct?
   a. Concerns about client privacy and security are addressed.
   b. Accommodations for advances in technology are included.
   c. The existing ethical framework is reaffirmed as the basis for CCM practice.
   d. All of the above

18. As a client advocate, the CCM actively promotes the clinical trial as a potential care option for all clients. Which of the following activities would NOT be commonly included in the CCM's client care responsibilities?
   a. Completing the grant application to fund the trial
   b. Ensuring that the client and family members are prepared to provide informed consent
   c. Assisting the client to identify personal goals for the therapy
   d. Documenting all elements of the client's care

19. Which of the following is NOT a primary goal at the core of case management practice?
   a. Empower the client to engage in self-directed care.
   b. Provide service and care coordination.
   c. Enroll patients in all applicable government benefit programs.
   d. Create a pathway to functional stability.

20. Ryan is an entry-level case manager in a hospital that houses a number of orthopedic specialties. He is working with an older female patient who has undergone a hip replacement but wants to continue a chair yoga practice. Ryan tells her, "Oh no. You definitely cannot do that in your condition. Let's take a look at the list of medications you've been prescribed." What would have been a better response from Ryan?
   a. "Let's discuss that in a few months."
   b. "It's wonderful that you want to stay active! Let's set up a time to talk with the physical therapist and rehab team to see how we can best approach this safely."
   c. "There may be other things in your life to prioritize first, such as walking comfortably."
   d. "I am deeply concerned about your safety as you recover from this operation, so I must tell you I do not think that is a good idea. I hope you can understand that I just want your recovery to happen quickly and safely."

21. Which of the following is a factor in access to high-quality health care?
   a. Location of the facility
   b. Health insurance coverage
   c. Technology-driven operations
   d. All of the above

22. Kenny works for a local government. The local government contracts with a national insurance company and offers three different health insurance plans to the company's employees. Each of these insurance plans has benefits specific to what the HR department has selected. Which kind of health care delivery plan is this?
   a. Managed care
   b. Tailored care
   c. TRICARE
   d. Obamacare

23. People who are poor, uninsured, live in low socioeconomic areas, or are unable to access quality health care (such as those who live in rural and remote areas) are described as what sort of population?
   a. Unemployed
   b. Fringe
   c. Vulnerable
   d. Off the grid

24. Which part of Medicare provides coverage for most prescription drugs?
   a. Part A provides coverage.
   b. Part B provides coverage.
   c. Part D provides coverage.
   d. Medicare does not allow coverage for prescription drugs; these must be paid for through supplementary insurance.

25. Which are the eligibility requirements for Medicare?
   a. Patients must be sixty-five years of age or older, have been diagnosed with end-stage renal disease, and/or have an eligible disability.
   b. Patients must be nineteen years of age or younger and/or have an eligible disability.
   c. Patients must be active duty, reserved, or retired military or an immediate family member of someone who falls into one of these categories.
   d. Patients must have an income below 85 percent of their state's median income.

123

26. What is an important consideration during the interview process?
    a. Encouraging empowerment
    b. Client's health literacy
    c. Environment
    d. Client's history of substance use

27. Which of the following is the BEST definition of spirituality?
    a. Belief in something larger than self or a higher power
    b. Belief in a divine or higher being and in the accompanying doctrine
    c. Belief in life after death
    d. Attending church regularly

28. Which of the following terms describes a case manager's ability to appreciate a client's cultural and religious background while being aware of individual biases?
    a. Cultural competency
    b. Spiritual awareness
    c. Multiculturalism
    d. Collectivism

29. Which of the following is typically NOT a barrier during the case management process?
    a. Client's religious background
    b. Client's primary language
    c. Client's overall culture
    d. Client's financial history

30. Which of the following types of assessments may case managers provide during the treatment process?
    a. Psychological evaluations
    b. Neuropsychological evaluations
    c. Personality assessments
    d. Informal psychological assessments

31. Which of the following tools is used to determine an appropriate caseload for a case manager?
    a. Case Lite Professional
    b. Case Load Capacity Calculator
    c. Case Works Pro
    d. Case Management Software

32. Case management programs that attain accreditation do which of the following?
    a. Pay their staff below market value to help manage costs
    b. Make sure that only clinical staff have well-defined roles
    c. Demonstrate their ability to deliver and facilitate quality health care
    d. Ensure that only nonclinical staff have clearly outlined responsibilities

33. Which of the following items does NOT factor into determining a case manager's caseload?
    a. Complexity of the cases
    b. Regulatory requirements
    c. Experience of the case manager
    d. A new company culture initiative

34. The CCM understands that which of the following questions is a priority question that must be included in the functional capacity evaluation?
    a. How much will the assistive devices cost?
    b. How long will the client be required to use the devices?
    c. What is the client's perception of their ability to improve with the assistive devices?
    d. What happens if the client refuses to use the assistive devices?

35. Which of the following correctly identifies the necessary sequence of assessments for the determination of the rehabilitative plan of care?
    a. Assessment of the nature of the injury, identification of appropriate assistive devices and specific client needs, and the functional capacity assessment
    b. Identification of the nature of the injury, identification of the associated financial arrangements, assessment of the client's willingness to participate, and completion of the functional capacity assessment
    c. Assessment of the client's recovery potential and the influence of any preexisting conditions and completion of the functional capacity assessment
    d. Assessment of available resources to meet the client's needs and completion of the functional capacity assessment

36. Which of the following is NOT consistent with the designation of workplace injuries?
    a. Acute
    b. Minor/mild
    c. Moderate
    d. Severe

37. Which of the following is an example of noncompulsory services?
    a. Family planning
    b. Outpatient hospitalization
    c. In-home care
    d. Podiatric care

38. Which of the following is the employer's responsibility for compliance with the Americans with Disabilities Act (ADA) following a workplace injury?
    a. Funding training/education for alternative work
    b. Making reasonable accommodation for the client's return to work
    c. Aiding the client's family in making the home environment safe for the client
    d. Setting a time frame for the client's return

39. The CCM managed the care of a client who required referrals to several specialty providers. The CCM received notice of a malpractice suit filed by the client against one of the specialty providers. The CCM was charged in the same complaint with a negligent referral. Which of the following referral policies is the CCM's primary defense against this complaint?
    a. The specialty providers were approved by the health care agency.
    b. All specialty providers were approved by the client's PCP.
    c. The PCP also communicated directly with the specialty provider.
    d. The CCM maintained meticulous case records for all clients.

40. Which of the following identifies a special circumstance associated with the Employee Retirement Income Security Act of 1974 (ERISA)?
   a. Individuals receiving Medicare are not eligible under this statute, as this is intended as disability insurance for elderly clients.
   b. Insurers use a legal loophole in this law to deny claims.
   c. The law was originally intended to protect mentally challenged adults.
   d. Treatment caps for mental health therapy are outlined in this law.

41. Breanna experiences a sudden muscular spasm in her neck and near her shoulder blade when she is lifting weights at the gym. She stops briefly, stretches, and is able to complete her workout. When she returns home, however, she has extreme shoulder pain and limited range of motion. She takes some ibuprofen and ices her shoulder and tries to sleep it off. In the morning, the pain has gotten worse, and she cannot move her arm without pain, although she can walk around and drive her car. Which type of care would best address this situation?
   a. Emergency care
   b. Urgent care
   c. Respite care
   d. Trauma care

42. Mitchell goes into cardiac arrest at a restaurant. Luckily, emergency services arrive quickly and transport him to the hospital in an ambulance. He makes a full recovery but has to stay in the hospital for two weeks. Which level of care did the emergency services provide for Mitchell?
   a. Urgent care
   b. Trauma care
   c. Short-term stabilization
   d. Long-term care

43. Under which category of care do nursing homes, assisted-living facilities, and hospice homes fall under?
   a. Urgent care
   b. Short-term care
   c. Long-term care
   d. Elder care

44. In which type of care organization are primary care providers utilized for all initial visits during which they can give a documented referral to a specialist for further treatment?
   a. Managed Care Organization
   b. World Health Organization
   c. Preferred Provider Organization
   d. Patient Specialist Organization

45. What type of care organization offers the most flexibility in terms of provider selection and availability?
   a. Managed Care Organization
   b. Health Maintenance Organization
   c. Patient Selection Organization
   d. Preferred Provider Organization

46. Which type of care organization provides access to services based on geographical region?
    a. Managed Care Organization
    b. Health Maintenance Organization
    c. Preferred Provider Organization
    d. State-Based Unionized Care

47. Which type of plan combines characteristics of HMO benefits and PPO benefits?
    a. Fee-for-service plans
    b. Point-of-service plans
    c. Private insurance plans
    d. Obamacare marketplace plans

48. According to the CCMC, which of the following is NOT an element of CCM competence?
    a. Knowledge of statutory laws
    b. Educational preparation
    c. Clinical expertise
    d. Ongoing professional development

49. The CCM accompanies a colleague who is conducting an initial assessment of a new client. The client shares personal information with the CCM that has possible legal implications, and the client voices concerns about who might have access to that information. The CCM says, "Don't worry about the security of the information you have just shared. It is not relevant to your injury, so I won't be including the information in my documentation." The CCM recognizes that the colleague has violated which of the following standards of practice?
    a. Disclosure
    b. Protection of PHI
    c. Competence
    d. Legal compliance

50. The CCM is responsible for updating disease-specific registries. Which of the following is consistent with the functions of these registries?
    a. The purpose is to provide quality assessment data for specific PCPs for use by insurers.
    b. Most registries are limited to tracking diabetes.
    c. The focus is on making evidence-based guidelines readily available to PCPs at the point of care.
    d. Clients can refuse to allow their data to be included in any registry.

51. Which of the following is NOT a typical sign/symptom of physical abuse?
    a. Bruises or abrasions
    b. Missed doctor visits
    c. Being withdrawn, sad, or angry
    d. Bedwetting/enuresis

52. Which is the most accurate definition of abuse?
    a. Causing harm to another person that leads to distress and pain
    b. Behaviors or actions that contribute to bodily health
    c. Refusing to provide food and care for a dependent person
    d. When a client is in a physically dangerous situation or under excessive mental distress

53. Which is the BEST definition of the "Form a coalition" stage in Kotter's 8-step change model?
    a. A group of individuals collaborating to support an individual making a change
    b. Examining different areas of a client's life (physical, emotional, spiritual) to offer resources
    c. Ensuring a client receives support from friends, support groups, or family
    d. Creating a plan ahead of time in collaboration with a client to prevent crisis

54. Which of the following is a common sign of substance abuse by a client?
    a. Enuresis
    b. Vomiting
    c. Disheveled or unkempt appearance
    d. Incidences of anxiety or aggression

55. Which of the following terms BEST matches the definition, "encouraging clients to be involved and take control of, and be active participants in their treatment"?
    a. Client activation
    b. Client engagement
    c. Client empowerment
    d. Client self-care management

56. How can some individuals subsidize the cost of room and board plus amenities, specifically in assisted-living facilities?
    a. They could share a one-bedroom unit with another person in the community.
    b. They could use a Medicaid waiver.
    c. All members over seventy years old receive subsidies.
    d. They could apply through the Department of Housing and Urban Development for a voucher.

57. What demographics of patients might a case manager encounter in a group home?
    I. Children
    II. Adults
    III. Patients with chronic mental illnesses
    IV. Patients with chronic physical illnesses

    a. I and II
    b. I, III, and IV
    c. I, II, and III
    d. All of the above

58. Joanne is a case manager who is working with a brand-new patient. She reviews the patient's initial intake forms, notes certain conditions on the patient's medical forms, and has a meeting with both the patient and his caregivers to discuss the patient's condition and necessary next steps. In what step of the case management process is Joanne?
    a. Assessment
    b. Coordination
    c. Evaluation
    d. Planning

59. What factor typically results in the closing of a case?
    a. The case manager reviews the patient's condition holistically and decides the patient has achieved their best possible outcome.
    b. The patient becomes eligible for Medicare.
    c. The patient's income increases above the poverty level.
    d. The case manager takes a leave of absence.

60. Which of the following resources functions as the standard system of classification for mental disorders?
    a. The International Classification of Diseases
    b. *The Diagnostic and Statistical Manual of Mental Disorders*
    c. The World Health Organization disorder scale
    d. The Centers for Disease Control's neurological classes

61. Collecting and analyzing patient satisfaction surveys falls under which part of the case management process?
    a. Evaluation
    b. Planning
    c. Assessment
    d. Outcome

62. When is the riskiest time for patients, in terms of vulnerability, to experience poor health outcomes?
    a. During an operation of the lower body
    b. During intake
    c. During transitions between different points of care
    d. During their time in a waiting room

63. Peter is a case manager in a research hospital. He learns of a new treatment for a chronic condition his ninety-year-old patient has. However, it is a very costly trial for the hospital, and it primarily benefits from the collection of longitudinal data. What should Peter do in this situation?
    a. Nothing; since his patient is older, it is unlikely the trial will be able to collect longitudinal data from him, and this will not be a cost-effective use of resources for the hospital.
    b. Advocate for the patient's inclusion in the trial, as it may improve the patient's quality of life.
    c. Find a younger patient with the same condition and ask to be transferred to that patient's case.
    d. Have an honest discussion with the patient about the situation and see if the patient will refuse treatment voluntarily, which may be empowering for the patient.

64. Co-payments, fixed fees for services, deductibles, and coinsurance are all examples of what kind of business practice for insurance companies?
    a. Multiple streams of revenue
    b. Theoretical planning
    c. Cost containment
    d. Affordable Care Act standards

65. Which of the following types of insurance models contracts providers with insurance companies in order to give lower co-pays and deductibles to the patient?
    a. PPO models
    b. Life insurance contingencies
    c. Disability insurance
    d. Fee-for-service models

66. Implementing a blood pressure check during every continuing care visit as part of a company's case management program to align with an industry best practice is an example of which of the following?
    a. Performance improvement plan
    b. Benchmark
    c. Corrective action
    d. Metric

67. Which health risk assessment serves as a representation of a patient's perception of his health status, limitations, social support, and environment?
    a. MMSE
    b. RUDAS
    c. 30-point Folstein
    d. SF-36

68. Why do case managers utilize health risk assessments?
    a. To serve as an asset in the predictive modeling process
    b. To provide insight into a patient's past perception of his health status
    c. To review a patient's previous healthcare experience that is readily documented/accessible
    d. To disprove the classification of patients into risk categories or domains

69. Which of the following tools is used to determine best practices and distribute associated resources based on historical data?
    a. Predictive outcomes
    b. Scenario analysis
    c. Predictive modeling
    d. Demand forecasting

70. Which of the following functions is common to assessment instruments that measure cognitive function and executive function?
    a. Verbal fluency
    b. Inhibition
    c. Self-regulation
    d. Memory

71. What is the primary objective of assistive devices?
    a. To speed the client's return to work
    b. To decrease costs by limiting the client's recovery time
    c. To enhance the client's sense of self-confidence
    d. To prevent delays that might occur with additional injuries

72. Which of following therapies would be required for a client who has a work-related head injury that has damaged the Wernicke's area of the left cerebral hemisphere?
    a. Speech therapy
    b. Use of sign language and lip reading to accommodate hearing loss
    c. Assistive devices to aid ambulation
    d. Syntax treatments

73. Which of the following work-related injuries would require management by the CCM?
    a. Hand laceration with a severed tendon
    b. Severe high ankle sprain
    c. Dislocated shoulder
    d. Grade 2 pectoral muscle tear

74. How many steps are there in Kotter's change model?
    a. Three
    b. Five
    c. Seven
    d. Eight

75. Which of the following is a typical component of a crisis plan?
    a. Client goals that were developed in collaboration with the case manager
    b. Relaxation strategies
    c. Assessment tools to determine crisis severity
    d. Resources that address spiritual and social needs of the client

76. What is the BEST definition of de-escalation?
    a. Working with participants of a conflict to find a solution that satisfies everyone
    b. Helping a client manage heightened emotions during a crisis
    c. Helping a client with pain management
    d. Helping a perpetrator of abuse develop anger management skills

77. Which of the following is a typical aspect of physical care during end-of-life services?
    a. Physical therapy treatments
    b. Neuropsychological assessments
    c. Newest Vital Sign assessments
    d. Assistance with sleep and appetite issues

78. Which of the following terms BEST matches the definition, "all care given between diagnosis of a terminal illness and death"?
    a. Palliative care
    b. Hospice care
    c. End-of-life care
    d. Withdrawal of care

79. Which of the following techniques is typically used in health coaching to help assess a client's capacity to implement change?
    a. Teaching goal-setting skills to the client
    b. Motivational interviewing
    c. Using open-ended questions
    d. Administering the Thomas–Kilmann Instrument

80. Which of the following is typically used to assess a client's health literacy?
    a. Newest Vital Sign assessment
    b. Thomas–Kilmann Instrument
    c. Thematic Apperception Test
    d. Multiphasic Personality Inventory

Use the following passage to answer questions 81 and 82:

Mary is a forty-five-year-old woman that is approximately 75 pounds overweight according to heathy weight guidelines. She has sought services at Agency B for health coaching at her doctor's recommendation. Mary seems uncomfortable as she begins her first session by telling her coach why she is there.

81. What is the first step in the health coaching process with Mary?
    a. Client engagement
    b. Asking Mary to step on a scale to verify baseline weight
    c. Working with Mary to set achievable goals
    d. Providing Mary with education about weight loss

82. What is the BEST technique to determine Mary's willingness and ability to make changes?
    a. Motivational interviewing
    b. Negotiation
    c. Client activation
    d. Informed decision-making

83. Which of the following BEST explains the importance of assessing a client's health literacy level?
    a. If a client cannot follow the instructions or understand the treatment recommendations of a health care provider, it could interfere with treatment effectiveness.
    b. A client's literacy level is not important if a capable family member can assist with health concerns.
    c. A clients is more likely to go to the doctor if they understand medical terminology.
    d. A client will have less dependence on the case manager if the health literacy score is high.

84. What is a common barrier to interpersonal communication within a group treatment setting?
    a. Rigid and overly restrictive rules create an oppressive group setting.
    b. One member of the group monopolizes the session.
    c. The group facilitator asks too many closed-ended questions.
    d. One member of the group is shut down due to group dynamics.

85. What type of questions would a case manager typically use when gathering demographic information?
   a. Open-ended questions
   b. Closed-ended questions
   c. Clarifying questions
   d. Collaborative questions

86. Which is the purpose of an acuity-level rating?
   a. To rate a medical center's quality standards
   b. To rate a patient's satisfaction with treatment upon discharge
   c. To rate the level of intensive care a center can provide
   d. To rate a patient's level of illness or disability severity

87. Gene's twenty-six-year-old daughter has recently been diagnosed with severe schizophrenia induced by a traumatic event. She is unable to properly care for herself, and so he places her in an assisted-living facility near the family home. Before the event, Gene's daughter had a stable job and had built up some savings in addition to buying a home. What is the best way for Gene to manage his daughter's assets?
   a. Freeze all accounts and apply for short-term leave with her company.
   b. Apply for legal guardianship to create and manage a special-needs trust and apply for government benefits on his daughter's behalf.
   c. Simply use her bank accounts to pay her bills in her name.
   d. Apply for Medicare.

88. What is the primary purpose of a viatical settlement?
   a. It allows patients with terminal illnesses to sell their life insurance policies for immediate cash to relieve financial burdens.
   b. It allows patients to quickly mediate and settle medical malpractice suits.
   c. It allows case managers the funds to protect themselves from patients who claim negligence.
   d. It allows the next of kin of a deceased patient to make funeral, legal, and other administrative arrangements.

89. Which of the following is TRUE regarding the Utilization Review Accreditation Commission's performance measures?
   a. They are all mandatory measures.
   b. They only provide value to consumers.
   c. They only provide value to purchasers.
   d. They are divided into mandatory and exploratory categories.

90. Which of the following is NOT considered to be a measurement that falls under URAC's case management domain for accreditation?
   a. Employees who fail fitness-for-duty exams
   b. Percentage medically released to return to work
   c. Medical readmissions
   d. Disability and workers' compensation

91. Which of the following is NOT a reason for a health plan to seek NCQA accreditation?
    a. Wellness and health promotion programs
    b. Support in receiving market advantage
    c. Effective transition management
    d. Assistance with request-for-proposal requirements

92. Under NCQA, an organization that is required to provide a report for disease management purposes falls under which level of accreditation?
    a. Provisional accreditation
    b. Accredited with performance reporting
    c. Accredited
    d. Lifetime Mastery Accreditation

93. Which of the following statements is TRUE regarding the time period for agencies earning NCQA accreditation?
    a. Agencies that earn accredited status do so for a five-year period.
    b. Agencies that attain provisional accreditation do so only for a two-year period.
    c. Agencies that earn accredited status perform at such a high level that they are awarded this status for the life of their business.
    d. Agencies that attain provisional accreditation must act within twelve months in order to achieve status.

94. Adherence to statins is an example of which type of quality measure under the National Quality Forum?
    a. Process
    b. Structure
    c. Outcomes
    d. Composite

95. What does the mission of the National Quality Forum entail?
    a. The design of a set of nationally recognized safety goals for patient care
    b. The creation of guidelines for personnel charged with handling a crisis management response
    c. The maintenance of a portfolio of performance measures that have a direct impact on the ability to deliver high quality care
    d. The means for reporting on the unnecessary costs associated with case management

96. Which of the following is NOT one of the board of directors' committees that is responsible for facilitating the National Quality Forum's activities?
    a. National Priorities Partnership
    b. The Manager Network
    c. Health IT Advisory Committee
    d. Consensus Standards Approval Committee

97. Why is the National Guideline Clearinghouse (NGC) valuable?
    a. It contributes checklists and toolkits to organizations to aid in the prevention of healthcare-associated infections.
    b. It enables the reporting of quality measures that best align with the improvement of patient outcomes.
    c. Its research provides insight into patient safety threats and the impact of medical errors.
    d. It gives healthcare professionals access to a wide variety of clinical practice guidelines.

98. The CCM is aware that there is legislation to protect pregnant women from discrimination in the workplace. Which of the following is a provision of the ADA concerning pregnant women?
    a. An employer cannot refuse to hire a pregnant woman with a pregnancy-related condition as long as the woman is able to perform the functions of the position.
    b. A woman cannot be fired or denied a position because she is, or may become, pregnant.
    c. A pregnant woman with medical complications may qualify for a disability determination.
    d. An employer cannot force a pregnant woman to stop working and use maternity leave at any point in the pregnancy.

99. The CCM understands that the initiation of the ACA has influenced the health insurance industry in the United States. At the same time, the ACA has affected the use of workers' compensation insurance. Which of the following statements is consistent with the relationship between the ACA and workers' compensation insurance?
    a. Employers no longer receive benefits for preventive care programs.
    b. There are fewer new claims for workers' compensation insurance.
    c. There are more full-time employees due to available insurance coverage.
    d. Workers' compensation insurance premiums have increased less rapidly since the implementation of the ACA.

100. Ethically speaking, the CCM is required to support the client's autonomy. In practice, which of the following statements regarding autonomy and consent best describes the relationship between the two elements?
    a. When clients consent to treatment, they relinquish a degree of autonomous control over their situation.
    b. The greatest threat to client autonomy is paternalism.
    c. Although the CCM is charged with protecting and supporting client autonomy, the degree to which the CCM is successful is minimal.
    d. Litigation has made providers more sensitive to the support of the client's autonomy.

101. The CCM is managing the care of a client who stopped at a local pub on his way home and was subsequently a passenger in a car involved in a multiple-vehicle accident. He admits to consuming several alcoholic beverages. The client now has a fractured hip, possible abdominal trauma, and a bruised spleen. The patient says to the CCM, "Do you think I'll be here very long? I need to get home." It is clear from his remark that he does not comprehend the severity of his injuries. The client's wife arrives and asks to speak to the CCM. "I can't have him in the hospital. This is not a good time for me. My mother is ill, and our son was suspended from school today. Can't you hurry up and get him out of here?" Which of the following is the CCM's priority in this situation?
   a. Protecting the client's PHI and not discussing this with his wife
   b. Contacting the PCP in order to see if they can speed up the patient's recovery process
   c. Contacting the orthopedic surgeon for orders for pain management so that he can leave now
   d. With the client's consent, discussing the severity of his injuries and plan of care with the client and his wife

102. The CCM must understand the relationship between adhesive contracts and the ACA. Which of the following is consistent with this relationship?
   a. The adhesive contract is another descriptor for policies offered under the ACA.
   b. Medicaid insurance contracts are considered adhesive contracts.
   c. A legal loophole in the ACA allows the sale of substandard insurance policies.
   d. Adhesive means that the level of care is the same as other ACA-sanctioned contracts.

103. One of the models that conceptualizes moral decision-making by the CCM is the quadrant model of moral judgment. The four major quadrants, which surround the client and support system, are client preferences, medical and clinical indications, contextual features, and quality of life. Which of the following is consistent with the definition of contextual features as identified in this model?
   a. Knowledge of the client's belief system and other personal characteristics helps the CCM establish rapport with the clients and their support systems.
   b. The CCM will examine the success possibilities of available treatments and resources.
   c. The CCM understands that mentally competent adults have the right to make medical decisions that are ill-advised decisions.
   d. The CCM is responsible for fostering the client's quality of life in a manner consistent with the client's definition.

104. The CCM is a master's prepared nurse who is self-employed as a case manager in the community. The CCM visits Mrs. R. to check on the status of her chronic heart failure. Mrs. R. also has a venous stasis ulcer on her left calf. Mrs. R. tells the CCM that the visiting nurse left an hour ago, but "there's still something wrong with the dressing because it just doesn't feel right." The CCM rewraps the bandage around the calf and makes a note to contact the home care agency. How would the home care nurse most likely respond?
   a. "Thanks very much for making Mrs. R. more comfortable."
   b. "Thank you for letting me know, but it would have been better if you had contacted me before removing and replacing the dressing."
   c. "Has the drainage from the open areas increased?"
   d. "Please don't intervene on my behalf again."

136

105. Which of the following is an essential element of CCM professional practice but is not included in the identification of the standards for the case management process as published by the CCMC?
    a. Adherence to relevant state and federal laws
    b. Consideration of all ethical principles and standards as identified by the CCMC
    c. Compliance with accreditation and regulatory standards
    d. Applied cost-effectiveness for all interventions

106. When discussing strategies to meet moral standards, which of the following personal characteristics is identified as most useful for the CCM?
    a. Moral courage
    b. Stamina
    c. Stubbornness
    d. Perseverance

107. Which social program provides health insurance to disabled people, children, the elderly, and low-income and/or pregnant women who have no other form of health insurance?
    a. Medicare
    b. Medicaid
    c. SNAP
    d. TANF

108. Nancy is a case manager working with a breast cancer patient who recently underwent a mastectomy. The patient has been adhering to care protocols and regularly returning for follow-up appointments to make sure there are no new lesions. She appears to be very healthy and has made positive lifestyle changes but always seems sad and anxious at visits. The patient has never verbally expressed any concerns, however. What is one way Nancy can help her patient?
    a. Say nothing in order to avoid making the situation awkward for the patient during her exams.
    b. Tell the patient she is available to talk over coffee one morning.
    c. Encourage the patient to make an appointment with the counselor on her care team for a simple follow-up evaluation.
    d. Tell the in-room technicians to be gentler during visits.

109. What type of care provides services for both the patient who is receiving direct medical care and the patient's family members?
    a. Inpatient
    b. Hospice
    c. Ambulatory
    d. Emergency

110. What type of care can be provided at any stage during an illness but only is offered to the patient in order to relieve chronic or painful symptoms?
    a. Hospice
    b. Palliative
    c. Ambulatory
    d. Emergency

111. Mel has been diagnosed with stage IV lung cancer and has been given six weeks to live. He is immediately placed into hospice care. What are some tasks Mel's case manager should definitely work through with him?
   a. Ensuring advanced directives and/or a living will have been created
   b. Reviewing Mel's personal "bucket list" and helping him experience whatever is possible in the short term
   c. Reading audiobooks to Mel during his waking hours
   d. Ensuring Mel receives a medical marijuana card to avoid opioids for his pain

112. How do most people in the United States receive health insurance?
   a. They purchase it through yearly government-sponsored open enrollment periods.
   b. They receive it through their employer.
   c. They receive it as a result of a universal provision through social programs.
   d. The majority of people in the United States are uninsured.

113. Micah is a welder who slips on-site due to issues with his personal protective equipment. He goes to the hospital and will likely need to rest at home for a total of three weeks. What type of insurance will Micah probably utilize?
   a. Life insurance
   b. Social Security
   c. Medicare
   d. Short-term disability

114. Which of the following regulations extended health insurance to individuals in the United States who may not have been able to receive it or afford it through their employer?
   a. The Consolidated Omnibus Budget Reconciliation Act
   b. The Emergency Medical Treatment and Active Labor Act
   c. The Affordable Care Act
   d. The Anti-Kickback Statute

115. What are primary goals case managers should work on with patients who are receiving workmen's compensation?
   a. Engaging in behaviors and showing demonstrated progression toward returning to work
   b. Filling out job applications for less dangerous positions
   c. Shifting reimbursement over to federal Social Security
   d. Encouraging patients to enjoy their time off and plan activities with family members

116. What is one reason a workmen's compensation claim might be denied?
   a. The patient has already met their personal health insurance deductible.
   b. The patient was found to be under the influence of a substance at the time of the incident.
   c. The patient had put in a resignation notice.
   d. The patient is over the age of sixty.

117. Anna is a hospital case manager who previously spent ten years working as a general surgical registered nurse before she moved into case management. Prior to going to school for a nursing degree, Anna worked in the human resources department as a risk management specialist of a company that manufactured nutritional supplements. What types of cases would best benefit from her work experience?
    a. Workmen's compensation
    b. Pediatric
    c. Malpractice
    d. Postnatal

118. What is a method insurance companies can utilize to minimize their risk of bankruptcy caused by catastrophic claims filed by people covered by the company's plans?
    a. Risk mitigation
    b. Claims mitigation
    c. Reinsurance
    d. Reassurance

119. Sina was recently in a catastrophic car accident in which she lost her right leg. She has been fitted with a prosthetic leg and is adjusting to using it. Her day begins with her doctor checking the area of her former wounds to ensure that skin healing and scarring is occurring normally and that she is not in pain. Then, Sina works with a physical therapist and an occupational therapist who specializes in prosthetics for the remainder of the morning. At mealtime, a registered dietitian talks to her about different food choices that will promote tissue healing, muscular strength, and mental wellness. Finally, she has a twice-weekly appointment with a therapist who focuses on Sina's mental and emotional health. What type of care is Sina receiving?
    a. Focused
    b. Interdisciplinary
    c. Amputee adherence
    d. Respite

120. Joe's son was born with a muscular degeneration disease. Though he is able to walk as a toddler, he loses almost all ability to walk as he nears puberty and has to use a wheelchair. Which of the following is a service for Joe's son that would be covered by long-term disability insurance?
    a. The insurance would cover tuition for a private special-needs school.
    b. Weekly chair yoga classes would be covered.
    c. The insurance would cover ramp installations for Joe's car and the entryways to his house.
    d. Since Joe's son is under sixty-five, he does not qualify for long-term disability insurance.

121. Interdisciplinary care teams are described to have more of which of the following qualities when compared to conventional care teams?
    a. Comprehensive and cost effective
    b. Niched
    c. Higher quality and more expensive
    d. Argumentative and costly

122. Which of the following types of conflict resolution lets the more powerful person get their way?
    a. Collaboration
    b. Compromise
    c. Accommodation
    d. Competition

123. During crisis management, what should be the case manager's biggest concern?
    a. Client economic status
    b. Client safety
    c. Client substance use
    d. The reason the client is in crisis

124. Which of the following factors determines the extent of a client's suicidal ideation and risk?
    a. The client had a previous suicide attempt and was hospitalized.
    b. The client seems very agitated and knows how to use a weapon.
    c. The client has a plan and a way to carry out the plan.
    d. The client has had a conflict with a family member and is crying uncontrollably.

125. Which of the following areas is typically assessed during a psychological evaluation?
    a. Memory/language
    b. Intellectual functionality
    c. Health literacy
    d. Client motivation to change

126. Which step is the "Build on the change" step in Kotter's 8-step change model?
    a. Second
    b. Fourth
    c. Seventh
    d. Eighth

127. What does a case manager need to be familiar with when working with clients that are uninsured or underinsured?
    a. The client's family dynamics
    b. Related community and state resources
    c. The client's medical history
    d. The name and address of the client's doctor

128. Which of the following is a situation where pastoral counseling would be a likely treatment recommendation?
    a. The client's health literacy needs to be assessed.
    b. The client needs a psychological evaluation.
    c. The client has been diagnosed with a terminal illness.
    d. The client needs help developing positive health behaviors.

129. What is the primary purpose of a support group?
    a. To encourage client empowerment
    b. To help clients develop interpersonal communication skills
    c. To assist clients in locating and accessing needed resources and services
    d. To allow individuals with common challenges to feel less isolated and receive encouragement from others

130. Which of the following is a likely benefit of exercise?
    a. Better conflict resolution skills
    b. Higher score on health literacy tests
    c. Better client engagement
    d. Improved mental health

131. What is the first stage in the Transtheoretical Model of behavioral change?
    a. Preparation
    b. Precontemplation
    c. Creating urgency
    d. Unfreezing

132. What term best matches the description, "the time period when recently implemented changes are sustained"?
    a. Refreezing
    b. Anchoring the change
    c. Maintenance
    d. Termination

133. Which of the following is a vital aspect of client empowerment?
    a. A focus on a client's strengths
    b. Maintenance of confidentiality
    c. A client's level of involvement in his own treatment activation
    d. A client's willingness to make positive changes

134. Which of the following is a component of the client engagement process?
    a. Health literacy testing
    b. Personality assessment
    c. Goal setting
    d. Assessing motivation to change

135. Which statement BEST describes the Caseload Matrix?
    a. Case managers can proactively use the matrix to adjust assignments based on changes in acuity.
    b. The schematic chart provided by the CMSA and the NASW Concept Paper is divided into five categories.
    c. Case managers utilize the matrix to be reactive when following their patients throughout the continuum of health care.
    d. A change to an element in one category of the matrix does not have an impact on the remaining categories.

136. Which of the following tasks can managers use to document cost savings as well as case status?
    a. Weekly reports that detail service costs and fees
    b. Daily email communications regarding inactive cases
    c. Case management reports that show patients moving along the continuum of care
    d. A listing of the costs associated with only managing cases without intervention

137. Which statement BEST describes the Adjusted Clinical Groups (ACG) System?
    a. The model focuses on physician centered care.
    b. It can better identify individuals who will be high cost utilizers.
    c. The system only supports commercial healthcare programs.
    d. It does not incorporate the ICD-9 and ICD-10 codes.

138. Which of the following lists contains the correct order of the steps in a CQI program?
    a. Employ a corrective action plan (CAP), identify the problem, reinforce required process changes, observe and monitor the CAP, review and evaluate outcomes
    b. Identify the problem, employ a corrective action plan (CAP), observe and monitor the CAP, review and evaluate outcomes, reinforce required process changes
    c. Review and evaluate outcomes, identify the problem, reinforce required process changes, employ a corrective action plan (CAP), observe and monitor the CAP
    d. Identify the problem, reinforce required process changes, employ a corrective action plan (CAP), observe and monitor the CAP, review and evaluate outcomes

139. Which statement is TRUE regarding the PDSA model?
    a. It focuses on slow and steady improvement within the healthcare setting.
    b. It challenges users to ask themselves five fundamental questions before starting.
    c. It operates independent of existing quality improvement models that are in place.
    d. It is divided into two parts: fundamental questions and four stages.

140. Why does the PDSA model specifically work well for pilot programs?
    a. It allows for small-scale testing before a large-scale implementation.
    b. It enables medical professionals to identify variances.
    c. It helps managers to identify process gaps that lead to performance inconsistencies.
    d. It encourages employees to become more innovative in their daily tasks.

141. An example of an industry benchmark that is MOST appropriate for managed care organizations is which of the following?
    a. Average time spent in emergency department before being admitted
    b. Percentage of patients who develop serious blood clots post-surgery
    c. Average time for a patient to receive an electrocardiogram
    d. Number of skilled nursing bed days per thousand

142. Which of the following tools is used by most of America's healthcare plans to provide insight into the ongoing effort to prevent illness?
    a. CAHPS
    b. HEDIS
    c. Benchmarking
    d. NCQA

142

143. The CCM is managing the care of an individual with the recent onset of altered mentation prior to a head injury related to a fall at home. The client's wife is concerned about all of the proposed diagnostic testing because her husband tires so quickly. She asks the CCM if there is a way to make the appropriate diagnosis without "all of those questions." Which of the following instruments would be appropriate for this client, and why?
   a. Visual Analog Scale
   b. SF-36
   c. Stroop test
   d. Mini-Cog test

144. What is the correct order of the for an employee seeking accommodations in the workplace?
   a. Making the accommodation, identify potential accommodations, requesting accommodations, identify functional limitations, monitoring effectiveness
   b. Requesting accommodations, identify functional limitations, identify potential accommodations, determine reasonable solutions, making the accommodation, monitoring effectiveness
   c. Requesting accommodations, identify potential accommodations, identify functional limitations, determine reasonable solutions monitoring effectiveness, making the accommodation
   d. Making the accommodation, determine reasonable solutions, identify potential accommodations, identify functional limitations, monitoring effectiveness

145. The CCM is managing the care of a thirty-eight-year-old male with a work-related spinal cord injury who will require long-term rehabilitative care. Which of the following is a priority action for the CCM in the care of this client?
   a. Inform the client weekly of the scheduled vocational training course.
   b. Frequently reevaluate the client's progress and needs.
   c. Schedule a test for the diagnosis of PTSD.
   d. Require alternative living arrangements to speed the client's recovery.

146. What is one of the primary differences in the CCM's responsibilities for the care of a client with chronic illness and disability and a client with workplace injuries that require rehabilitation?
   a. The care of clients with workplace injuries is focused only on the clients' return to work.
   b. Workers' compensation insurance only provides disability benefits for workplace injuries.
   c. The CCM is responsible for being knowledgeable about all forms of private insurance that vary significantly from one client to another.
   d. All workers' compensation insurance plans are the same from state to state, unlike private insurers.

147. Which of the following is a major distinction between the discharge teaching for a client being discharged to home versus a client being discharged to a rehab facility?
   a. The severity of the client's deficit will not affect the rehab admission process because there will be skilled nursing care available.
   b. The client's support system and home environment must be assessed prior to discharge.
   c. When discharged to home, all of the client's concerns will be addressed by home care providers.
   d. The rehab facility staff can access all of the information they need from the client's Epic record (an electronic medical record system).

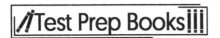

148. What is the CCM's responsibility for improving the efficiency of the identification process for clients who require case management?
   a. The CCM understands that the DRG-related census is sufficient in most cases.
   b. The CCM should strengthen the network of informed staff, including the admitting officer and managers on the nursing units.
   c. The CCM should lobby the agency for the creation of a client identification model in the health records database already in use in the agency.
   d. The CCM understands that the current system is sufficient, and any additional framework would not increase the overall efficiency of the existing system.

149. The CCM is responsible for the examination of all workplace injuries using root-cause analysis, which is a systematic mode of inquiry of an untoward event. Which of the following is consistent with the primary function of the CCM in this analysis?
   a. Identify procedural, institutional, or provider flaws at each point of the untoward event.
   b. Use the assessment as an integral part of employee evaluation.
   c. Identify the specific individuals who were responsible for the error to facilitate remediation.
   d. Understand that the results of the analysis are only applicable to institutional process revisions.

150. Which state agency is most commonly responsible for oversight of the workers' compensation insurance?
   a. The Department of Health and Human Services
   b. The Department of Labor
   c. The Department of Public Safety
   d. The Department of Public Works

Answer Explanations #1

1. C: Compliance and adherence to care are two separate components to patient care that are often confused with one another. Compliance refers to a patient simply following doctor's orders or a discharge plan, whereas adherence to care encourages patients to be involved in their care plan by discussing their limitations and strengths and engaging in other healthy behaviors that encourage good health outcomes (such as taking medications and incorporating lifestyle changes).

2. D: Joan is considered nonadherent because she voluntarily missed a scheduled post-appointment visit. Nonadherence to care is highly correlated with poor patient outcomes. It is possible that if Joan had adhered to her post-appointment schedule, any complications with her surgical site could have been discovered earlier, with fewer complications (or prevented entirely). She is described as having good medical knowledge, Choice *A*, was otherwise compliant in following at-home instructions for taking medications, Choice *B*, and financial issues, Choice *C*, were not prominently addressed, so the other options would not apply.

3. B: Communication skills are critical for health care case managers, who assess how well patients are adhering to care instructions. It requires detailing care instructions, ensuring that the patient understands them, and picking up on both obvious and subtle personal barriers to adherence the patient might present. This requires the case manager to have excellent listening and speaking skills. While the other options listed may be useful, those skills are often not the responsibility of the case manager (rather, they may be employed by other members of the interdisciplinary team).

4. B: The all-inclusive model allows residents in a continuing care retirement community, a type of residential community in which residents can receive various types of care for the duration of their time there, to receive both long-term care services and health care services. Other financial options include fee-for-service, where residents pay for specific services as they are used, and modified coverage model, in which residents get care based on an established maximum. These options may or may not qualify for certain tax advantages, Choice *A*, and may or may not be paid for using Medicare, a government-subsidized medical insurance plan for certain eligible individuals, Choice *C*. An IRA, Choice *D*, is a type of investment account that does not apply to the question presented.

5. A: Assisted-living facilities allow residents to live in apartment-style homes on their own and can provide services such as in-home help or medication assistance as needed. They are considered a middle ground between completely independent living and a nursing home and are more economical than full-time care. Senior apartment centers, Choice *B*, are communities geared toward older residents, but they do not offer assisted-living services. Health-aide housing, Choice *C*, and all-inclusive models, Choice *D*, are not real entities of the care system.

6. D: Unconditional positive regard is a part of client engagement. When clients feel safe and validated to disclose information, it leads to a better relationship and rapport building with the client.

7. A: Active listening and showing empathy are important parts of establishing rapport with a client, which contributes to client engagement. Choice *B,* making sure the client is truthful and makes eye contact, may come once rapport is established, but these client behaviors are not part of the clinician's job, which is establishing rapport; instead, they involve participation and trust from the client, which will hopefully come if good rapport is established. Choice *C,* focusing on what is good and hopeful in the

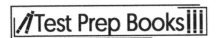

client, is a part of client empowerment, and Choice *D,* assessing and evaluating the client's problem, is another step in the client engagement process.

8. C: Informed decision-making is a critical part of client self-care management. The role of the case manager is to help educate clients, so they have a better understanding of their treatment options to better self-manage their care.

9. B: A case manager's role is to help clients find appropriate resources in different areas of a client's life, including emotional, social, spiritual, physical, and psychological.

10. B: The first step for a case manager in conflict resolution is to be respectful and display empathy with clients and family members. Other steps include use of eye contact, nodding, and active listening skills, Choice *A,* to accurately collect information from all parties, Choice *D,* and then identify the problem objectively, Choice *C.* Finally, it is important to note that case managers should ensure the client's needs are a priority at all times.

11. D: Genetic predisposition to the condition is the only answer choice that is not considered to be one of the variables that form the foundation of the Aggregated Diagnosis Groups (ADGs). The ADGs make up a system of thirty-two groups that are used to assign patients based on their health condition. It is possible for a patient to be assigned to multiple groups if they have more than one health condition. Specialty care involvement, Choice *A,* etiology of the condition, Choice *B,* and diagnostic certainty, Choice *C,* are all variables that form the foundation of the ADGs.

12. A: A survey is a tool that is used to evaluate a program to provide insight into how well it is operating, along with identifying opportunities for improvement. Choices *B, C,* and *D* are all options for obtaining customer feedback.

13. C: The statement that best explains the Six Sigma model that is used to measure quality improvement is, "It results in a renewed customer approach, costs savings, and/or the reduction or removal of defects." DMADV is used to develop a new process, or when an existing process requires more than an incremental improvement, Choice *A.* DMAIC is used when an existing process needs improvement because it is not meeting standards, Choice *D.* Six Sigma can lead to process backlogs, but that does not mean many people feel that it has a limited effect in the healthcare industry, Choice *B.*

14. A: The transitional care model is focused on the successful movement of the client to the next appropriate level of care, which may include the client's home, a rehabilitation unit, or an extended care facility. Although cost containment is a consideration, the primary functions of the transitional care model depend on proper client recruitment, comprehensive documentation, and evaluation.

15. B: A recent history of depression or psychiatric illness can alter the client's score on the depression scale, and the CCM must consider that history when using the scale as part of the care-planning process. The questions may be familiar, as noted in Choice *A;* however, the directions ask for a real-time assessment of the client's feelings, so any familiarity with the specific questions should not impact the results of the test. The scale is self-administered, so there is no technician to influence the results, Choice *C.* The intended use of the test is to assess the client for depression in order to complete the individualized plan of care. This means the intended use of the results, Choice *D,* is consistent with the function of the test and will not adversely affect the client's results.

16. D: The Frenchay (FAST) Index assesses four major areas of language, including verbal expression and comprehension, reading, and writing. This assessment can differentiate expressive and receptive

aphasia in addition to other common communication defects. Choice *A*, the Katz instrument, and Choice *B*, the Pfeffer Index, are appropriate for the assessment of the client's abilities related to ADLs. Choice *C*, the Stroop test, is designed to assess executive function, which may be used with the FAST Index to assess comprehension.

17. D: While unanimously reaffirming the existing ethical framework for practice, the commission identified privacy and security concerns, Choice *A*, and technological advances, Choice *B*, as critical issues currently affecting professional practice. Other issues addressed in the review included the need to adapt clinical practice to multiple care environments and a renewed call to avoid conflicts of interest. The CCM is charged with maintaining the code of ethics through rigorous attention to clinical practice and a life-long commitment to education. The existing ethical framework is reaffirmed as the basis for CCM practice.

18. A: The CCM is commonly responsible for providing client education so the client has all of the information required for making an informed decision, Choice *B*, and setting personal goals, Choice *C*. Once the therapy is begun, the CCM may be responsible for observing and documenting the results of the therapy, Choice *D*. However, the majority of case managers employed in acute-care or industrial settings would not commonly be responsible for grant applications.

19. C: While case managers may direct patients or provide resources relating to the government benefits for which they might be eligible, they are not responsible for enrolling patients directly into those programs. The other options listed are direct responsibilities of the case manager.

20. B: In this statement, Ryan acknowledges the patient's desires and takes action to involve specialists who can better equip the patient with evidence-based, expert knowledge about when and how to continue her yoga practice. The other statements ignore her wishes, Choice *A*, are limiting, Choice *C*, and are based off Ryan's personal opinions rather than a medical opinion, Choice *D*. Case managers should make every attempt to empower and involve patients in their own recovery and respect their wishes.

21. D: These are all factors that improve access to high-quality health care. A top-rated facility must be in a location accessible to patients, even those without personal transportation. Patients with comprehensive health insurance are also able to access quality health care with greater ease, as they do not experience the full financial burden. Finally, technology-driven processes optimize and standardize operations to minimize errors and increase quality.

22. A: Managed care systems are those where an organization contracts with another organization (usually a place of business or other operation) to provide a set of health care services to the group at a discounted rate. Tailored care, Choice *B*, is not a system. TRICARE, Choice *C*, is a type of insurance for military personnel. Obamacare, Choice *D*, is a colloquial name for the Affordable Care Act of 2010, which was passed during the Obama administration.

23. C: Vulnerable populations consist of the demographics listed, as they are at increased risk of poor health outcomes due to decreased access to care. Those who are uninsured or poor or cannot easily get to a health facility may face difficult financial burdens or other obstacles in order to treat simple health problems, which can then progress to more serious or chronic conditions.

24. C: Medicare Part D provides Medicare recipients with coverage for prescription drugs in order to reduce the financial burden for older and/or disabled people. Part A, Choice *A*, covers hospital visits. Part B, Choice *B*, covers additional, optional medical services and requires a premium to be paid. Choice

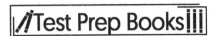

D is incorrect because Medicare Part D provides Medicare recipients with coverage for prescription drugs. Some patients choose to get supplemental drug coverage as well.

25. A: Medicare is government-sponsored health insurance for all people aged sixty-five years or older and people of any age who have end-stage renal disease or a disability. It is divided into three parts: one that covers health care without a monthly premium, one for other additional services (such as outpatient services) for a monthly premium, and one for prescription medications for a monthly premium.

26. C: It is important to make sure the client is comfortable in the environment where the interview is taking place. Adjustments should be made to the location, time, etc., to create the best environment for an effective interview. Choice *A*, encouraging empowerment; Choice *B*, the client's health literacy; and Choice *D*, the client's history of substance abuse, may occur or be discussed as part of the interview process but are not primary considerations.

27. A: Belief in something larger than self is the best definition of spirituality. Choice *B*, belief in a divine or higher being and the accompanying doctrine, is a possible definition of religion. It is important for a case manager to be aware of a client's spiritual and religious beliefs and respect and appreciate how their beliefs might affect services.

28. A: A case manager's ability to respect and appreciate a client's cultural background is called *cultural competency*. All case managers should strive to achieve cultural competency to effectively serve clients of different cultures. Choice *C*, the concept of multiculturalism, includes individuals from many different cultures and nations living together to form a society.

29. D: Financial history is not usually a barrier to the case management process. A client's overall cultural background, Choice *C*, including religion and spirituality, Choice *A*, and primary language, Choice *B*, may all serve as barriers to the case management process. Case managers should work to become culturally competent to minimize the effect of those barriers.

30. D: Case managers may provide informal psychological assessments during the case management process. Choice *A*, psychological evaluations; Choice *B*, neuropsychological evaluations; and Choice *C*, personality assessments, which are part of these evaluations, are performed by psychologists or neuropsychologists.

31. B: The Case Load Capacity Calculator is a free tool that is used to determine the appropriate caseload for a case manager. Case Lite Professional, Choice *A*, Case Works Pro, Choice *C*, and Case Management Software, Choice *D*, are simply fictitious names of tools that a case manager might use.

32. C: Case management programs that attain accreditation are able to demonstrate their ability to deliver and facilitate quality health care. These types of programs make sure that both clinical and nonclinical staff have well-defined roles and clearly outlined responsibilities, unlike Choice *B*, which says that case management programs make sure that only clinical staff have well-defined roles, and unlike Choice *C*, which says that case management programs ensure that only nonclinical staff have clearly outlined responsibilities. Case management programs also pay their staff at or above market value, unlike Choice *A*, which says that case management programs pay their staff below market value to help manage costs.

33. D: The only item in this list that would not factor into determining a case manager's caseload is a new company culture initiative. This type of initiative is undertaken to rebuild the culture in an

organization where morale is low, and employees are not engaged in their work and the overall mission. Complexity of the cases, Choice A, regulatory requirements, Choice B, and experience of the case manager, Choice D, are all factors that play a role into determining a case manager's caseload.

34. C: The functional capacity assessment is focused on the client's ability to perform basic tasks as well as job-specific tasks. The client's perceived ability for each of these behaviors will have a significant effect on the outcomes of the rehabilitative plan of care; therefore, Choice C is correct. Although it is an important consideration of the overall plan of care, the cost of the devices, Choice A, is not an element of the functional capacity assessment. The functional capacity assessment is focused on assessment of the need for the devices rather than identifying an estimate of the duration of the use of the devices, Choice B. The client's opinions are an important part of the functional capacity assessment that is used to identify appropriate assistive devices rather than to enforce punitive measures for noncompliance, Choice D.

35. A: The functional capacity assessment is an essential element of the rehabilitation plan, and successful completion of that plan is contingent on the identification of the nature of the injury, the appropriate assistive devices related to the injury, and the specific patient needs. Based on those findings, the functional capacity assessment then evaluates the client's abilities to complete daily and job-related tasks. The financial assessment, Choice B, is not a part of this sequence. Choice C (recovery potential and preexisting conditions) is also incorrect because it does not include the nature of the most recent injury, which is an essential step in the creation of the rehabilitation plan. Resource identification, Choice D, is also an important element of the overall care plan, but it is not one of the steps in this primary sequence.

36. A: Acute is not a descriptor used for categorizing the degree of injury. The descriptors are used to assess and plan for the client's specific needs. The remaining choices, B (minor/mild), C (moderate), and D (severe), are used to plan care.

37. D: The CCM understands that federal law dictates access to designated compulsory services. State laws regulate the provision of services that are designated as noncompulsory. This means the CCM must be aware of all state-mandated services available to the client. Choice D is a noncompulsory service that may or may not be available to the client, depending on applicable state laws. Choices A (family planning), B (out-patient hospitalization), and C (in-home services) are compulsory services required by federal law.

38. B: The functional assessment provides the basis for the determination of the client's injury as a disability. A disabled client requires the employer to make reasonable accommodations in the work environment to facilitate the client's return to work. The employer is not responsible for funding training for an alternative position or renovating the client's home environment; therefore, Choices A and C are incorrect. The client's care team is responsible for working with the client to determine the optimum time frame for the client's return to work. Therefore, Choice D is incorrect.

39. D: Experts agree that accurate documentation that is completed in a timely manner is the CCM's best defense against charges of negligent referral and all other charges as well. Case reports that are comprehensive, complete, and accurate provide the "paper trail" that creates an objective view of the CCM's performance. The activities identified in Choices A, B, and C may be subject to agency policy, but they do not provide an objective view of the management performance of the CCM.

40. B: ERISA was originally enacted to protect individuals with disabilities. Modifications of the original legislation allow insurers to deny all appeals for services not covered that are received more than sixty days after the notification of denial is received. The CCM should assist the client to actively pursue all appeal remedies within the stated time frame. Choice *A* is incorrect because the law provides coverage for disability care rather than health care. ERISA was initially intended to standardize basic coverage for disabled persons, not specifically mentally challenged adults; therefore, Choice *C* is incorrect. Choice *D* is incorrect because this law does not outline treatment caps for mental health therapy.

41. B: Breanna's injury is muscular in nature, limiting, and near an important structure (her cervical spine), but she is still able to provide at-home care measures for herself and move around. She requires immediate care due to her extreme discomfort and the fact that the pain is not subsiding at home, but this is likely not a life-threatening situation that requires emergency care, Choice *A*, or a chronic condition that would require respite care, Choice *C*, or trauma care, Choice *D*.

42. C: Short-term stabilization provides immediate care to stabilize patients with threatening conditions in order to transfer them to more appropriate services. In this case, Mitchell experienced a life-threatening event requiring immediate intervention (such as defibrillation, medication, and assisted ventilation) to keep him alive until he was in an environment where he could receive comprehensive medical care. Urgent care, Choice *A*, refers to treatment that is not life sustaining but still is required quickly. Trauma care, Choice *B*, takes place in a full medical environment and cannot be effectively delivered in an ambulance. Mitchell received short-term stabilization in transit and therefore did not receive long-term care, Choice *D*.

43. C: Long-term care facilities are those where ongoing support is provided for complex conditions in which patients cannot adequately care for themselves. They are not necessarily limited to elderly patients, as a number of patients under the age of sixty-five may need long-term care due to congenital conditions or catastrophic events.

44. A: Managed Care Organizations encourage their members to see primary care providers first and specialists only with a referral. This promotes health care that is more affordable and brings costs down across the board by limiting specialty visits unless absolutely necessary.

45. D: Preferred Provider Organizations allow patients to select from a large range of in-network providers as well as out-of-network providers for whom a portion of services will still be covered. Patients can also see specialist doctors without a referral, which can save time and empower them to select the providers they want rather than be referred to someone they may not have selected otherwise.

46. B: Health Maintenance Organizations provide access to health care services in a select region, such as by state or region of the country (i.e., the southeast). These types of organizations may even be managed by physicians, therefore opening access to patients who are in the geographical vicinity of these providers and would, consequently, be able to use their services.

47. B: Point-of-service plans combine the better aspects of HMO plans and PPO plans by leveraging an in-network primary care provider who can refer patients to specialists that are both inside and outside the network. While the overall plan may be cheaper, deductibles are expensive, and administrative processes can be cumbersome.

48. A: According to the CCMC, Choices *B* (educational preparation), *C* (clinical expertise), and *D* (ongoing professional development) are specific elements of competence, while knowledge of statutory laws is required but is identified as a legal and benefits system requirement.

49. A: The CCM has violated the professional obligation of disclosure. The client must be informed that all data will be documented and shared with the appropriate personnel. In this example, the issue of the possible legal implications also means the CCM is obligated to inform the client of the use of the data.

50. C: The registries are focused on providing current, relevant data to primary care practitioners at the point of care. The registries are often accommodated by existing EHR software and can be stored on desktop computers and/or agency servers. The CCM understands that the data is not intended for insurance providers, Choice *A*, and many of the registries are regional in scope. The registries are used to guide the treatment of many chronic diseases, including diabetes, Choice *B*, in addition to rare diseases and regional diseases such as Lyme disease in the northeast United States. In most instances, the client's consent for care allows the collection of PHI, but the CCM is still responsible for full disclosure. The CCM is responsible for identifying the registries that are relevant to assigned client populations in order to enter the appropriate data.

51. B: Choice *A*, having bruises, abrasions, or other evidence of physical trauma, and Choice *C*, presenting as withdrawn, sad, or angry, are all indicators of physical abuse. Choice *D*, bedwetting/enuresis, is also an indicator of possible physical abuse. However, missed doctor visits are a more likely sign of client neglect.

52. A: The best definition of abuse is causing harm to another person that leads to physical, emotional, and psychological distress and/or pain. Choice *B*, behaviors or actions that contribute to bodily health, are better related to behavioral health concepts. Choice *C*, refusing to provide food and care for a dependent person, is a better definition of neglect. While Choice *D*, a client that is in physical danger or under excessive mental distress, may be an abusive situation, it is a better definition of a crisis.

53. A: During the "Form a coalition" stage, case managers, service providers, and the client's family come together and collaborate to support the client's change process. Choice *B*, looking at different areas of a client's life to offer appropriate resources, and Choice *C*, ensuring the client receives support from friends, family, and support groups, are part of locating community resources. Choice *D*, creating a plan with clients ahead of time to prevent a possible crisis, is a part of crisis intervention.

54. D: Displays of anxiety or aggression are more commonly possible signs of substance abuse or addiction, along with slurred speech, and a change in sleeping pattern. Choice *A*, enuresis; Choice *B*, vomiting; and Choice *C*, disheveled or unkempt appearances, are more likely indicators of abuse and neglect.

55. C: When case managers help clients become empowered, they focus on client strengths, not weaknesses, and use the client's resources to help take an active role in treatment. Choice *A*, client activation, is related to tapping into a client's motivation so they can be an active participant in treatment. Choice *B*, client engagement, happens during the beginning stage of the treatment process and involves encouraging the client to buy into the treatment process. Choice *D*, client self-care management, involves helping clients achieve ongoing involvement and management of their care.

56. B: Some individuals in specific states can receive a Medicaid waiver to apply to their room, boarding, and amenity costs. Most assisted-living facilities operate as for-profit companies, and usually subsidies

are not an option. It is not expected that elder residents who need care will crowd multiple people into a single-bedroom unit, Choice *A*. All members over seventy do not qualify for subsidies, Choice *C*. Any low-income individual can apply for HUD vouchers, Choice *D*, but HUD units are not assisted-living facilities.

57. D: Group homes may house patients of any age (although they are generally divided between children and adults) and often serve those with illnesses that are difficult to manage with a single, untrained caregiver.

58. A: The assessment process usually consists of reviewing a new patient's information, including medical history and information provided directly by the patient or the patient's caregivers. The assessment process may also include a series of additional tests to determine health literacy or health risk factors. These processes allow the case manager to holistically work with the patient and ensure the best health outcomes in the long run.

59. A: Once the case manager has reviewed factors such as the patient's health stability, ability to use resources to help their condition, risk for readmission, level of available social support, and ability to adhere to care and determined that the patient will be able to maintain their highest level of functioning, the patient's case will typically be closed. The other options do not result in case closure, as the patient may still need case management during any of these events. A case may also be closed due to death, lack of payment or benefits, lack of service availability, or if the patient/caregiver declines services.

60. B: The *Diagnostic and Statistical Manual of Mental Disorders* (currently in its fifth edition) functions as the standard system of classification of mental disorders. It provides diagnostic classification, criteria, and descriptive texts. It is widely used by health care and allied health professionals. The International Classification of Diseases, Choice *A*, is used for all types of diseases, not just mental disorders. Choices *C* and *D* are not real entities.

61. D: Patient satisfaction surveys can be one way to collect outcomes data. Outcomes are critical to understanding whether treatments and interventions are working as desired. Other methods to measure outcomes include collecting data relating to quality, provider service times, costs, and business metrics.

62. C: During transitions between different points of care, ranging from between-care facilities or simple nursing staff transitions, patients are especially vulnerable to medical or administrative errors. This often occurs due to incomplete or inaccurate communication about the patient's health status or care needs. Case managers play a role in ensuring all necessary caregivers and interdisciplinary team members have accurate and complete information about a patient in order for transitions to occur smoothly.

63. B: Case managers should always place advocacy for their patients as a top job priority, even if this puts them in a tough position against the organization for which they work. Patient advocacy is a fundamental component of this role; case managers should always support and empower choices that are in the patient's best interest and optimize the patient's chances for positive health outcomes.

64. C: Cost containment is the practice of providing comprehensive services at the least cost. Co-payments, fixed fees, deductibles, and coinsurance shift some of the financial burden onto the patient, therefore serving as a cost containment measure for the insurance company. These do not count as

multiple streams of revenue, Choice *A*, for the insurance company, as the payments are going to the provider. This is not a form of theoretical planning, Choice *B*, and the question is not relevant to legal provisions such as the Affordable Care Act, Choice *D*.

65. A: PPOs, or preferred provider organizations, group networks of providers that accept specific types of insurance. Patients with this insurance have to go to the listed providers in order to use their insurance benefits, but it does result in lower costs for the patient.

66. B: This is an example of a benchmark, which companies establish internally to monitor the overall effectiveness of case management within the organization. Companies can also use the data to compare their performance to that of other organizations. A performance improvement plan, Choice *A*, is used to help employees who are experiencing performance deficiencies to succeed. Corrective action, Choice *C*, is used to help coach an employee who is displaying unacceptable behavior. A metric, Choice *D*, is used to measure performance toward a goal.

67. D: The SF-36 health risk assessment serves as a representation of a patient's perception of his health status, perceived limitations, social support, and environment. The MMSE, Choice *A*, provides an assessment of cognitive impairment. The RUDAS, Choice *B*, provides an assessment of dementia, and the 30-point Folstein, Choice *D*, is another name for the MMSE assessment.

68. A: Case managers utilize health risk assessments to serve as an asset in the predictive modeling process. Case managers are not interested in a patient's past perception of his health status, Choice *B*, and they are able to review a patient's healthcare experience that is readily documented and accessible on their own, Choice *C*. Finally, case managers do not desire to disprove the classification of patients into domains or risk categories, Choice *D*.

69. C: Predictive modeling is a tool that is used to determine best practices and distribute associated resources based on historical data. The remaining answer options, Choices *A, B,* and *D,* are incorrect because none of the terms are nationally recognized in this arena.

70. D: Cognitive function and executive function are often used interchangeably in the literature; however, there are common factors and differences that emerge from the item descriptions. Memory is common to both assessments, while verbal fluency, Choice *A*, is assessed with cognitive functioning instruments such as the Mini-Mental State Examination, and inhibition, Choice *B*, and self-regulation, Choice *C*, are assessed with executive functioning instruments such as the Stroop test.

71. C: The primary purpose of the assistive devices is to increase the client's self-confidence, which in turn positively affects the rehabilitation process because client participation will be enhanced. This view is supported by the theory of self-efficacy, which proposes that individuals do not participate in new behaviors unless they have a sense that they will succeed. Choices *A, B,* and *D* may also result from the client's enhanced self-confidence; however, none of the choices is the primary purpose for the use of assistive devices.

72. A: Damage to Wernicke's area results in receptive aphasia, which means the client is unable to comprehend the spoken word. Intensive speech therapy is used to improve comprehension. Choices *B* (sign language and lip reading) and *C* (assistive devices) are not appropriate to the stated injury. In contrast, damage to Broca's area results in expressive aphasia, which is treated with syntax therapy, Choice *D*, that may include word-finding treatments.

73. B: The client with a high ankle sprain will most likely be treated with self-care at home; the injury will not have a significant impact on the client's ability to return to work. The injuries identified in Choices *A*, *C*, and *D* (hand laceration, dislocated shoulder, and grade 2 pectoral muscle tear) will potentially require surgery, rehabilitation, and possible accommodations to return to work. The CCM would be involved in the planning process for transitional care and rehab.

74. D: There are eight steps in Kotter's 8-step change model. They include creating urgency, forming a coalition, creating a vision, communicating the vision, removing obstacles, creating short-term wins, building on the change, and anchoring the change.

75. B: When case managers collaborate with clients to create crisis plans, one component of the plan should include possible methods to help the client cope with the crisis, such as relaxation strategies and a plan to call upon and utilize the client's support system. Choice *A*, client goals, is a part of client empowerment, and Choice *D*, resources for spiritual and social needs, is a part of referring the client to community resources. Assessment tools to determine crisis severity, Choice *C*, would be important in establishing an appropriate crisis plan, but it is not a component of the plan itself.

76. B: Helping a client de-escalate or effectively manage emotions during a crisis is a critical step in crisis management. One method of de-escalation is encouraging the use of relaxation techniques. Another is the intervention of an uninvolved participant to help stabilize the crisis. Choice *A*, working with participants to find a solution that is satisfactory to everyone, is the collaboration style of conflict management, and Choice *C*, helping with pain management, is a part of end-of-life care. Choice *D*, helping a perpetrator of abuse develop anger management skills might be a helpful step in the long-term, but it is not the definition nor a major component of de-escalation.

77. D: A typical focus during end-of-life care is assisting clients with sleep and appetite issues, which are common symptoms of clients diagnosed with a terminal illness. Other typical symptoms include digestive issues, nausea, and fatigue. Choice *A*, physical therapy, and Choice *B*, neuropsychological assessments, are not typical parts of end-of-life care. Choice *C*, the Newest Vital Sign test, is a health literacy assessment.

78. A: Palliative care includes all care given between the diagnosis of a terminal illness and death. This type of care could go on for an extended period of time, especially with the improvements in the treatment of terminal illnesses. Choice *B*, hospice care, is more time limited and typically takes place during the last stage of a person's terminal illness. Choice *C*, end-of-life care, incorporates all aspects of treatment for an individual diagnosed with a terminal illness. Choice *D*, withdrawal of care, is making the decision to remove means of artificial life support for a person diagnosed with a terminal illness.

79. B: Motivational interviewing is a technique utilized in wellness coaching. This type of interviewing assesses a client's desire to make positive changes. It also helps to identify what motivates a client to make changes or prevents a client from making changes.

80. A: The Newest Vital Sign assessment is an assessment that uses a sample nutritional label to test a client's health literacy. Choice *B*, the Thomas–Kilmann Instrument, is used to assess conflict resolution skills. Choice *C*, the Thematic Appperception Test, and Choice *D*, the Multiphasic Personality Inventory, are used in psychological evaluations.

81. A: Client engagement, including rapport building, is the first step in wellness coaching, much like it is with other types of client services. Choice *C*, assisting with goal setting, and Choice *D*, providing education, are later steps in the wellness coaching process.

82. A: The health coach should utilize motivational interviewing to assess Mary's desire and willingness to make positive changes. It would also help to identify what internally motivates Mary and to identify reasons she may have difficulty making the desired positive changes. Choice *B*, negotiation, is a type of conflict resolution style where everyone gives a little and gets a little. Choice *C*, client activation, is the level of involvement clients have in their treatment. Choice *D*, informed decision-making, is a vital part of self-care management.

83. A: Health literacy is important, as a client's inability to understand the information given by medical professionals, such as medication instructions or treatment recommendations, can affect the success of treatment.

84. D: A possible barrier to successful group communication is one group member feeling uncomfortable expressing himself due to oppression by other members. All members of a group should feel they are being heard and their opinions are welcomed. This can be achieved by ensuring rules and expectations of the group are clear to the members.

85. B: Close-ended questions are typically used to collect basic information from a client, including name, address, and age. Choice *A*, open-ended questions, will allow case managers to get more in-depth information from the client's perspective. Choice *C*, clarifying questions, are used to gain more information from a client and encourage better self-expression.

86. D: An acuity-level rating indicates how severe a patient's disability or illness is. It is given based on factors determined by the organization in which the patient is seen; the patient is normally rated upon intake. While this practice is not standardized, general commonalities appear to be widely considered when providing acuity-level ratings.

87. B: A special-needs trust allows a legal appointee to manage assets on behalf of someone who is mentally or physically unable to do so alone. Through obtaining legal appointment, Gene can also file for government benefits (such as Medicaid) on behalf of his adult daughter. In these instances, a case manager may need to provide documentation for the potential guardian. Otherwise, Gene cannot legally freeze his adult daughter's account, Choice *A*, or pay bills in her name using her bank account, Choice *C*. Even if she is eligible for Medicare, Medicare benefits, Choice *D*, would not allow Gene to manage his daughter's assets.

88. A: A viatical settlement is when an individual chooses to sell a personal life insurance policy in order to pay for medical treatments or other situations that may be causing a financial burden. The sale amount is often contingent on the reason for selling as well as the person's prognosis.

89. D: The Utilization Review Accreditation Commission's performance measures are divided into mandatory and exploratory categories, unlike Choice *A*, which says that they are all mandatory measures. Value is provided by these performance measures to both purchasers and consumers, unlike Choice *B*, which says they provide value only to consumers, and unlike Choice *C*, which says they provide value only to purchasers.

90. A: Employees who fail fitness-for-duty exams is not a measurement that falls under the Utilization Review Accreditation Commission's case management domain for accreditation. An employee may be

asked to take a medical exam, which is known as a fitness-for-duty exam, when an employer is questioning if they are psychologically or physically able to perform their job. Percentage medically released to return to work, Choice B, medical readmissions, Choice C, and disability and workers' compensation, Choice D, are measurements that fall under URAC's case management domain for accreditation.

91. C: Effective transition management is not one of the reasons that a health plan would seek accreditation from the National Committee for Quality Assurance (NCQA). Rather, the Utilization Review Accreditation Commission's case management accreditation program focuses on enabling health plans to manage transitions effectively. An example of this deals with reducing the risk for inpatient admissions to support the Affordable Care Act. Wellness and health promotion programs, Choice A, support in receiving market advantage, Choice B, and assistance with request-for-proposal requirements, Choice D, are all reasons for a health plan to seek NCQA accreditation.

92. B: When an organization receives a level of disease management accreditation known as "accredited with performance reporting" from the National Committee for Quality Assurance, its program meets or exceeds the NCQA's standards, and it is required to provide a report for disease management measures. When an organization receives a level of disease management accreditation known as "accredited," Choice C, its program has obtained the highest rating. Finally, when an organization receives a level of disease management accreditation known as "provisional accreditation," Choice A, its program has failed to meet some of the NCQA's standards, and it will be required to take some action in the next twelve months to achieve status. NCQA does not provide a level of accreditation that is known as lifetime mastery, Choice D.

93. D: Agencies who attain provisional accreditation under the NCQA must act within twelve months to achieve a higher status. They are not provided provisional accreditation for a two-year period, as is stated in Choice B. Agencies that earn the highest level of accreditation do so for a three-year period, not five years, as is stated in Choice A. Agencies that meet NCQA standards earn accreditation for a two-year period. Finally, there are no agencies that are awarded accreditation status for the life of their business based on their high level of performance, as stated in Choice C.

94. A: Adherence to statins is an example of a process quality measure under the National Quality Forum. An example of a structure NQF quality measure, Choice B, is the adoption of medication e-Prescribing. Acute stroke mortality rate is an example of an outcomes quality measure under the National Quality Forum, Choice C. Finally, an example of a composite NQF quality measure, Choice D, is comprehensive diabetes care: hemoglobin A1c (HbA1c) testing.

95. C: The mission of the National Quality Forum entails the maintenance of a portfolio of performance measures that have a direct impact on the ability to deliver high quality care. These quality measures fall into various groups including: composite, outcomes, structure, and process. Choices A, B, and D are not relevant.

96. B: The Manager Network is not one of the board of directors' committees that is responsible for facilitating the National Quality Forum's activities. The four committees include: The Leadership Network, National Priorities Partnership, Choice A, Health IT Advisory Committee, Choice C, and Consensus Standards Approval Committee, Choice D.

97. D: The National Guideline Clearinghouse (NGC) is valuable because it gives healthcare professionals access to a wide variety of clinical practice guidelines. Clients and healthcare professionals can access

these easy-to-understand guidelines that provide equal access to research treatment options and associated risks. The HAI Program contributes checklists and toolkits to aid in the prevention of healthcare associated infections, Choice *A*. AHRQ's core measures enable the reporting of quality measures that best align to the improvement of patient outcomes, Choice *B*. AHRQ also performs research that provides insight into patient safety threats and the overall impact of medical errors, Choice *C*.

98. C: The ADA allows reasonable accommodation for women with complications of pregnancy who qualify for disability. For instance, a client required to maintain bedrest may be offered a position in the employer's call center. The interpretation of this provision of the ADA has been inconsistent, and the definition of disability in this client population has varied significantly from one jurisdiction to another. Choices *A, B,* and *D* are provisions of the Pregnancy Discrimination Act, which is a subsection of title 7. The act protects pregnant women from discrimination with regard to employment policies.

99. B: According to government data, prior to the introduction of the ACA, individuals with no insurance or with plans with limited coverage tended to file workers' compensation claims instead. This means there is currently a reduction in the number of claims, which may or may not continue. Under the ACA, employers still continue to receive discounts on health care costs for the successful implementation of wellness initiatives in the workplace, Choice *A*. In addition, the ACA has resulted in increased numbers of part-time employees because individuals are able to work fewer hours as a result of their lowered insurance costs, Choice *C*. Choice *D* is incorrect because it's not that the premiums for workers' compensation have increased less rapidly since the implementation of the ACA; it's that the number of workers' compensation claims have declined.

100. A: The consent to treatment document is rarely itemized, which means the client is entrusting the providers with wide discretion to implement the plan of care. Although the client can refuse treatment at any point, most commonly, a degree of autonomy is given up in favor of the plan of care. Choice *B* (paternalism) is a less common influence of autonomy than it was several years ago. The provider–client relationship has more often become a partnership, with decisions being influenced by the opinions of all concerned. CCMs vigorously support the client's autonomy and are most often successful in ensuring the client is making informed decisions, Choice *C*. Obviously, the success or failure of these efforts depends on the particular situation; however, educated decision-making is always preferable to the alternative. Litigation, Choice *D*, concerns are the basis for defensive medicine, which is not publicly identified as a common practice. The literature indicates that most physicians (two-thirds of those polled) would not resort to defensive medicine, while the remaining one-third consider it to be an appropriate approach in certain circumstances.

101. D: All of the listed interventions are appropriate; however, It is clear that the client and his wife do not understand the implication of the client's injuries. The CCM has concerns about the couple's ability to comprehend the information due to his wife's anxiety and his recent intake of alcohol. While protecting the client's PHI, Choice *A*, contacting the PCP, Choice *B*, and contacting the orthopedic surgeon for pain management orders, Choice *C*, are appropriate for this client, the CCM's main concern is the client's comprehension of the severity of his situation. It is critical that both the client and his wife understand the CCM's presentation of the facts.

102. C: Adhesive contracts are often called *take it or leave it* contracts. This term was used to describe the often substandard health insurance policies that prompted the development of the ACA. Policies in compliance with the requirements of the ACA are moderately priced and allow the client to choose from the available options. Recent independent oversight of compliance with the ACA indicates that, although

the individual states are responsible for implementation and enforcement of the ACA, the existing consumer protection laws are often inadequate to provide legal recourse to consumers against the insurers of the adhesive contracts. For instance, in most states, consumer protection laws do not apply to insurance, and breach of contract laws only apply to insurance policies that incorporate all of the required elements of the ACA. All of this means that adhesive contracts can still be sold to uneducated consumers, and dissatisfied consumers most likely will not have legal recourse against insurers in most states. Therefore, Choices *A, B*, and *D* are incorrect.

103. A: The model suggests that identifying internal client contextual characteristics, such as religious beliefs and other personal interests, can facilitate the development of a rapport among the client, the client's support system, and the CCM. In addition, external client contextual characteristics, such as issues surrounding the availability of resources and the constraints placed on care due to insurer regulations, will also affect the CCM's care plan and associations with the client and the support group, Choice *B*. The severity and characteristics of the client's specific condition will affect the CCM's response to the other quadrants of the model.

For instance, in many societies and in at-risk populations, access to health care is rationed or scarce due to the lack of resources. The CCM's response to these conditions will dictate the approach to care planning. Supporting client preferences for care planning is similar to supporting the client's autonomy. The essential element of this support is the CCM's acknowledgment of the client's right to make a poor decision, which is the definition of autonomy, Choice *C*. The moral dilemma of recognizing and supporting the client's quality of life is one of the CCM's ongoing challenges. The difficulty stems from the inevitable differences among the clients and the members of their support systems, and at this point, the CCM is required to meet the client's needs if at all possible with available resources, Choice *D*.

104. B: The CCM has violated the CCMC standard of representation of practice, qualifications, and competence. The CCM has not actively practiced clinical nursing for some period of time as a self-employed case manager. This means the CCM is practicing outside of boundaries of the job description for case management. In this example, there was no harm done to the client; in fact, the client was probably grateful for the intervention. However, the fact remains that a professional standard for practice has been violated. The response of the home care nurse in Choice *B* indicates a dissatisfaction with the CCM's decision to intervene. Choices *A* and *C* appear to indicate that the home care nurses agreed with the CCM's decision to intervene. The nurse's response in Choice *D* is a similar sentiment as Choice *B* but written in a less professional manner. Practicing within the bounds of one's licensure, job description, and educational preparation is essential to the CCM's professional practice.

105: D: Although cost-effectiveness is most commonly identified as an essential element of CCM practice, the CCMC did not include it on the priority list. The remaining choices were included as primary elements of the case management process.

106. A: The CCMC specifically identifies moral courage as a useful personality characteristic for dealing with ethical dilemmas that arise in the relationships in the health care environment. Choices *B, C*, and *D* (stamina, stubbornness, and perseverance) would be useful in all forms of nursing practice.

107. B: Medicaid is government-sponsored health insurance for vulnerable populations. Additionally, SCHIPs (which vary by state) provide health insurance for children whose household incomes are too high for Medicaid but who have no other access to health insurance. Medicare, Choice *A*, provides coverage for older adults and some young adults with specific disabilities. SNAP, Choice *C*, provides food

assistance to people whose income falls below certain limits. TANF, Choice *D*, provides temporary cash assistance to needy families.

108. C: Case managers have a responsibility to assist with behavioral health concerns, including mental and emotional concerns. In this situation, Nancy does well to notice outward signs of sadness and anxiety in her patient, which is often a common response for cancer survivors. By suggesting she make an appointment with the counselor, Nancy is serving as a liaison to better resources for her patient as well as utilizing the full benefits of having an interdisciplinary team on hand. She also suggests in a general manner, without making it too uncomfortable or direct for the patient.

109. B: Hospice care attends to the needs of a terminal patient by providing comfort measures and end-of-life counseling. However, this type of care is unique in that it also provides counseling, education, bereavement resources, and respite services for family members and caregivers. A number of hospice institutions train family members to be more effective caregivers as well so they may be more involved in their loved one's end-of-life treatments. Inpatient, Choice *A*, ambulatory, Choice *C*, and emergency, Choice *D*, treatments are delivered strictly by trained clinicians.

110. B: Palliative care can be administered at any time to provide comfort to a patient who is experiencing unbearable suffering. It is holistic care that may focus on nutrition, exercise, spiritual counseling, psychotherapy, or a combination of different treatments to ease the patient's discomfort. It is typically used for patients with chronic, debilitating, or painful conditions, such as cancer or dementia. Hospice, Choice *A*, is typically only offered at the end of life; ambulatory, Choice *C*, and emergency, Choice *D*, treatments normally treat acute conditions.

111. A: Legal and administrative documents, such as advanced directives and living wills, are important components of hospice care, as patients are terminal. Medical staff and family will need to know the patient's wishes for end of life, such as funeral wishes and asset division. While the other tasks listed may occur in hospice care, it is highly unlikely that a case manager would help with these specific tasks. Rather, family members or medical staff would assist with emotional and physical comfort measures a patient might want at the end of life.

112. B: The majority of people in the United States receive health insurance through their employer; often, employers pay a portion of the premium and offer this as a benefit to employees. The Affordable Care Act opened health insurance benefits to a large number of previously uninsured people, Choice *A*, but this is still not the primary means of obtaining health insurance for the majority of the population. The United States does not provide health care as a universal social program, Choice *C*; however, most people do have some form of health insurance, Choice *D*.

113. D: Short-term disability insurance provides benefits (such as a percentage of pay) for a period of time where an individual is deemed medically unable to work. In this case, Micah would likely receive it for the three weeks he is unable to work; however, short-term disability insurance can sometimes last for up to two years. Life insurance, Choice *A*, is used in the case of death. Social Security, Choice *B*, and Medicare, Choice *C*, are social benefit programs rather than insurance.

114. C: The Affordable Care Act was passed in 2010 to make health care more accessible to citizens, including provisions such as removing preexisting condition clauses, statewide marketplaces, and tax subsidies based on income. The Consolidated Omnibus Budget Reconciliation Act, Choice *A*, includes a provision that allows some employees to retain insurance coverage upon termination or loss of employee benefits. The Emergency Medical Treatment and Active Labor Act, Choice *B*, includes

provisions relating to emergency department admissions. The Anti-Kickback Statute, Choice *D*, focuses on unethical medical practices.

115. A: Case managers should ensure that patients on workmen's compensation are setting and meeting clear goals that bring them closer to returning to work, such as physical rehabilitation, healthy lifestyle choices, and maintaining technical skills. Case managers should ensure these patients are adhering to proposed care protocols and limiting behaviors that would prevent them from returning to work, such as engaging in high-risk activities like substance abuse.

116. B: Finding out that an employee was under the influence of a substance at the time of injury is a common reason for a workmen's compensation claim to be denied. Most organizations and states require immediate drug testing when treating an employee who has been injured on the job. The other options listed would not interfere with an injury someone received while legally employed and on the job.

117. A: Case managers with a background in medical surgical settings are able to comprehensively represent the needs of both the patient and the workmen's compensation organization. In this example, Anna also has a strong human resources background, which likely gives her additional experience and/or knowledge with injuries that might occur on the job. She may be able to support patients falling into the other categories listed, but her prior expertise is focused on worker support and medical care.

118. C: Reinsurance provides additional coverage to insurance companies and is provided by designated reinsurance carriers. It acts as an insurance plan for the insurance company, so the company is not bankrupted by too many claims or claims that are too high.

119. B: Sina is receiving care from an interdisciplinary team that is taking a collaborative approach to provide mental, physical, and emotional care for her after a life-changing event. Not only is she receiving care that aids her physical healing; she is also receiving care to support any adjustment stress she might be facing. Focused, Choice *A*, and amputee adherence, Choice *C*, care are not specific types of care found in medical settings. Respite care, Choice *D*, provides temporary assistance to nonmedical caregivers, such as family.

120. C: Long-term disability insurance will typically cover installations necessary for the patient's quality of life, such as a ramp for someone in a wheelchair to access a vehicle or home. They won't usually cover elective benefits such as specialized schooling, Choice *A*, or recreational activities, Choice *B*. Additionally, most patients who use long-term disability insurance are under the age of sixty-five, Choice *D*.

121. A: Interdisciplinary care teams work collaboratively and can include a wide array of medical and allied health specialists. These professionals work as a group to develop a comprehensive care plan that addresses any possible wellness needs of the patient. This can sometimes lead to conflicting opinions, but the care team is expected to resolve conflicts in a professional manner that puts the patient's needs first. On the whole, this approach is shown to be the most comprehensive, effective, and cost-efficient method of care.

122. D: The competition style of conflict resolution is when the participants compete, and the conflict ends with the stronger person getting what he or she wants. Choice *A*, collaboration, occurs when all participants work together to find an outcome that is in everyone's best interest. It is likely the best outcome but may not be possible given the time constraints and the level of conflict. Choice *B*,

compromise, requires all participants to give a little and get a little. Choice *C*, accommodation, occurs when one participant gets what they want because the other gives in; this is not an effective method in most cases, as it can cause ongoing problems.

123. B: Client safety should always be the case manager's biggest concern. After the case manager ensures that the client is safe, further assessment can take place to determine the next course of action.

124. C: Determining whether the client has a realistic plan and method for carrying it out are the factors to determine the suicide ideation level.

125. B: Intellectual functionality is typically tested during a psychological evaluation. Choice *A*, memory

and language, are assessed during a neuropsychological evaluation. Case managers can test for health literacy, Choice *C*, during service provision, and typically health coaches assess a client's motivation to change, Choice *D*, during motivational interviewing.

126. C: "Build the change" is the seventh step in Kotter's model. During this stage, the individual begins building on the small changes created in the sixth step, "Create short-term wins," and uses that as a stepping-stone to make larger and more permanent changes. Choice *A*, Kotter's second step, is "Form a coalition" when the treatment team and client's support system collaborate to assist the client in making a change. Choice *B*, the fourth step, is "Communicate the vision," or share the plan with all participants. Choice *D*, the eighth step, is "Anchor the change," which is when changes become an integrated part of a client's life.

127. B: A case manager needs to be knowledgeable about state and local community resources to assist a client in accessing health care costs assistance, insurance, prescription assistance, and other related resources.

128. C: Pastoral counseling would be a likely recommendation when a client has been diagnosed with a terminal illness, as pastoral counselors are trained to provide mental health care and spiritual guidance. These clients are likely to be concerned about spiritual care as they are facing end-of-life concerns. Choice *A* is related to health literacy; Choice *B*, psychological evaluations, are performed by psychologists; and Choice *D*, developing positive health behaviors, is related to wellness coaching.

129. D: Support groups bring together individuals facing common challenges, illnesses, and psychosocial or substance use issues. Individuals can receive support and understanding from others facing similar problems. Choice *A*, encouraging client empowerment; Choice *B*, helping clients develop interpersonal communication skills; and Choice *C*, assisting clients in locating and accessing needed resources and services, may be indirect benefits of support groups but are not their primary purpose.

130. D: Exercise can improve mental health, increase energy levels, and contribute to healthy weight maintenance. Exercise may benefit other areas but are not as likely to affect conflict resolution skills, Choice *A*, health literacy scores, Choice *B*, or client engagement levels, Choice *C*.

131. B: During this precontemplation stage, an individual has yet to acknowledge that a change needs to be made. Choice *A*, the preparation stage, is when an individual begins making plans or preparing for the upcoming change process. Choice *C*, creating urgency, is the first step in Kotter's 8-step change model, and Choice *D*, unfreezing, is the first step in Lewin's model.

132. C: During maintenance, in the Transtheoretical Model, an individual maintains the changes that took place in earlier stages. Choice *A*, refreezing, is the last step in Lewin's change management model when the newly instituted changes become integrated into an individual's behavior. Choice *B*, anchoring the change, is the last stage in Kotter's change model when the client makes recent changes permanent. Choice *D*, termination, is the final stage in the Transtheoretical Model when the client no longer feels tempted to return to the pre-change behavior.

133. A: Client empowerment focuses on a client's strengths to help the client take control of treatment. Choice *B*, maintenance of confidentiality, is important throughout services but is not a unique component of the empowerment process. Choice *C*, the client's level of involvement in treatment, is better matched with activation, and Choice *D*, a client's willingness to make positive changes, is related to wellness coaching.

134. C: Collaborative goal setting between the case manager and client is a part of client engagement along with establishing rapport and making treatment recommendations. Choice *A* assesses health literacy. Choice *B*, personality assessments, are part of psychological evaluations, and Choice *D*, assessing motivation to change, is a part of wellness coaching.

135. A: The statement that best describes the Caseload Matrix is, "Case managers can proactively use the matrix to adjust assignments based on changes in acuity." The chart is divided into four categories, unlike in Choice *B*, which states that the chart is divided into five categories. Case managers do not want to be reactive in nature, unlike in Choice *C*, which states that case managers utilize the matrix to be reactive when following their patients through the continuum of health care. Finally, a change to an element in one category does have an impact on the remaining elements/categories, unlike in Choice *D*, which states that a change to an element in one category of the matrix does not have an impact on the remaining categories.

136. C: Case management reports that show patients moving along the continuum of care is a tool that managers can use to document cost savings as well as case status. Case managers would send out quarterly reports that detail service costs and fees, not weekly ones, as stated in Choice *A*. Case managers would send out updates for active cases, not inactive cases, as stated in Choice *B*. Case managers would send out a comparison of the costs associated with case management intervention versus the costs of managing a case without intervention, rather than sending out a listing of the costs associated with only managing cases without intervention, as stated in Choice *D*.

137. B: The Adjusted Clinical Groups (ACG) System can better identify individuals who will be high cost utilizers. This model focuses on patient-centered care, not on physician-centered care, as stated in Choice *A*. It can support both commercial and Medicaid managed care programs, not just commercial healthcare programs as stated in Choice *C*. Finally, this model does incorporate the ICD-9 and ICD-10 codes, which is the reverse of what is listed in Choice *D*.

138. B: The correct order of the steps in a CQI program is as follows: Identify the problem, employ a corrective action plan (CAP), observe and monitor the CAP, review and evaluate outcomes, reinforce required process changes. Continuous quality improvement programs are used in an effort to remove any barriers and improve the overall quality of healthcare delivery. Answer Choices *A*, *C*, and *D* simply do not list the steps in the CQI program in the correct order.

139. D: The statement that is true regarding the PDSA (Plan-Do-Study-Act) model is "it is divided into two parts: fundamental questions and four stages." This model fast-tracks improvements within the

healthcare setting, unlike Choice *A*, which states that the model focuses on slow and steady improvement within the healthcare setting. The model challenges its users to ask themselves three fundamental questions prior to beginning ("What are we trying to accomplish?" / "How will we know a change is an improvement?" / "What changes can we make that will result in an improvement?"), unlike Choice *B*, which states that the model challenges its users to ask themselves five fundamental questions before starting. Finally, this model operates in conjunction with quality improvement models that are already in existence and supplements them, unlike Choice *C*, which states that the model operates independently of existing quality improvement models that are in place.

140. A: The PDSA (Plan-Do-Study-Act) model works well for pilot programs because it allows for small-scale testing prior to large-scale implementations. Answer Choices *B*, *C*, and *D* are not relevant.

141. D: The number of skilled nursing bed days per thousand is an example of an industry benchmark that is most appropriate for managed care organizations. The average time spent in the emergency department before being admitted, Choice *A*, the percentage of patients who develop serious blood clots post-surgery, Choice *B*, and the average time for a patient to receive an electrocardiogram, Choice *C*, are three benchmarks that would be most appropriate for a midsized community hospital facility.

142. B: The Healthcare Effectiveness Data and Information Set (HEDIS) is the tool that is used by most of America's healthcare plans to provide insight into the ongoing effort to prevent illness. The Consumer Assessment of Healthcare Providers and Systems (CAHPS), Choice *A*, is only one component of HEDIS, and is a survey that allows patients to rate their experiences with health care in the United States. Benchmarking, Choice *C*, is used to compare an organization against an industry standard. Finally, the National Committee for Quality Assurance (NCQA), Choice *D*, utilizes HEDIS to monitor the quality of healthcare delivery and to provide accreditation to organizations.

143. D: Cognition is the CCM's primary concern in this initial diagnostic phase. Although the Mini-Mental State Examination (MMSE) is used most frequently to assess this dimension, there is recent evidence that the Mini-Cog test has equivalent psychometric properties. In addition, the Mini-Cog T test is shorter than the MMSE, and the administration of the test is less difficult, which may be more appropriate for this client. The Visual Analog Scale, Choice *A*, is the assessment of the client's pain, which is not currently a priority for this client. The SF-36 scale, Choice *B*, measures the client's self-perception of health, which will not provide useful information for this client at this time. The Stroop, Choice *C*, tests executive functioning, which may be indicated after the initial assessment of the client's current cognitive status because executive function is one of the dimensions of cognitive functioning. However, initially, the CCM must first establish the baseline status of the client's cognitive functioning prior to assessing this form of higher-order thinking.

144. B: The correct order of the process for an employee seeking accommodations is: the employee requests the accommodation; the employer and employee identify the employee's functional limitations; the two identify potential accommodations; they determine reasonable solutions for implementing the accommodation(s); they make the accommodation; they continually monitor the effectiveness of the accommodation. Choices *A*, *C*, and *D* do not reflect this correct order and are therefore incorrect.

145. B: The CCM can maximize the client's progress by the frequent reevaluation of his needs and circumstances. This oversight can increase cost-effectiveness by reassessing the use of resources and addressing the ongoing needs of the client during the recovery period. Choices *A* and *D* appear to be punitive in nature; however, although the client will require vocational training at some point in his

recovery, frequent reminders of a specific time frame for each phase of the recovery would be stress provoking in most clients. Similarly, alternative living arrangements may be therapeutic at some point, but this decision should be made with active input from the client. The question does not raise the issue of PTSD, and without concerns related to this disorder, routine orders for testing would be inappropriate. Therefore, Choice *C* is not cost-effective and would only be appropriate in specific circumstances.

146. C: The insurance coverage of the two types of clients is different. This requires the CCM to be familiar with all benefits due the client, whether the coverage is workers' compensation insurance, which tends to be consistent within an individual state, or one of many private insurers or Medicare. The care of the client following a workplace injury is focused on recovery of their maximum level of functioning, including ADLs and return-to-work activities, Choice *A*. Workers' compensation insurance provides medical benefits and disability and indemnity benefits, in addition to death benefits., Choice *B*. The plan is managed by the individual states, and although common services are offered in all states, Choice *D*, as noted previously, the CCM must be aware of, and in compliance with, all of the state-specific elements.

147. B: The CCM understands that discharging a client to the home environment requires a comprehensive assessment of the details of the home in order to ensure the successful transition from acute care, in addition to all of the additional details that are common to all discharges. Choice *A* incorrectly states that the client's specific deficits do not affect the discharge process. The CCM is responsible for providing services that are appropriate to the client's specific needs, which means the client's condition is very much an integral determinant of the rehab facility. The CCM also cannot assume that the home care nursing providers will address all of the client's needs without proper communication and coordination with the CCM prior to the client's discharge, Choice *C*.

148. C: In order to ensure proper identification of clients requiring case management, the CCM must make every effort to be sure the agency system is "state of the art." Independent queries can be created in the comprehensive medical record databases, such as ERIC, that are currently available. It is imperative that a standardized procedure is used to prevent errors of omission. The remaining responses support the status quo and do not represent an active approach to this potential problem.

149. A: The CCM is responsible for root-cause analysis, which is a fact-finding framework focused on tracing each individual step of any untoward event in order to identify institutional, personnel, or procedural issues that contributed to the identified errors. The identification of personnel issues may be related to the function of a specific individual, or it may refer to the involvement of an employee with the inappropriate skill set. For instance, if an unlicensed assistive person gives aid to a client and an error occurs, the analysis will consider if the outcome would have been the same in each instance if a registered nurse had provided the care. The focus of the investigation is to identify errors and ways to modify procedures in order to avoid the same error in the future. The results are not used for employee evaluation, Choice *B*, and the process is not punitive, Choice *C*. As previously stated, the process is intended to evaluate any procedural issue and are not just applicable to institutional process revisions. Therefore, Choice *D* is incorrect.

150. B: Individual states vary in the oversight of the workers' compensation insurance; however, the Department of Labor in each state is the most common agency responsible for the plan. Choices *A* (the Department of Health and Human Services), *C* (the Department of Public Safety), and *D* (the Department of Public Works) are less common.

CCM Practice Test #2

1. What type of illness is the common cold?
   a. Acute
   b. Chronic
   c. Urgent
   d. Emergent

2. Which of the following is an example of comorbid chronic diseases with a direct relationship to one another?
   a. A patient who has breast cancer and the flu
   b. A patient who has terminal brain cancer and depression
   c. A patient who has sinusitis and a respiratory infection
   d. A patient who has osteoporosis and a pulled muscle

3. Patients with multiple chronic illnesses have a higher risk of experiencing which of the following?
   a. Financial discrimination
   b. Mental illness
   c. Asthma
   d. Heart arrhythmias

4. Emmanuel has type 2 diabetes and cardiovascular disease. In addition to a number of lifestyle recommendations, he has been prescribed medication to support insulin breakdown and manage his cholesterol levels. While he commits to an exercise routine to support his wellness goals, he does not refill his prescriptions due to financial issues. This behavior is an example of which of the following?
   a. Medication reconciliation
   b. Preventive care
   c. Big Pharma
   d. Medication therapy management barriers

5. John is a stay-at-home parent of three children, and his wife is in the air force. Sadly, she passes away while on duty. What is John's best course of action for maintaining health insurance for his children and himself?
   a. Shop around in his state's health insurance marketplace, as he now qualifies for a special enrollment period.
   b. Start applying for jobs that offer health insurance as a benefit.
   c. Remain on TRICARE Prime, his wife's policy.
   d. Apply for Medicaid.

6. What is a key benefit of TRICARE Prime for all covered individuals?
   a. There are no deductibles, enrollment fees, or copayments.
   b. It is accepted internationally.
   c. All members only pay if using point-of-service options.
   d. There is an assigned case manager who handles referrals, copayments, and filing claims.

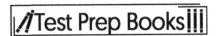
7. What is a key benefit of TRICARE for Life?
    a. It covers extra prenatal services, such as a postpartum doula.
    b. It has low out-of-pocket costs for services received at a VA hospital.
    c. It covers partners of eligible members, even if they are not married.
    d. It provides Medicare wraparound coverage for eligible members.

8. Danny is an active military service member who has a twenty-two-year-old son. Danny plans to stay in the military until he is able to retire. He and his son are both TRICARE participants. Which of the following life events would disqualify Danny's son for coverage?
    a. He is charged with a DUI.
    b. He marries.
    c. He moves out of state.
    d. He has a child.

9. What is a unique feature of the Patient-Centered Medical Home care model?
    a. Family members are trained as part of the care team.
    b. The patient's home environment is replicated in the medical setting to provide comfort.
    c. It is led by a nurse practitioner.
    d. It is led by a case manager.

10. Which regulation requires accountable care organizations to maintain a minimum of five thousand Medicare beneficiaries for five years?
    a. The Health Insurance Portability and Accountability Act of 1996
    b. The Social Security Amendments of 1965
    c. The Affordable Care Act of 2010
    d. The Medicare Prescription Drug, Improvement, and Modernization Act of 2003

11. Which of the following types of quality indicators is used to assess the number of readmissions and emergency room diversions?
    a. Productivity
    b. Financial
    c. Clinical
    d. Client experience

12. If a case manager treats seven patients per day and spends 30 minutes documenting each of those visits, what is his measure of productivity for time spent charting per day?
    a. 47.98%
    b. 35.10%
    c. 26.25%
    d. 43.75%

13. A goal, such as decreasing patients' stays in the hospital following knee replacement surgery, would be established during which step of the DMAIC approach to process improvement?
    a. Define
    b. Measure
    c. Analyze
    d. Improve

14. What approach to quality improvement focuses on reducing or eliminating waste to ultimately increase value?
   a. Six Sigma
   b. Root cause analysis
   c. Lean
   d. FMEA

15. Which of the following is NOT considered to be a performance improvement measurement?
   a. Process
   b. Structure
   c. Change
   d. Outcomes

16. The percentage of patients who receive a flu shot in a nursing home facility is an example of which type of performance improvement measurement?
   a. Capacity
   b. Process
   c. Outcomes
   d. Structure

17. Which of the following is used to pinpoint concerns with quality of care and compare care between various facilities and geographic locations over time?
   a. Process improvement indicators
   b. Documentation indicators
   c. Medical review indicators
   d. Quality indicators

18. The redesigned approach is integrated into the existing process during which phase of the PDSA model?
   a. Act
   b. Plan
   c. Study
   d. Do

19. Which of the following organizations provides accreditation in the areas of durable medical equipment, opioid treatment programs, and aging services?
   a. URAC
   b. AHRQ
   c. CARF
   d. Joint Commission

20. How is the Delphi technique used to gather information that is needed to assess quality indicators?
    a. Six to twelve participants suggest all of the ideas they can come up with in a given period of time.
    b. Individuals complete questionnaires and participate in rounds until a point in time when they are able to reach a group consensus.
    c. Options are presented on a whiteboard and participants vote individually on their top five to help narrow down the list.
    d. Participants write down ideas independently, ideas are presented one at a time, and participants silently rank order the ideas after group discussion.

21. Which of the following is a likely consideration when assessing family dynamics?
    a. Conflict resolution skills
    b. Health literacy skills
    c. Goal-setting skills
    d. Knowledge of community resources

22. Which of the following is NOT a component of wellness coaching?
    a. Education
    b. Goal setting
    c. Emotional support
    d. Psychological support

Use the following to answer questions 23 and 24:

John is a sixteen-year-old boy that is having behavioral problems in school and has frequently skipped class. John's family is seeking assistance to help him improve his school performance and attendance. During the session, John's mother, Allison, and father, Jake, begin to argue over resources being offered and the direction of treatment suggested by the case manager. Jake stands up and begins yelling at John's mother and the case manager. John's mother seems upset and quietly agrees with Jake's demands.

23. What technique does the case manager need to utilize in this situation?
    a. Crisis intervention strategies
    b. Conflict resolution strategies
    c. Client activation skills
    d. Establishing rapport

24. What should be the case manager's primary goal?
    a. Making sure Jake calms down
    b. Accommodating all parties involved
    c. Ensuring John's needs remain the priority
    d. Creating a crisis plan

25. Why is it vital for case managers to have effective interpersonal skills?
    a. To be able to communicate with clients and service providers
    b. To assess clients' ambivalence about change
    c. To be able to acquire a DNR from clients with terminal illnesses
    d. To be skilled at motivational interviewing

26. Which of the following tests provides a streamlined assessment that utilizes a nutritional label to determine a client's literacy?
    a. Health literacy scale
    b. Health Literacy Skills Instrument
    c. Newest Vital Sign assessment
    d. Thematic Apperception Test

27. What is the highest priority goal of the client interview?
    a. Developing client self-care management
    b. Determining health literacy
    c. Helping the client set realistic goals
    d. Collecting pertinent information to create a client treatment plan

28. What is the goal of a clarifying question during the client interview process?
    a. Determining how motivated clients are to make positive changes
    b. Helping clients learn effective conflict resolution skills
    c. Identifying if clients are experiencing any communication deficits
    d. Helping clients better and more effectively express themselves

29. Which of the following types of cultural belief involves community and familial involvement in health care decision-making?
    a. Individualistic
    b. Collectivist
    c. Multiculturalism
    d. Western American

30. Which assessment, used in psychological evaluations, consists of 567 questions and provides scores on 10 scales?
    a. Wechsler Adult Intelligence Scale (WAIS)
    b. Multiphasic Personality Inventory (MMPI)
    c. Thematic Apperception Test (TAT)
    d. Rapid Assessment of Adult Literacy in Medicine (REALM)

31. Dr. Thompson is a private-practice cardiologist who is bundling a payment for her patient's heart procedure. What is one benefit of the bundled payment system for Dr. Thompson?
    a. Payments are received after care has been completed.
    b. Complications from the procedure might result in unanticipated costs.
    c. A smooth procedure with no complications may result in a net profit.
    d. Patients prefer this system over all others.

32. Which of the following reimbursement mechanisms are used by the Medicare system?
    a. Retroactive payment systems
    b. Prospective payment systems
    c. Fee-for-service plans
    d. Sliding-scale payment systems

33. The Value-Based Purchasing Program drives reimbursements by placing a high emphasis on which aspect of health care operations?
    a. Revenue cycle management
    b. Green initiatives and sustainability
    c. Leadership development
    d. Quality

34. Billy is a case manager in the emergency department of a local hospital. A patient arrives at the hospital saying he feels like he cannot breathe and is extremely anxious. The patient is checked in, and all vital signs appear normal. The patient's medical history shows he is on anti-anxiety medication. Billy recognizes that the patient most likely had a panic attack. What should Billy's next steps be?
    a. Providing a liaison to the on-site therapist and ensuring the patient is discharged when he feels stable
    b. Ensuring the patient receives as much care as his insurance covers
    c. Asking the attending physician to perform an MRI on the patient's brain to ensure there are no neurological issues
    d. Telling the patient to leave and take another dose of the anti-anxiety medicine, as additional care is not really necessary

35. Managed case care managers are often tasked with process and quality improvement initiatives that ultimately lead to a reduction in which of the following?
    a. Self-paying (or uninsured) patient admissions
    b. The number of days a patient has to stay in the hospital
    c. Medicaid patients
    d. The number of medications a patient is prescribed

36. Emery is a clinical case manager at a nonprofit that serves undocumented, uninsured families. She also has worked extensively in her state's public health department and developed and implemented programs to support public health nursing initiatives. What is a task her employer could assign for which Emery could be a great fit?
    a. Grant writing to raise funds for the organization
    b. Enrolling families into private or state-sponsored health insurance plans
    c. Calling state and federal representatives for policy reform
    d. Payroll processes for the other staff members

37. George is a case manager who handles home health care cases. His patient, Louis, has been diagnosed with chronic obstructive pulmonary disease (COPD) and will need to be on a ventilator long term. Louis is expected to be discharged from the hospital within the next few days. What will George need to focus on as Louis leaves the medical setting?
    a. Making sure billing receives a full list of the services Louis received
    b. SBAR handoffs
    c. Making sure Louis' residence is safe and there are no obstacles to his ventilation support system
    d. Making sure the ventilation system meets quality engineering standards

38. Community-based case managers typically work with which demographic of patients?
    a. Pediatric patients
    b. Low-income or Medicaid and Medicare recipients
    c. First-time mothers
    d. Patients that set up virtual medical appointments

39. A stage III lung cancer patient's interdisciplinary team is likely to include a primary care physician, an oncologist, a therapist, a registered dietitian, and which of the following?
   a. A dentist
   b. A pharmacist
   c. A physical therapist
   d. A podiatrist

40. What is the primary difference between a psychologist and a therapist?
   a. Psychologists primarily work with affected individuals; therapists primarily work with the family members of the affected individuals.
   b. Psychologists work with children in school settings; therapists work with adults in work settings.
   c. Psychologists can prescribe medications; therapists cannot prescribe medications.
   d. Psychologists conduct evaluations and assessments to gauge a person's state of well-being; therapists provide counseling modalities that support or balance dysfunctions.

41. The CCM is caring for a client who sustained a catastrophic work-related injury. The client and his family voice their financial concerns to the CCM. The CCM's response is based on the knowledge that which of the following assistive devices is available free of charge to all individuals with a physician's certification of need?
   a. Modified automobile
   b. Residential structural modifications
   c. Assistance with relocation expenses to a more favorable climate
   d. Captioned telephone with enhanced volume controls

42. The CCM is aware that the International Classification of Functioning, Disability, and Health (ICF) is a framework for addressing multiple aspects of personal functioning and disability. Which of the following elements is NOT consistent with this framework?
   a. The ICF was originally initiated to track the incidence of HIV.
   b. The framework facilitates the implementation of health information systems by providing a universal coding scheme.
   c. The framework allows diverse entities to compare the incidence and characteristics of individual disabilities.
   d. The database associated with the framework is a resource for members of the public, health care providers, and researchers.

43. Which of the following statements is consistent with the client's FMLA status with regard to workers' compensation and COBRA health insurance coverage?
   a. Employers often send COBRA continuation notices prematurely.
   b. Employers are responsible for COBRA expenses for employees.
   c. Workers' compensation leave can create a "qualifying event" that requires the client to access COBRA coverage.
   d. COBRA coverage is always required for long-term rehabilitation for clients with work-related injuries.

44. When the CCM assigns low-, moderate-, or high-risk labels to individual clients, the CCM is demonstrating which of the following case management functions?
- a. Screening
- b. Planning
- c. Implementation
- d. Risk stratification

45. Which of the following CCM activities is most closely identified with rehabilitative care?
- a. Skilled communication
- b. Leadership
- c. Risk management
- d. Utilization review

46. Which of the following is the primary focus of transfer skills analysis?
- a. Physical therapy approach to bringing clients to their preinjury level of functioning
- b. Providing a comprehensive program aimed at learning new skills
- c. Assessment of the client's current skill level aimed at appropriate job placement
- d. Determination of the most appropriate rehabilitation approach

47. The implementation of the "meaningful use" criteria is associated with incentives and is subject to penalties. Which of the following is a common incentive associated with these criteria?
- a. Cash payments to participating providers
- b. Decreases in the required number of patients "connected" with the patient portal that is necessary to demonstrate compliance with criteria
- c. Altered time frames for compliance
- d. Increased reimbursement for select diagnoses

48. Which of the following is one of the broad-based objectives of the meaningful use criteria?
- a. To increase the cost-effectiveness of the primary care practice
- b. To decrease clients' reliance on face-to-face medical appointments
- c. To provide the optimum platform for providers to document the need for specialty care
- d. To decrease health disparities

49. In what way can the electronic health record be used to protect patient privacy and health information?
- a. Server-side data should be encrypted.
- b. Need-to-know limitations on accessible information can be established with password-protected computer access to specific information.
- c. Only registered or licensed personnel should have access to the data.
- d. Informed consent should be obtained prior to any data entry.

50. Which of the following is a violation of the Affordable Care Act?
- a. Medicaid clients are exempt from penalties.
- b. The plan network will not be available to the patient until after the plan has been chosen.
- c. A patient diagnosed with type 1 diabetes fifteen years ago is unable to get coverage.
- d. Several comparable plans are available to every individual.

CCM Practice Test #2

51. What is the primary benefit of documenting the use of evidence-based practice in the EHR?
    a. It is useful for the ongoing evaluation of the client's progress.
    b. This documentation validates the collaborative development of the plan of care.
    c. Auditing agencies require the information.
    d. It eliminates most of the errors in patient care.

52. Which of the following is NOT one of the issues addressed in "how" questions on an incident report?
    a. Procedural error
    b. Human error
    c. Administrative error
    d. Technical error

53. Which of the following is the primary purpose of risk management?
    a. Evaluation of employee compliance
    b. Identification of actual and potential errors
    c. Substitution of costly procedures
    d. Elimination of liability

54. Which of the following conditions differentiates the focus of the incident report from the root-cause analysis?
    a. The incident report confirms the sentinel event.
    b. Root-cause analysis focuses on prevention.
    c. A near-miss event will be investigated with root-cause analysis.
    d. Incident reports must be completed within 24 hours of the event, while root-cause analysis must be completed within two weeks of the incident.

55. CCMs use several frameworks to manage the care of clients with varied needs. Which of the following statements is consistent with the difference between clinical pathways and treatment guidelines?
    a. Clinical or critical pathways are used by the interdisciplinary team.
    b. Treatment guidelines are used only in critical-care units.
    c. Clinical pathways are used to set only short-term outcome criteria.
    d. Treatment guidelines are most useful for identifying time frames that facilitate evaluation of client outcomes.

56. The CCM is discussing the individualized plan of care with Mr. G., who sustained a severe workplace injury two days ago. Mr. G. is reluctant to "sign off" on the proposed plan of care. He says, "I don't think I'm going to go through all of this. I don't feel good, and maybe it should wait for a month or two." The CCM understands that rehab begins the day of the injury. What is the CCM's best response to Mr. G.?
    a. "Your insurance won't pay for your needs for two months."
    b. "Why don't you want to participate in your recovery?"
    c. "Tell me more of how the last two days have been for you."
    d. "I think you need to discuss this with your family."

57. Which of the following laws contains provisions for vocational training and job placement only for disabled clients who sustained job-related injuries and are unable to return to their previous employment?
    a. Americans with Disabilities Act (ADA)
    b. Workforce Innovation and Opportunity Act of 2014 (WIOA)
    c. The Health Insurance Portability and Accountability Act of 1996 (HIPAA)
    d. Workers' compensation insurance

58. The CCM is visiting a client, Mrs. B., who has been hospitalized frequently for the treatment of chronic heart failure. Mrs. B. tells the CCM, "I'm having quite a time with my son and daughter-in-law. I know that my heart is getting weaker, and I also know that I'm ready to die. I'm eighty-seven! But they will have none of it. I guess they want to keep me around, but I'm tired." Mrs. B. confirmed her "no code" status; however, when her family arrived, they demanded that full resuscitative efforts be reinstated. Which of the following represents the CCM's primary responsibility in this case?
    a. Ensure that the client's resuscitation preferences remain in force.
    b. Discuss the family's point of view with Mrs. B. in order to change her mind about the order.
    c. Rescind the "no code" order because if Mrs. B. is not resuscitated, the family can sue the agency for ignoring their request.
    d. Refer the issue to the agency attorney and the risk management team.

59. The CCM is reviewing the results of a recent root-cause analysis of an error that resulted in client harm. Several contributing factors were identified, and recommendations for correction and prevention of the error were addressed. Which of the following strategies is the CCM's most effective approach to remediating nursing behaviors that have been identified as contributing factors by the root-cause analysis?
    a. Notify the individual involved in the incident that a specific program of remediation will be required within the next two weeks.
    b. Notify all nursing personnel that a mandatory review will be conducted on each shift this week.
    c. Provide a comprehensive self-paced learning module for the nursing staff that awards two CEUs upon completion.
    d. Submit a list of all nursing staff identified in the analysis to the appropriate nursing administrator.

60. The CCM is employed part time in an acute-care agency in addition to being employed full time as a case management auditor for a large insurance company. The CCM is preparing to admit a new client and notes that the client is covered by the same insurance company. The principle of veracity requires that the CCM must do which of the following first?
    a. Request reassignment to a different client.
    b. Inform the insurance company that the CCM cannot audit the client's account.
    c. Inform the client of all the details related to the CCM's employment.
    d. Proceed with the assessment.

61. Josie is a case manager who is working with a patient, Moe, who is obese and experiencing a number of comorbidities as a direct result of his obesity. Josie sets up an information-gathering session for Moe, where a registered dietitian talks to him about healthy food choices; an exercise physiologist talks to him about a starting point for a daily, 30-minute exercise plan; and a behavioral therapist talks to him about reflecting on possible behaviors that may have led to his obesity. After the session is over, Josie asks Moe to develop two actions he can perform daily for the next thirty days that will benefit his health. Moe decides he will walk for 30 minutes daily and eliminate eating while distracted (such as while driving or watching TV). What approach is Josie using to support Moe?
    a. Peer-to-peer coaching
    b. Medical modeling
    c. Self-management support
    d. Patient home care

62. The chronic-care model is positively associated with which of the following outcomes?
    a. Weight maintenance
    b. Increased peer-to-peer support
    c. Decreased emergency room visits
    d. Medication management

63. Jack is a case manager working with an insurance company to negotiate rates for palliative care for a cancer patient. At a meeting with a representative from the insurance company and the patient, the insurance company says they cannot approve payment for an experimental trial for the patient; the patient will need to pay out of pocket. Upon hearing this, the patient becomes enraged and starts screaming at both the insurance representative and Jack. What does Jack need to do next?
    a. Leave the room while the two involved parties work it out.
    b. Focus on calming the patient down before talking further with the insurance representative.
    c. Ask his supervisor to transfer him to a different case.
    d. Calmly ask the insurance representative if there are other options to pursue for reimbursement.

64. A cluster of physical changes, such as unstable moods, unpredictable appetite and sleep patterns, fatigue, and pain, are most likely indicative of which of the following?
    a. A uterine tumor
    b. Lyme disease
    c. Aging
    d. Mental illness

65. Melanie is conducting intake on a new patient, Tina, a forty-five-year-old woman with liver cancer. After completing personal information and documenting the patient's medical history, Melanie asks Tina questions about how many hours she sleeps at night, how often she drinks alcohol weekly, how happy she feels at her job, and how often she exercises weekly. What component of care is Melanie delivering?
    a. A clinical inquiry
    b. A behavioral health assessment
    c. Daily-living mapping
    d. SBAR handoff

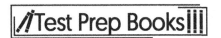
66. Which type of program influences more than 80 percent of drug coverage?
    a.   Health Maintenance Organization
    b.   Pharmacy benefits management
    c.   Activities of daily living
    d.   Medicare Part D

67. Doug contracts with a large company to provide consulting services and obtains health insurance through his state-run marketplace during the yearly open enrollment period. At the end of his first year as a contractor, the company offers him an internal position with benefits, including group health insurance, which he accepts. What type of health insurance does Doug now have?
    a.   Individual-purchased insurance
    b.   Marketplace insurance
    c.   Catastrophic health insurance with an HSA
    d.   Employer-sponsored health insurance

68. Maya is a sixty-three-year-old woman that has had a double knee replacement and lives alone. Her private insurance covers the cost for Lilly, a registered nurse, to support Maya with wound care, physical therapy exercises, dressing, grooming, and grocery shopping for three months after Maya's discharge date. What is this type of benefit called?
    a.   Home care benefits
    b.   Group insurance benefits
    c.   Vulnerable population coverage
    d.   Elder care coverage

69. Boris voluntarily quits a full-time job with health benefits to move out of state in order to care for an aging aunt. Which of the following laws would allow Boris to keep his existing health insurance plan for a period of time?
    a.   The Affordable Care Act of 2010
    b.   The Consolidated Omnibus Budget Reconciliation Act of 1986
    c.   The Family and Medical Leave Act of 1994
    d.   The Worker Adjustment and Retraining Notification Act of 1988

70. Nick unexpectedly passes away, leaving a wife and son who survive him. Nick's family was on a health insurance plan sponsored by his employer. If his family remains on the plan under COBRA continuation, how long can they keep this plan before needing to find new health insurance coverage?
    a.   They can keep it for eighteen months.
    b.   They can keep it for twenty-nine months.
    c.   They can keep it for thirty-six months.
    d.   Unfortunately, once the employee dies, all coverage benefits are terminated for additional covered family members.

71. Which of the following are typical forms of abuse?
    a.   Physical, sexual, financial, emotional
    b.   Physical, psychological, medical, financial
    c.   Psychological, emotional, financial, mental health
    d.   Psychological, educational, mental health, financial

72. Which of the following is NOT a type of emotional abuse?
    a. Manipulation
    b. Humiliation
    c. Forced sex acts
    d. Threats

73. A perpetrator of abuse is NOT likely to be which of the following?
    a. In a power position over the victim
    b. A stranger to the victim
    c. Older than the victim
    d. A person in a relationship of trust with the victim

74. What are Lewin's management model's three stages of change?
    a. Unfreeze, change, refreeze
    b. Unfreeze, create urgency, refreeze
    c. Freeze, activate, refreeze
    d. Unfreeze, create a vision, refreeze

75. What occurs during the refreeze stage in Lewin's change management model?
    a. Changes become solidified and an integrated part of the client's behavior.
    b. The client becomes firmly involved in their own treatment.
    c. The client becomes fearful, regresses, and leaves treatment.
    d. The client anchors the change, making it a part of life.

76. What is a likely first step in substance abuse treatment?
    a. Detox and inpatient treatment
    b. Building rapport with client—client engagement
    c. Providing educational resources
    d. Asking nonjudgmental questions

77. Which of the following is NOT an example of a behavioral health disorder?
    a. Substance abuse
    b. Mental illness
    c. Obesity
    d. Ineffective communication

78. Why is maintaining confidentiality an integral part of client engagement?
    a. It encourages the client to like the case manager.
    b. It creates better boundaries in the client—case manager relationship.
    c. It helps build trust.
    d. It makes the client more satisfied with services.

79. Why is client activation important?
    a. It leads to better treatment outcomes and reduced treatment costs.
    b. It makes the client feel more intelligent.
    c. It encourages collaboration from the client's support system.
    d. It builds rapport with the client.

80. Who coined the term unconditional positive regard?
    a. Rogers
    b. Lewin
    c. Kotter
    d. Ross

81. Susan is laid off from her job as a procurement specialist. She and her two children were on employer-sponsored health insurance. The COBRA cost to continue this coverage was extremely expensive, but Susan found comparable state-sponsored health insurance through her state's marketplace that was cheaper. Since she qualified for a special enrollment period, she obtained insurance through the marketplace. However, Susan later found out that no provider within 75 miles of her home accepted the state-sponsored health insurance plan. Since she is still within the sixty-day window in which she can enroll in COBRA, Susan returned to her old employer's human resources department to complete the paperwork. What will the human resources department likely tell Susan?
    a. She needs to first provide a signed affidavit from the state-sponsored insurance program saying her family's coverage has been formally terminated.
    b. She will be fined a one-time 5 percent fee for not enrolling on the date of her termination.
    c. She cannot enroll in COBRA, as she has already enrolled in another insurance plan.
    d. She will need to pay the full cost of premiums plus an administrative fee.

82. Barbara, a US citizen, immigrated to the Netherlands at age thirty-one to pursue a business venture. When she is sixty-seven years old, she faces a debilitating financial event and cannot maintain her life abroad. She decides to move back to the United States to live with her daughter in the state of Maine. On her first day back, she applies for a Maine driver's license, registers to vote, and applies for Supplemental Security Income (SSI). What will be one obstacle Barbara faces to receiving SSI?
    a. She is considered a naturalized citizen of the Netherlands.
    b. She is living with her daughter, which automatically disqualifies her from SSI.
    c. She does not appear to be disabled, which is a requirement of receiving SSI.
    d. She has not yet lived in the United States for a consecutive thirty days since turning sixty-five years old.

83. Individuals who are not yet of retirement age, have paid into Social Security for enough years, and have severe or long-term health limitations that prevent them from working enough to support their basic needs may qualify for which of the following public benefits?
    a. Medicare
    b. Social Security Disability Insurance
    c. Supplemental Security Income
    d. Social Security Pension Fund

84. Which component of Medicare covers hospital visits and nursing care such as hospice?
    a. Medicare Part A
    b. Medicare Part B
    c. Medicare Part C
    d. Medicare Part D

85. How do people who qualify for Medicare Part B typically pay for it?
   a. They pay out of pocket through a checking or savings account only.
   b. They purchase supplemental private insurance that Medicare then reimburses.
   c. They pay through automatic Social Security payment deductions.
   d. Medicare Part B does not require additional payments from the recipient; it is fully funded by Social Security taxes paid over one's career.

86. Which regulation enacted Medicaid?
   a. The Affordable Care Act of 2010
   b. The Social Security Amendments of 1965
   c. The Benefits Embargo of 1975
   d. The Consolidated Omnibus Budget Reconciliation Act of 1986

87. What is the source of Medicaid funding?
   a. Citizens must pay a portion of their income as an annual tax that is specifically used for their family should anyone in their family ever need Medicaid support.
   b. The source is federal and state funds.
   c. The source is federal funds only.
   d. Business entities must pay a corporate tax that is used for their employees' Medicaid benefits upon job loss.

88. What was a key component of Medicaid expansion under the Affordable Care Act of 2010?
   a. Undocumented immigrants could qualify for Medicaid benefits.
   b. Medicare Part D became available to Medicaid recipients in the US territories.
   c. Private insurers became required to offer plans that did not exceed 10 percent of a family's household income.
   d. States could elect to offer Medicaid benefits to all low-income individuals under age sixty-five.

89. Although the federal government is responsible for establishing the guidelines for Medicaid programs, what responsibilities do states have regarding these programs?
   a. Defining eligibility criteria and choosing program services
   b. Procuring and distributing all necessary funds
   c. Ensuring all constituents have comprehensive health insurance plans to avoid fines and penalties
   d. Completing waivers that allow some medical facilities to refuse Medicaid patients

90. Which of the following services is least likely to be covered by state Medicaid programs?
   a. Prenatal care
   b. Physical therapy
   c. Well-visit vaccinations
   d. Hospice care

91. Which of the following pieces of legislation allows patients, or individuals they appoint, to obtain access to their medical records electronically and share this information with other medical providers in this format?
   a. HITECH Act
   b. E-Sign Act
   c. HIPAA
   d. Electronic Communications Privacy Act

92. Which of the following falls under the category of patient safety indicators (PSIs) under the Agency for Healthcare Research and Quality Indicators?
   a. Urinary tract infection admission rate
   b. Hip fracture mortality rate
   c. Pressure ulcer rate
   d. Cesarean delivery rate, uncomplicated

93. What statement best describes the category of prevention quality indicators (PQIs) under AHRQ's Quality Indicators?
   a. They uncover risks for volumes of procedures, excessive surgeries, and high mortality in hospital settings.
   b. They form the foundation for evaluating community-based programs and determining where gaps exist.
   c. They focus on errors and complications that affect those in the pediatric population.
   d. They provide opportunities for comparative public reporting and pay-for-performance initiatives.

94. Why do organizations track the productivity of their case managers?
   a. To watch employees to ensure they are behaving
   b. To analyze the level of associated supplies being utilized
   c. To justify the hourly wage employees are earning
   d. To demonstrate the need of services and validate staffing models

95. Which of the following types of quality indicators is used to track general behaviors and trends of the population being served?
   a. Utilization indicators
   b. Clinical indicators
   c. Client experience indicators
   d. Financial indicators

96. An experienced case manager can conduct 35, 30-minute intake interviews during a 40-hour work week. If a newly hired case manager conducts 25 intake interviews per week, what is their measure of productivity?
   a. 71.4%
   b. 43.8%
   c. 31.3%
   d. 25.0%

97. Which of the following groups focuses on improving Americans' health through making evidence-based recommendations about services such as healthcare screenings and counseling treatments?
   a. AHRQ
   b. USPSTF
   c. NQF
   d. NGC

98. Which statement BEST describes the goal of the Agency for Healthcare Research and Quality (AHRQ)?
    a. To improve the health care that individuals on Medicare receive
    b. To provide accreditation to medical rehabilitation companies
    c. To develop better guidelines for services delivered to Medicaid beneficiaries
    d. To improve the quality, safety, and accessibility of health care

99. Which of the following is true regarding healthcare-associated infections?
    a. They can be prevented by using toolkits to improve patient safety in long-term care facilities.
    b. They are the least common complication associated with patient stays in the hospital.
    c. One out of every 250 hospitalized patients in the United States will contract such an infection.
    d. They are known to be an inevitable hazard of hospitalization or receiving care in nursing homes.

100. Which of the following falls under the category of inpatient quality indicators (IQIs) under the Agency for Healthcare Research and Quality's Quality Indicators?
    a. Bacterial pneumonia admission rate
    b. Post-operative sepsis rate
    c. Acute stroke mortality rate
    d. Transfusion reaction rate

101. Which of the following is NOT a part of client engagement?
    a. Active listening
    b. Establishing rapport
    c. Maintaining confidentiality
    d. Encouraging self-directed care

102. What is the case manager's role in self-care management?
    a. Ensuring the client has access to emotional and psychological services
    b. Helping build trust with the client by ensuring confidentiality
    c. Supporting the client through education, skills, and confidence development
    d. Supporting and collaborating with the client to set their own goals

103. What domains of a client's life should a case manager consider when finding resources?
    a. Emotional, family, social
    b. Physical, spiritual, social
    c. Social, family, emotional
    d. Psychological, financial, social

104. Which of the following is NOT a typical way conflicts may arise in the case management process?
    a. Conflict about the treatment process
    b. Conflict about the way services are being provided
    c. Conflict between the client and providers
    d. Conflict between the client and law enforcement

105. What is the purpose of the Thomas–Kilmann Instrument?
    a. It is used to determine what type of substances a client uses.
    b. It helps find the community resource needs of a client.
    c. It is used by case managers to tell whether a client is being abused.
    d. It identifies and assesses types of conflict resolution strategies.

181

106. Which of the following conflict resolution strategies leads to participants each getting a little of what they want?
    a. Collaboration
    b. Compromise
    c. Accommodation
    d. Competition

107. What is the BEST definition of a crisis?
    a. When a client is unable to pay his bill
    b. When a client has a severe history of alcohol abuse
    c. When a client is in extreme physical, psychological, or emotional danger
    d. When a client has a current substance addiction

108. Which of the following is the third step in Kotter's 8-step change model?
    a. Create urgency
    b. Form a coalition
    c. Create a vision/strategy
    d. Remove obstacles

109. What is a typical focus of end-of-life care?
    a. Helping the client with depression or other mental health disorders
    b. Assisting the client to become empowered
    c. Assessing the client's suicidal ideation
    d. Working with the client to develop informed decision-making skills

110. Which of the following terms BEST matches the definition, "the decision is made by an individual or an individual's family member to stop artificially sustained life support"?
    a. Hospice care
    b. Withdrawal of care
    c. DNR
    d. Palliative care

111. What type of approach should be used with a client that has a chronic illness or disability?
    a. Multicultural approach
    b. Neuropsychological approach
    c. Biopsychosocial approach
    d. Interpersonal approach

112. A case manager must provide which of the following types of care when working with a client that has a chronic illness or disability?
    a. Interpersonal care
    b. Hospice care
    c. End-of-life care
    d. Whole-person care

113. Which of the following resources can case managers and clients use to help find health insurance options based on income and other individual factors?
    a. Affordable Care Act
    b. 211 helpline
    c. Health Insurance Marketplace
    d. Client's employer

114. How should a case manager approach a client's spirituality during care?
    a. A case manager should not discuss spirituality with clients.
    b. A case manager should acknowledge and respect a client's spiritual view during treatment.
    c. A client's spiritual beliefs should not be a consideration during care.
    d. A case manager should discourage a client from following spiritual beliefs if it could be detrimental to care.

115. What type of counseling assists clients that have experienced loss?
    a. End of life
    b. Bereavement
    c. Crisis
    d. Abuse and neglect

116. Jane is a case manager who is coordinating care for her patient, Simon, who recently suffered a stroke. Simon is able to understand everything that is spoken to him, but he struggles with speaking properly. Luckily, he is able to type many of his thoughts on his laptop. Jane explains to Simon that he will see a primary care physician, a vascular specialist, and a speech therapist daily. Simon begins to type on his laptop. Jane reaches over and takes the laptop away, saying gently, "Don't worry. I have it all under control for you. You'll get everything you need. Just get some rest!" What is the key issue with Jane's response in this situation?
    a. She should have been firmer in her command rather than speaking so gently, as she no longer seems confident in her job duties.
    b. She should have asked the primary care physician to relay this information to Simon.
    c. She should have allowed Simon to finish typing his thoughts and responded after he was done.
    d. She should have told his caregivers this information rather than burdening Simon when he could have been resting.

117. Which of the following aspects is most critical for resulting in positive patient outcomes when transitioning between different levels or settings of care?
    a. Clear and direct communication between involved staff members and between staff members and the patient
    b. Whether or not all institutions involved in the transition are accredited by the Joint Commission
    c. Whether there is a 7:1 ratio of staff members to patient within the institution
    d. Whether there is a quality initiatives team within the institution

118. Which of the following groups mainly focuses on addressing problems associated with transitions of care?
    a. The Joint Commission
    b. The Nursing Alliance for Quality Care
    c. The National Transitions of Care Coalition
    d. The American Pharmacists Association

CCM Practice Test #2

119. Which process determines the medical necessity for hospital admissions and procedures?
    a. Case management
    b. Triage
    c. Reimbursement mechanism
    d. Utilization management

120. Nicole has just given birth to her first baby. It was a healthy delivery with no complications. Nicole is wheeled from the labor and delivery room into an overnight suite, which is on the same ward but has more space for visitors and for her partner to spend the night with her and their baby. What is this an example of?
    a. Transition of care
    b. FMLA reform
    c. Utilization management
    d. Hospital hospitality, a cultural term coined by millennial parents

121. What term is used to describe individuals or families who earn too much to qualify for Medicaid but whose personal expenses are too high to afford private health insurance?
    a. Middle class
    b. Categorically needy
    c. Vulnerable
    d. Medically needy

122. What is the procedure for developing a life care plan (LCP)?
    a. Scheduling follow-up appointments, home visits, medication management
    b. Interview client, consult treatment experts, research costs and sources
    c. Around-the-clock nurse monitoring, consulting with doctors, implement plan
    d. Medication management, interview client, home visits

123. Which of the following is a component of maintaining good health?
    a. Frequent visits to a wellness coach
    b. Attending religious or spiritual services
    c. Regular doctor visits
    d. Practicing effective conflict resolution skills

124. Which of the following is a possible result of a high level of self-disclosure by a case manager?
    a. It improves the client and case manager relationship.
    b. It creates boundary confusion between the client and case manager.
    c. It encourages client activation.
    d. It increases the client's trust of the case manager.

125. Which of the following types of client may be more likely to adhere to treatment recommendations and to practice healthier habits outside of treatment?
    a. An empowered client
    b. A client with effective interpersonal communication skills
    c. A client that participates in support groups
    d. An activated client

184

This material is provided for exam preparation purposes only and does not indicate an endorsement of any specific scientific, political, or religious point of view. © TPB Publishing. You have been licensed one copy of this document for personal use only. Any other reproduction or redistribution is strictly prohibited. All rights reserved.

126. Which of the following is an effective method of increasing client activation?
    a. Education and skills training
    b. Ensuring confidentiality
    c. Helping a client create a crisis plan
    d. Referral to services based on different areas of a client's life

127. What should precede a psychological evaluation?
    a. Health literacy test

    b Medical exam
    c. Health coaching
    d. Motivational interviewing

128. What is a benefit of using the Delphi technique?
    a. It is the least time-consuming data collection method.
    b. It allows participants to directly confront one another.
    c. Its flexible design can be changed while collecting data.
    d. It enables geographically dispersed professionals to participate.

129. Figuring out why patients who undergo knee replacement surgery on Friday do not fare as well as patients who undergo knee replacement surgery Monday–Thursday would take place during which step of the DMAIC approach to process improvement?
    a. Analyze
    b. Measure
    c. Control
    d. Improve

130. How have the HCAHPS survey measurements been impacted by the Affordable Care Act?
    a. The survey results are no longer publicly reported on the internet.
    b. There are fewer categories for patients to report on after being discharged.
    c. Survey results are used to calculate government incentive payments for eligible hospitals.
    d. A sliding scale of 1 to 10 is used for ratings, instead of selecting words like "never" and "always."

131. Which of the following is NOT one of the areas covered by URAC's case management standards?
    a. Organizational structure
    b. Research and development
    c. Review of marketing and sales material
    d. Clinical staff credentialing

132. Which of the following is a primary function of the Quality Improvement Organization (QIO) program under CMS?
    a. Keeping patients' health information safe and secure
    b. Improving care for the expectant mother population
    c. Promoting the health literacy of consumers
    d. Ensuring Medicare pays for services that are necessary/reasonable

133. The following verbiage is typically included by a case manager in which type of patient report?
        -Before Intervention: Patient ambulates 6 feet using a rollator walker
        -Current Status: Patient ambulates 20 feet using a four-pronged cane

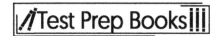

-Intervention Goal: Patient will ambulate 100 feet using a straight cane

a. Justification of continuation of intervention
b. Cost-benefit analysis
c. Justification of more costly intervention
d. Summary of interventions

134. Which choice BEST explains the relationship between validity and reliability in data interpretation?
a. Reliable data is always valid.
b. Only validity must be taken into consideration.
c. Reliable data is accurate; valid data measures what is intended.
d. Only reliability must be taken into consideration.

135. The CCM is managing the care of a client who sustained a work-related injury. The client is a recent immigrant from eastern Europe who does not speak or understand the English language. He has a supportive family; however, no one in the family is fluent in English. The acute-care agency does not employ an interpreter who is fluent in the client's native language. The CCM is responsible for providing culturally competent care that guarantees the client's informed consent for care. Which of the following would be the best approach to the care of this client?
a. Consult with local colleges and universities to identify individuals that could serve as interpreters.
b. Use hand gestures and props to indicate points of care.
c. Ask the family to identify any community members who might act as an interpreter.
d. Use clipart charts to communicate with the client.

136. The CCM is caring for a thirty-two-year-old woman who sustained a work-related injury and is unable to return to work. Her husband asks the CCM to explain what will happen with the family's health insurance coverage that has been provided to date by his wife's employer. Which of the following statements is the CCM's best response?
a. "Your family's out-of-pocket costs for COBRA will be lower than your costs for your employer-sponsored health care plan."
b. "If your wife is eligible for Family Medical Leave Act coverage, you will continue to receive your current insurance coverage for the next twelve weeks."
c. "You will need to apply for COBRA immediately."
d. "You don't need to worry about COBRA coverage because there are no limits on catastrophic care."

137. The CCM is mentoring a newly certified CCM. They are reviewing the record of a client on an acute-care nursing unit. After their discussion is concluded, the newly certified CCM copies the client's medical record to use as a study guide for appropriate agency documentation. Which of the following represents the CCM's assessment of this behavior?
a. An appropriate way to prepare for data entry because incidental use is allowed in this institution
b. Necessary incidental use needed to plan the client's care
c. An appropriate way to learn case management using personal health information
d. A HIPAA violation

138. The CCM is reviewing the admission orders for a client, Mr. J., who sustained a crush injury to the right lower leg. The surgeon has informed the client that surgery will be necessary to verify the integrity of the vascular supply to the leg. The CCM prepares to discuss the preoperative plan when the client says, "I'm not going to do all of this—it's crazy. I just cut my leg. I'm out of here as soon as my wife gets here with some clothes." The CCM informs the client that he is considered leaving against medical advice, and there are forms to be signed to waive the hospital's liability. Mr. J. replies, "I'll sign anything you want—I'm just not going to stay here, because I don't need to." Which of the following is the CCM's best response to Mr. J.'s comments?
   a. "Mr. J., if you leave, you will jeopardize your health because of the risk of the development of compartment syndrome in the affected leg, and you will also be denied workers' compensation insurance coverage."
   b. "If you leave, you will have to apply for COBRA immediately."
   c. "Be sure to keep checking for a pulse on the top of your right foot to compare it with the unaffected side."
   d. "At least take the prescribed antibiotics and see your PCP this week."

139. Which of the following disorders would require long-term accommodations from an employer according to the Americans with Disabilities Act?
   a. An acoustic neuroma
   b. Meniere's disease that is not responding to conservative treatment
   c. Hearing deficit resulting from blasting and excavation for a new building
   d. Diminished hearing acuity due to post-concussion syndrome

140. The CCM is on a team project for the acute-care agency. The CCM noticed that a colleague's behavior in the team meetings and one-to-one exchanges had changed. The CCM understands that the priority reason for self-identifying the manifestations of burnout is which of the following?
   a. Employer satisfaction rating
   b. The function of the care team
   c. Impressions of client families
   d. Protection of physical and emotional health

141. The CCM is managing the care of a forty-three-year-old male client who sustained a severe workplace injury yesterday. The care team has presented the proposed plan of care to the client and his wife. They both agreed to the plan, and the treatments and referrals were initiated. The next day, the client's brother, a physician, confronted the CCM demanding to review the care plan while loudly denouncing the client's care to that point. The client approved his brother's request to view the medical record. Which of the following is the CCM's priority action in this situation?
   a. Protect client confidentiality.
   b. Deny the brother's request to view the medical record.
   c. Contact the agency risk management team.
   d. Contact the primary care provider.

142. The CCM is the safety officer for a large manufacturing company. One employee whose job requires him to wear specialized safety gloves refuses to use any personal protective equipment (PPE). The employee has been injured several times due to this failure to comply with the PPE requirements. Which of the following is NOT consistent with OSHA requirements in this situation?
    a. Offer non-leather PPE to Hindu or Muslim employees.
    b. Allow employees to choose their PPE from an employer-supplied catalog.
    c. Dismiss the client for refusal to wear PPE.
    d. Inform employees that they are legally responsible for any harm or injury.

143. The CCM is mentoring a colleague going through the certification process who was severely injured in an automobile accident last year. The injuries required an extended rehab and the use of opioid medications for pain relief. This person's recent attendance has become erratic, work assignments have not been completed in a timely manner, and she has not been willing to discuss any of these concerns with others. Today the CCM received a well-founded complaint about this colleague from a client. Which of the following is the CCM's priority intervention?
    a. Follow the agency chain of command for communicating the client complaint.
    b. Refer the impaired colleague for therapy.
    c. File a complaint with the Committee on Ethics and Professional Conduct of the Commission for Case Manager Certification (CCMC).
    d. Discuss the concerns with the colleague.

144. The CCM is providing a workshop for new RNs on a surgical unit. The unit is currently involved in a safety initiative to decrease the incidence of falls by postoperative clients. Which of the following Agency for Healthcare Research and Quality (AHRQ) toolkits would be useful for this workshop?
    a. CANDOR
    b. TeamSTEPPS
    c. SHARE
    d. RED

145. The CCM understands that the AHRQ collects and analyzes outcome data from many sources. Which of the following is the primary purpose of these efforts?
    a. Identify detailed outcomes assessment for primary care providers.
    b. Penalize agencies that do not meet client satisfaction outcomes.
    c. Increase the dissemination of evidence-based research.
    d. Focus on national disease-specific outcomes.

146. The CCM is aware that which of the following care management activities requires the client's consent?
    a. Conducting care planning
    b. Contacting providers and clients with relevant treatment alternatives
    c. Evaluating provider outcomes
    d. Sharing PHI with a provider not associated with the care of the client

147. The CCM understands that, under HIPAA, there are requirements that must be met before the PHI can be shared among covered entities without the client's consent. One of those requirements is that only the information required to address the current health care concern can be shared. Which of the following is another of the requirements?
   a. Each of the covered entities must have a current or past relationship with the client.
   b. The current health concern is the basis for that relationship.
   c. The client previously consented to the sharing of PHI among the covered entities.
   d. The covered entities, including their employees, must be revealed to the client.

148. The Office of the National Coordinator for Health Information Technology (ONC) publishes tools to assess the administrative, technical, and physical security of PHI in the possession of covered entities. Which of the following is an administrative responsibility related to PHI security?
   I. Assessing the need for video monitoring to control facility access procedures
   II. Maintaining policies and procedures to secure access to workstations
   III. Developing sanction policies and procedures related to security awareness
   IV. Documenting safeguards that are enforced to limit access to PHI as necessary
   a. I, III, IV
   b. I, II, and IV
   c. II, III, and IV
   d. I, II, III, and IV

149. The CCM is employed by a large manufacturing company and is responsible for oversight of the safety and health program as required by OSHA. The guidelines dictate that health and safety must be a cooperative effort between employer and employees. Which of the following strategies would be most successful in accomplishing improved health and safety in the workplace consistent with these guidelines?
   a. Employers provide employees with a website URL that identifies the latest health and safety updates.
   b. Employees design a policy for reporting dangerous situations or near misses in the workplace.
   c. The CCM creates a series of health and safety posters for the employee lunchroom.
   d. Attendance at mandatory monthly safety seminars is monitored by the employer.

150. The CCM understands that which of the following is a violation of title II of the Americans with Disabilities Act?
   a. A county government refused to hire a client with epilepsy as a probation officer only because of his condition.
   b. A large university declined to reassign two qualified employees to satisfy a reasonable accommodation.
   c. Individuals with intellectual and developmental disabilities were inappropriately segregated in sheltered workshops and integrated day services by the state of Rhode Island.
   d. An employer failed to provide a website listing employment opportunities that met the Web Content Accessibility Guidelines (WCAG).

Answer Explanations #2

1. A: The common cold occurs suddenly and lasts for a short period of time—the definition of an acute illness. Colds do not last for longer than seven to ten days, so they cannot become chronic, Choice B. It rarely becomes life threatening, Choice C, unless it presents in severely immunocompromised individuals. An emergent illness, Choice D, refers to a new illness that has been seen in a population; it inherently would not be described as common.

2. B: Brain cancer is a chronic condition; cancer, in general, often results in depression in patients. Brain cancer, in particular, can affect mood and personality. These two are occurring simultaneously, and one is impacted by the presence of the other. The other options listed all include one or more acute rather than chronic conditions; not all pairs of conditions could be considered to have a direct relationship either.

3. B: Patients with chronic illnesses often experience a diminished quality of life and situations such as job loss, isolation, fatigue, exhaustion, and feeling overwhelmed due to the need to manage their conditions. Constant doctor appointments, medication management, and physical discomfort can all result in mental illnesses, such as high levels of anxiety and depression, and feelings of hopelessness and overwhelming stress.

4. D: Medication therapy management has to do with obtaining and taking required medications. Due to his financial situation, Emmanuel fails to take his medications. In this situation, the case manager would need to identify this barrier and support Emmanuel in finding resources to support obtaining and taking his prescriptions. Since his prescriptions are accurate, he is not having issues with medication reconciliation, Choice A. Emmanuel is not engaging in preventive care, Choice B, as he is actively treating his existing conditions. He is on medications, but this case does not otherwise relate to the pharmaceutical industry, Choice C.

5. C: TRICARE Prime is health insurance that exceeds the requirement of the Affordable Care Act and is extended to all military and their families; it remains intact for survivors of those who die in duty. While John could potentially follow through with the other options listed, it would be a lot of extra work for him, and there is no guarantee any of those will work out to provide health insurance for him and his family.

6. D: Each recipient of TRICARE benefits has an assigned case manager who handles administrative processes on behalf of the members. This eliminates some health care administrative processes, such as filing reimbursement claims. TRICARE Prime covered family members may pay deductibles, enrollment fees, and copayments, Choice A, and the benefits are not accepted internationally, Choice B.

7. D: TRICARE recipients who receive Medicare Part A and Part B are also eligible to receive TRICARE for Life as a Medicare-wraparound coverage. It is typically used by members who are sixty-five years of age or older, so prenatal services, Choice A, are not the main focus. Since VA providers cannot bill Medicare, out-of-pocket costs are usually higher for members who use TRICARE for Life at VA facilities, Choice B. Unmarried partners, Choice C, are normally not covered.

8. B: Unmarried adults between the ages of twenty-one and twenty-six years old can remain active in TRICARE as long as their sponsor remains eligible. If Danny's son marries before twenty-six, he will lose

coverage for which he otherwise would have remained eligible. He can still remain covered on Danny's plan if the other events occur.

9. A: Patients receive comprehensive care from an interdisciplinary team; in addition, their family members are trained to support the development and implementation of care. This allows the family members to feel more involved and supportive and can serve as an important comfort measure and source of positivity for the patient. The patient still receives care in a medical facility, Choice *B*, led by a primary care physician or other physician specialist, Choices *C* and *D*.

10. C: The Affordable Care Act required accountable care organizations to maintain this minimum in order to provide adequate care at reasonable rates. This provision was included to try to combat inefficient payment systems. Case managers have an important role in managing this within accountable care organizations to keep costs down through practices such as avoiding services that are not medically necessary. The Health Insurance Portability and Accountability Act of 1996, Choice *A*, includes provisions for medical privacy. The Social Security Amendments of 1965, Choice *B*, relate to social benefit programs. The Medicare Prescription Drug, Improvement, and Modernization Act of 2003, Choice *D*, introduced Part D.

11. B: Financial quality indicators are used to assess the number of readmissions and emergency room diversions. Productivity indicators, Choice *A*, are used to track the efficiency of case managers. Clinical indicators, Choice *C*, assess the efficiency of case management programs' assessments and plans of care. Finally, client experience indicators, Choice *D*, are used to track cultural sensitivity and trustworthiness.

12. D: To determine the case manager's measure of productivity for charting, first determine the number of times per day the task is completed, multiplied by the time to complete the task:

$$7 \text{ patient visits} \times 30 \text{ minutes to document each visit} = 210$$

Next, calculate the number of hours in a workday, multiplied by the number of minutes in a workday

$$8 \text{ hours in a workday} \times 60 \text{ minutes in an hour} = 480$$

Finally,

$$\frac{210}{480} \times 100 = 43.75\%$$

Answer Choices *A*, *B*, and *C* are simply incorrect values for the case manager's measure of productivity for charting.

13. A: Scopes of projects and goals are determined during the Define step of the DMAIC approach to process improvement. Answer Choices *B*, *C*, and *D* are not relevant.

14. C: The Lean approach to quality improvement focuses on reducing/eliminating waste for the purpose of increasing the value to the customer. Six Sigma, Choice *A*, focuses on eliminating defects, while root cause analysis, Choice *B*, centers on identifying the root cause or initial source of problems. Finally, Failure Modes and Effects Analysis (FMEA), Choice *D*, identifies all possible failures in a design.

15. C: Measurements for process improvement consist of process, structure, and outcomes. Therefore, change is not considered to be a performance improvement measurement. Process, Choice *A*, deals with the guidelines that case managers follow and the steps that are conducted when providing care.

191

Structure, Choice *B*, deals with a managed care organization's ability to have everything in place to meet the needs of its members. Finally, outcomes, Choice *D*, deals with patients' health statuses as a reflection of the health care that they receive.

16. B: The percentage of patients who receive a flu shot in a nursing home facility is an example of a process performance improvement measurement. An example of a structure performance improvement measurement, Choice *D*, is staffing ratios, and an example of an outcomes performance improvement measurement, Choice *C*, is patient mortality rates. Capacity, Choice *A*, is not a type of performance improvement measurement.

17. D: Quality indicators are used to pinpoint concerns with the quality of care and compare care between various facilities and geographic locations over time. Choices *A*, *B*, and *C* are not relevant.

18. A: The redesigned approach is integrated into the existing process during the Act phase of the PSDA model. The Plan stage, Choice *B*, is used for identifying a process that has resulted in outcomes that are less than ideal. A new approach is developed during the Study phase, Choice *C*, and key performance attributes are measured during the Do stage, Choice *D*.

19. C: The Commission on Accreditation of Rehabilitation Facilities (CARF) is an organization that provides accreditation in durable medical equipment, opioid treatment, and aging services. The Utilization Review Accreditation Commission (URAC), Choice *A*, serves as the case management credentialing body. The Agency for Healthcare Research and Quality (AHRQ), Choice *B*, provides quality indicators to oversee various aspects of healthcare. Finally, the Joint Commission, Choice *D*, provides accreditation that is required as a condition for healthcare organizations to receive reimbursements from Medicare and Medicaid.

20. B: The Delphi technique gathers information by having individuals complete questionnaires and participate in rounds until a point in time when they are able to reach a group consensus. Six to twelve participants brainstorm by suggesting all of the ideas they can come up with in a given period of time, Choice *A*. Criticism of ideas is not allowed, and all of the ideas are recorded. Multivoting can be used following a brainstorming session to narrow down a long list of ideas. Options are presented on a whiteboard and participants vote individually on their top five to help narrow down the list, Choice *C*. Finally, the nominal group technique allows for interaction without restricting the independent thinking of participants. They write down ideas independently, ideas are presented one at a time, and they silently rank order the ideas following group discussion, Choice D.

21. A: Determining a family's conflict resolution skills will help a case manager assess a family's ability to help a client during treatment or to what extent they may be a barrier to treatment. Other typical aspects to consider are family expectations and emotionality and crisis management skills. Choice *B*, health literacy skills, are an important consideration when providing resources of an appropriate level and when disseminating information verbally. Choice *C*, goal-setting skills, is better matched with health coaching and client empowerment. Choice *D*, knowledge of community resources, is a part of helping a client find appropriate resources.

22. D: Psychological support is not typically a focus of wellness coaching. Wellness coaching helps individuals develop healthier habits and behaviors that lead to an increase in overall health and wellness. Components of health coaching include Choice *A*, education; Choice *B*, client-led/coach-assisted goal setting; and Choice *C*, ongoing emotional support.

23. B: The case manager needs to use conflict resolution strategies. Jake and Allison disagree with the treatment direction. The case manager would begin employing conflict management steps, including treating everyone with respect and active listening. Choice *A*, crisis intervention, is used when a case manager must assist a client that is in danger emotionally or physically. Choice *C*, client activation, is the level of involvement clients have in their treatment, and Choice *D*, establishing rapport, is a part of the client engagement process.

24. C: The case manager in this situation should incorporate steps in the conflict resolution process by treating all members of the family with empathy and using active listening skills to help manage the conflict. The primary goal, however, should always be to ensure the client's needs are the treatment priority.

25. A: The ability to effectively communicate is essential for case managers. Successful treatment administration depends on a case manager's ability to communicate with clients, their support systems, and other providers. Choice *B*, to assess clients' ambivalence about change, and Choice *D*, to be skilled at motivational interviewing, are better associated with wellness coaching. Choice *C*, to be able to acquire a DNR, is related to end-of-life care issues.

26. C: The Newest Vital Sign assessment is a simple assessment that uses a few questions and a sample nutritional label to determine and assess a client's health literacy. Choice *A*, the health literacy scale, is an electronic health literacy assessment. Choice *B*, the Health Literacy Skills Instrument, tests a client's understanding of electronic health information. Choice *D*, the Thematic Apperception Test, is used in psychological evaluations.

27. D: The primary goal during the client interview is to collect client information in order to develop a treatment plan. The interview process can also function to build rapport and to begin the client engagement process. Choice *A*, developing self-care management; Choice *B*, determining health literacy; and Choice *C*, helping set realistic goals, may all take place during client assessment and treatment but are not the primary goals of the interview process.

28. D: Clarifying questions allows the interviewer to get additional information from a client. An example would be asking the client to further explain or give more information about an earlier statement. Choice *A*, determining how motivated clients are to make positive changes, is motivational interviewing in health coaching, and Choice *B*, helping clients learn effective conflict resolution skills, is related to conflict resolution during case management.

29. B: If a client has a collectivist cultural view, he may believe his family, community, and/or other members of his support system should be involved in treatment and health care decisions. Choice *A*, individualistic, is when a person believes the individual is the primary decision maker, and confidentiality and privacy are priorities. Choice *C*, multiculturalism, includes individuals from many different cultures and nations living together to form a society.

30. B: The MMPI is an objective computer-evaluated test used to assess personality during psychological evaluations. Choice *A*, WAIS, is used during psychological evaluations to test intelligence. Choice *C*, the Thematic Apperception Test, assesses a client's perception of vague images. Choice *D*, the Rapid Assessment of Adult Literacy in Medicine, is a straightforward test that uses a short-answer format, pharmaceutical labels, and other real-world health forms to assess health literacy.

31. C: When bundling payments, providers charge a single, flat fee for a service rather than invoicing line items individually. If the procedure goes smoothly, the difference between the cost of the procedure and the payment is a profit for the practice. On the other hand, if complications occur, Dr. Thompson might lose money. Choices *A* and *B* are cons to this system, and there is no evidence to show patients prefer this system over others, Choice *D*.

32. B: In the prospective payment system, procedures are reimbursed a flat rate by diagnosis code or another categorization. This can sometimes result in a mismatch between actual service cost and reimbursement rate. Accurate diagnosis by the provider and accurate billing by the institution (which can often be a responsibility of the case manager) are critical components of ensuring this system works as intended.

33. D: This system reimburses based on how well established quality standards are met. These standards typically cover best practices, standard operating procedures, and process improvements over specific periods. Reimbursement mechanisms that pay based on the other indicators listed currently do not exist.

34. A: This situation is an example of a patient in an acute-care setting in which the case manager is ensuring the patient's needs are met but medical resources are used sparingly. Billy advocates for the patient by making sure the patient receives necessary care (such as therapy services) but avoids unnecessary time in the emergency department, Choice *B*, and needless procedures, such as the MRI, Choice *C*. Choice *D* would not help the patient feel cared for and may not safely address the problem.

35. B: Managed care case managers often work on improvements that support their employer's business operations, visions, and goals. A key task for these case managers is reducing the amount of time a patient has to stay in the hospital; this can be achieved through eliminating unnecessary tests and ensuring thorough patient education. Case managers may also work to reduce inpatient admissions and delays in discharge while still providing adequate patient care and meeting patient needs. The other options listed are not ways that promote patient advocacy or fully meet their needs for care.

36. A: Due to her public health experience developing new programs, Emery likely has worked with grants and found adequate funding for the programs she developed and implemented. She can use this experience to do similar work for her employer, as nonprofits often rely on external funding sources. The other choices are not in the scope of her experience or would not have probable outcomes (i.e., undocumented individuals are not legally eligible for private or state-sponsored health insurance plans).

37. C: Since Louis has a severe, long-term condition, George will be tasked with ensuring Louis' residence poses no hazard to him or his equipment. George may also need to follow up with Louis regularly to ensure he transitions smoothly and does not have any questions or concerns that come up once he is home. George is not responsible for billing, Choice *A*, in this case (typically handled through electronic medical record systems), SBAR handoffs, Choice *B*, (a transition for medical staff if they are changing shifts or personnel), or the mechanism of the ventilation device, Choice *D*, (certified internally through medical device manufacturing companies and externally through the FDA).

38. B: Community case managers typically work with low-income, Medicaid, and/or Medicare recipients; they may also serve nonprofits, government and social agencies, and other organizations that support underserved or vulnerable communities. While pediatric or first-time mothers, Choices *A* and *C*, may fall into these categories, community case managers do not focus solely on these demographics. Virtual medical appointments, Choice *D*, are not a commonly utilized resource in general; moreover,

194

community case managers are not likely to come across them due to the socioeconomic statuses of the populations they serve.

39. B: Any cancer patient likely needs the services of a pharmacist to provide counseling and direction regarding medications such as chemotherapy and those used for pain management. A lung cancer patient is unlikely to need the services of a dentist, Choice *A*, physical therapist, Choice *C*, or podiatrist, Choice *D*, as these professionals specialize in areas not relating to lung cancers. An effective case manager must be able to gauge what health needs each of their cases might have and coordinate the appropriate care within the medical organization.

40. D: Psychologists are trained to assess and evaluate individuals to determine their overall state of well-being and identify areas that may be causing problems. Therapists are trained in counseling modalities that support the individual in addressing and solving personal issues. Both can work with individuals or small groups, Choice *A*, and both can work in various settings and with patients of all ages, Choice *B*. Neither psychologists nor therapists are legally allowed to prescribe medications, Choice *C*.

41. D: All individuals with a hearing deficit certified by their physician are eligible for a captioned telephone at no cost. The program is managed by the state and is not dependent on the client's insurance coverage. The program commonly provides for in-person installation and a review of the functions of the phone. Choices *A* and *B* (automobile and residential modifications) and Choice *C* (relocation assistance) may be covered with limitations after an extensive assessment of the individual client's needs; however, there are usually some limitations imposed on the dollar amount provided.

42. A: The ICF has only recently received funds to increase the surveillance of cancer and HIV infection as the source of individual disability. Therefore, Choice *A* is correct because HIV surveillance was not the original intent of the framework. The remaining choices are consistent with the ICF, which has set the international standard for the consistent definition of individual disabilities.

43. C: The literature indicates that employers often do not notify employees in a timely manner that COBRA coverage will become necessary, which puts an undue burden on the employee. The exact circumstances, or qualifying events, that require COBRA coverage are dictated by the specific terms of the employer's insurance contract. Most commonly, COBRA costs are the responsibility of the employee, not the employer, Choice *B*, and the COBRA coverage may or may not be required for long-term rehab, Choice *D*, depending on the employer's contract. Choice *A* is incorrect because employers don't typically prematurely alert employees of the need for COBRA coverage; the issue is that they often fail to do so in a timely fashion.

44. D: Risk stratification is an essential preliminary step for planning the appropriate interventions for each client, while screening, Choice *A*, is the process of identifying clients who will need case management of their illness or injury. Planning, Choice *B*, is focused on the identification of specific objectives for the plan of care, and implementation, Choice *C*, involves the coordination of care that is necessary for meeting the objectives.

45. A: Successful case management of the client with an acute workplace injury or illness that requires rehabilitative care is dependent on the communication skills of the CCM. Numerous details must be discussed among all of the members of the care team and the client and the family. The CCM will coordinate the implementation of the care plan. Choices *B* (leadership) and *C* (risk management) are principles of CCM practice, while utilization review, Choice *D*, is an element of the health care reimbursement issues.

46. C: Transfer skills analysis is used to provide an accurate assessment of the client's postinjury abilities. This assessment is critical if the client can no longer fill their preinjury position or if the position is no longer available when the client is able to return to work. The most common physical therapy objective is to return clients to their maximum potential level of functioning, and depending on the severity of the clients' injuries, this is rarely their preinjury level of functioning, Choice *A*. The results of the transfer skills analysis may be used to implement Choice *B* (comprehensive learning program) or as an element of Choice *D* (rehab approach); however, the original analysis is focused on assessment rather than instruction and planning.

47. A: Providers who meet implementation deadlines can qualify for cash payments. Increasing the number of patients who connect with the patent portal, Choice *B*, is one of the criteria for compliance; however, it is not associated with incentives. Choice *C* (altered time frames) is not an incentive or a penalty. Decreased reimbursement, Choice *D*, for select diagnoses is often imposed as a penalty for noncompliance.

48. D: Choices *A, B*, and *C* are commonly identified as uses for the meaningful use criteria; however, Choice *D* is the single broad-based objective among the choices.

49. B: All providers designate "need to know" employees in order to complete the functions needed to provide care. However, limiting the specific data that each individual has access to could potentially limit the exposure of patient-specific information. Choice *A* is incorrect because both PC and server-side encryption are already required, and anonymous data would be unworkable for routine data entry. Need-to-know employees, of necessity, may or may not be licensed, Choice *C*. The integrity of the employee rather than professional status is the most important consideration. The patient's consent for treatment by the PCP is obtained in accordance with the patient's insurance requirements, but no specific consent is obtained for EHR data entry, Choice *D*.

50. C: Insurance companies receive additional penalties if clients are refused coverage for a preexisting condition. Clients must be aware, however, that there are lifetime coverage limits associated with each of the plans. The remaining choices correctly identify additional features of the plan.

51. B: Comprehensive documentation that includes references for evidence-based care planning by all providers creates a more accurate view of the development of the care plan. Choices *A* and *C* are benefits of documentation; however, they do not represent the primary benefit. Choice *D* is an unrealistic outcome.

52. C: Administrative error is not addressed in this phase of the fact-finding process. The "How did it happen?" question that must be answered to complete the incident report focuses on three areas of potential error: procedural error, Choice *A*, human error, Choice *B*, and technical error, Choice *D*.

53. B: The purpose of risk management to identify and eliminate problems and to identify and prevent potential problems. Choices *A* (evaluation of employee compliance) and *C* (substitution of costly procedures) may also be included in the management process; however, Choice *D* (elimination of liability) is an unrealistic goal.

54. B: The root-cause analysis uses the information contained in the incident report to investigate preventive procedures. The sentinel event, Choice *A*, is identified by the root-cause analysis investigative team, who uses the data gathered for the incident report. This means the incident report is the foundation of the root-cause analysis and identification of the sentinel event; however, the incident

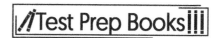

report does not specifically address preventive measures. Near-miss events, Choice *C*, are initially investigated by completing the incident report. Incident reports should be completed as soon as possible to gather data from all concerned parties. Root-cause analysis by the investigative team can take months to years to identify and implement the preventive measures, Choice *D*. The CCM recognizes that many of these preventive measures require institutional change, which means the CCM will play an integral part in the assimilation of these measures into clinical practice.

55. A: Treatment guidelines are best-practice algorithms for specific diseases used by direct care providers to treat illness. Critical pathways, Choice *B*, are used by the interdisciplinary team to set intermediate and long-term outcomes, Choice *C*, and a variance record allows deviations reporting. Treatment guidelines are used in multiple settings, and they are focused on the best-practice diagnosis and disease treatment, Choice *D*.

56. C: Mr. G. hasn't refused to participate in his care, but he is demonstrating a reluctance to cooperate with the specifics of the plan. The CCM understands that therapeutic communication is key to gaining Mr. G's acceptance and that Mr. G's current reluctance is most likely due to pain and anxiety related to the entire event. The technique of motivational interviewing is used very successfully in assisting the reluctant client to reach an informed decision, which will positively affect his health outcomes. The communication "tools" for this strategy are identified by the acronym OARS, which refers to open-ended questioning, affirmation, reflection or active listening, and summarization.

Choice *C* is an example of an open-ended question that allows Mr. G. to express himself and identify his concerns about the care plan as he copes with the events of the past two days. This provides more significant information for the CCM than the answers to multiple closed-ended yes or no questions. Choice *A* may be true, but at this point in Mr. G's recovery, it could be perceived as punitive. Mr. G will most likely perceive Choice *B* as threatening, and the CCM is aware that "why" questions generally are to be avoided because clients are most often unable to give a satisfactory response. Telling a client to discuss his decisions with his family, Choice *D*, may also be appropriate; however, the exact language in Choice *D* may be perceived as dismissive and threatening.

57. D: Employees who are unable to return to their previous position following a workplace injury receive twenty-four months of vocational training through coverage from the workers' compensation insurance. The ADA, Choice *A*, requires employers to make "reasonable accommodations" to allow injured employees to return to their original or comparable positions. The WIOA program, Choice *B*, is a vocational training program offered to a wide variety of individuals, which is aimed at strengthening the workforce and providing trainees with worthwhile employment. HIPAA, Choice *C*, requires that insurers cover the costs of "preexisting conditions" and sets standards for privacy and confidentiality of personal health information (PHI).

58. A: If the CCM finds Mrs. B. competent to initiate and understand the implications of this order, then the CCM is bound to support the client's decision against all challenges. Functioning as a client advocate is a requirement for ethical practice and is based on the principles of justice, autonomy, and veracity. Choice *B* may be a reasonable approach in some cases; however, Mrs. B. appears to clearly understand the implications of her decision, and therefore, her decision should be respected. The order cannot be rescinded, Choice *C*, by anyone other than Mrs. B. while Mrs. B. is competent. Referring the issue to the attorney and the risk management team, Choice *D*, is acceptable, but it is not the CCM's primary responsibility to Mrs. B.

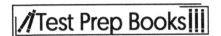

59. C: The CCM understands that, even though the focus of root-cause analysis is prevention rather than punitive action against personnel involved in the incident, remediation of nursing behaviors is a logical step in prevention. Therefore, Choice *C* presents the option with the greatest potential for long-term success because it is nonpunitive, presented in a flexible time frame, and rewarded with CEUs. Choice *A* will remediate the behavior of only one staff member. Choice *B* will most likely be met with some resistance from the nursing staff, and the time spent on the review will interrupt the work of the nursing unit for that period of time. Choice *D* may be perceived as punitive rather than preventive.

60. C: The principle of veracity requires the CCM to provide full disclosure and truthfulness to all assigned clients. This means the CCM's first priority is to disclose the employment details with the client. Choice *A* (reassignment) may well be the outcome, depending on the client's wishes and the agency's policies; however, veracity first requires disclosure to the client. The CCMs may have the option of recusing themselves in some, but not all circumstances, as indicated in Choice *B*. Choice *D* would be inappropriate without consulting with the client before proceeding with the assessment.

61. C: In this approach, which is widely used as part of the chronic-care model to support patients with chronic diseases, the patient is supported through empowerment and self-accountability. Josie provides various resources for Moe to learn from, but ultimately he chooses which steps he would like to take toward his wellness goals and chronic disease management.

62. C: Chronic-care modeling can be expensive to implement up front. However, decreased emergency room visits (and hospitalization in general) often result in cost savings and positive patient outcomes in the long term. These are the positive associations that have been shown with chronic-care modeling.

63. B: Case managers are often responsible for negotiations on behalf of the patient and other parties involved in care, such as insurance companies that reimburse for procedures. As a result, they may find themselves in negative or hostile situations. Case managers should always remain calm and do their best to ameliorate tense situations while advocating for the patient. In this situation, Jack's focus should be on making sure the patient is able to maintain emotional stability before pursuing new options with the insurance company, Choice *D*.

64. D: Mental illness often manifests in behavioral patterns, such as poor or increased appetite, poor or excessive sleep, mood instability, fatigue, and pain. Therefore, when examining a cluster of physical symptoms such as these, practitioners may want to inquire about emotional or mental stressors in the patient's life. While some of these symptoms might present with the other conditions, multiple symptoms are normally indicative of a mental illness such as depression.

65. B: Melanie is delivering a behavioral health assessment that evaluates the patient's level of functioning and substance abuse history. This provides insight as to what types of needs the patient may have or if additional interventions need to be included in the treatment plan. For example, if Melanie's patient, who has liver cancer, discusses a habit of heavy drinking, Melanie may need to coordinate a substance abuse intervention. The other options listed are not documented evaluative practices, although the SBAR handoff, Choice *D*, is a real transition technique between health care professionals.

66. B: Pharmacy benefits management programs heavily influence drug coverage benefits, and they are a critical component of health care decision-making processes. These programs develop pharmaceutical contracts with discounted rates to offer patients and make money through service fees. Health maintenance organizations, Choice *A*, focus on health care service delivery. Activities of daily living,

Choice *C*, determine how well a person can live independently. Medicare Part D, Choice *D*, is a payment system available to Medicare recipients for pharmaceuticals.

67. D: Doug now has health insurance through his employer. This is typically an advantageous benefit, as employers often pay a large portion of the premium and may offer other incentives, such as Health Savings Account deposit matching, in order to provide more coverage options than available or affordable through individual purchasing. Employers are able to provide benefits such as this due to the company size, which often makes the employer eligible for group discounts. Doug did not independently purchase this insurance plan, so it is not individual purchased, Choice *A*. Marketplace insurance, Choice *B*, refers to insurance plans available for individual purchase through state-run markets. Catastrophic health insurance plans, Choice *C*, are minimal plans that protect one from bankruptcy; they cannot be paired with an HSA and do not qualify as comprehensive coverage under Affordable Care Act requirements.

68. A: Home care benefits are a tailored insurance provision that allows the recipient to receive care in home rather than at a medical or care facility. Not all insurance plans offer this option, however, and it may come at a higher premium cost. The other options listed are not real benefit programs, nor do they accurately describe Maya's needs.

69. B: The Consolidated Omnibus Budget Reconciliation Act (COBRA) of 1986 requires organizations with twenty or more employees to offer individuals to keep, for up to eighteen months, health insurance plans in which they were enrolled while employed upon voluntary or involuntary termination or resignation. However, individuals often become responsible for the full premium amount and an administrative service fee at this point. This can be extremely cost prohibitive, especially if family members also remain covered. The Affordable Care Act, Choice *A*, includes provisions for standardizing health care operations and expanding insurance options to previously uninsured populations. The Family and Medical Leave Act, Choice *C*, includes provisions to ensure eligible employees are able to keep a job position with unpaid leave, even if they have to leave for a qualifying medical or family event. The Worker Adjustment and Retraining Notification Act, Choice *D*, is a protection act that requires companies to give a certain period of notice before mass layoffs or other terminating activities.

70. C: COBRA continuation for covered beneficiaries can last up to thirty-six months in the event of the primary insured's death. Nick's family members may be responsible for the full premium amount and an administrative service fee. The eighteen-month period, Choice *A*, applies to employees who have a reduction in hours. The twenty-nine-month period, Choice *B*, applies to people who become disabled during the eighteen-month period.

71. A: Physical abuse is typically the easiest to recognize and usually results in harm to the victim's body but could also include unreasonable confinements. Sexual abuse includes sexual acts or contacts that are forceful or with a person unable to legally consent. Financial abuse is typically carried out on the elderly or persons with disabilities and includes theft and/or inappropriate control or misuse of the victim's finances. Emotional abuse or psychological abuse includes manipulation of the victim and is typically subtler and harder to identify.

72. C: Forced sex acts are typically associated with sexual abuse. Choice *A*, manipulation; Choice *B*, humiliation; and Choice *D,* threats, are all types of emotional abuse. For reference, another example of emotional abuse is offering and then withdrawing affection.

199

73. B: Perpetrators of abuse are typically not strangers to the victim. Perpetrators of abuse are typically in positions of power over the victim, Choice *A*, older than the victim, Choice *C*, and in a relationship of trust with the victim, Choice *D*. It could be a family member, spouse, or another type of relationship.

74. A: The first stage, unfreeze, is when a client identifies the need for change or the behaviors that need to be changed. During the next stage, change, clients will begin to embrace the change and look for ways to achieve new behaviors. During the last stage, refreeze, behaviors become integrated into the client's behavior. Choice *B*, creating urgency, and Choice *D*, creating vision, are steps in Kotter's 8-step change model.

75. A: During the last stage, refreeze, behaviors become integrated into the client's behavior. Choice *B*, when a client becomes firmly involved in their treatment, is a component of client activation. Choice *D*, anchoring the change, is the last step in Kotter's 8-step change model.

76. A: A likely first step in substance abuse and addiction treatment is inpatient detox care. Choice *B*, building rapport, and Choice *D*, asking nonjudgmental questions, are a part of the client engagement process. Choice *C*, providing educational resources, is a general case manager role in assisting clients in locating and accessing community resources.

77. D: Ineffective communication by itself is not considered a behavioral health disorder. Choice *A*, substance addictions, and Choice *B*, mental Illness, are considered behavioral health disorders. Other challenges such as Choice *C*, obesity, and smoking may also be considered behavioral health disorders.

78. C: When clients feel safe to disclose personal information with confidence that the information will be kept confidential, they are more likely to develop trust in the case manager and the treatment process. This trust is a key factor in establishing rapport, which is the first step in client engagement.

79. A: Clients that are activated are better able to participate in their treatment, follow treatment plans, and advocate for themselves, which can lead to better treatment outcomes. Choice *C*, encouraging collaboration from a client's support system whenever possible, is crucial throughout service provision but not a likely outcome of client activation. Choice *D*, building rapport with the client, is related more directly to client engagement. Making the client feel more intelligent, Choice *B*, is not a main goal of client activation.

80. A: Unconditional positive regard, coined by Carl Rogers, is an integral part of client engagement. The term refers to a client's need to feel safe and validated in treatment when disclosing information.

81. C: Once Susan has enrolled in a different health insurance plan, she no longer has the COBRA choice, even if she remains within the sixty-day election period or offers to pay the full premiums. Susan could potentially shop around for other plans if she is still within her special enrollment period through the state; otherwise, she may simply need to wait until the next open enrollment period or find a new job that offers health benefits.

82. D: Barbara fits many of the requirements for receiving SSI (age sixty-five or older, limited income and assets, a resident of one of the fifty states, and a US citizen), but she has not yet been living in the United States for a consecutive thirty days. Once this period passes, she likely will be able to apply for and receive SSI. The other options listed are not requirements for receiving SSI.

83. B: The Social Security Disability Insurance program allows certain disabled or unwell individuals to receive Social Security payments, even if they are not yet of retirement age. This depends on how much

the individual has contributed into the fund via taxes over their lifetime, the length of disability (individuals cannot collect until they have been medically unable to work for five months or more), and the type of disability. Medicare, Choice *A*, is strictly for individuals over age sixty-five and younger individuals who have very specific conditions. They could apply for Supplemental Security Income, Choice *C*, but will only qualify if they are over the age of sixty-five or are blind or disabled. The Pension Fund, Choice *D*, is not a real option.

84. A: Medicare Part A covers hospital and nursing care services. Part B, Choice *B*, is optional and provides supplementary coverage in addition to hospital and nursing care services. Part C, Choice *C*, offers additional benefits through Managed Care Organizations, especially for individuals who suffer from diseases that require specialized care or those who are under sixty-five yet qualify due to certain disabilities. Part D, Choice *D*, provides coverage for prescription drugs.

85. C: Medicare Part B is an elective and supplementary option that covers additional doctor visits, preventive care, and other allied health services. While everyone who qualifies for Medicare Part A receives it, Medicare Part B is an additional charge. This charge for premiums is normally deducted from a recipient's Social Security payment each month.

86. B: The Social Security Amendments of 1965 created subsidized programs and public benefits for US citizens, including Medicaid. Medicaid supports low-income and vulnerable populations in accessing health care. The Affordable Care Act, Choice *A*, includes provisions for standardizing health care operations and expanding insurance options to previously uninsured populations. The Benefits Embargo, Choice *C*, is not a real act. The Consolidated Omnibus Budget Reconciliation Act, Choice *D*, includes provisions regarding employer-sponsored health insurance when an employee faces a reduction in hours.

87. B: Both federal and state funds, which are collected through a number of ways, including taxes, are used to fund Medicaid programs. Some states plan and implement statewide Medicaid programs; based on operating guidelines, they may not be eligible to receive federal dollars. This can be limiting for constituents of the state that would otherwise qualify for Medicaid services.

88. D: The Medicaid expansion encouraged states to offer Medicaid benefits to all low-income (falling below 138 percent of the federal poverty level) legal residents who are under the age of sixty-five rather than categorically needy populations only (including pregnant women, children under age six, and mothers with dependent children whose household income fell below 133 percent of the federal poverty level). So far, only thirty-three states have opted to expand Medicaid coverage, even though federal funding covers the expansion. Recipients would still need to be legal residents, Choice *A*. Medicare Part D, Choice *B*, is only available in the fifty states and the District of Columbia. Private insurer plan premiums are not capped at 10 percent of the family income, Choice *C*.

89. A: Federal guidelines establish a general overview for what state Medicaid programs should entail; however, each state focuses on setting eligibility criteria for services and determining administrative features, such as reimbursement rates, types of services, and coverage limits, for Medicaid recipients. They are not responsible for the other options listed; as they receive funds from the federal levels, Choice *B*, constituents are responsible for selecting their own health care, Choice *C*, and are fined individually, and states do not govern who can reject Medicaid payments, Choice *D*.

90. B: While the other options listed are required by federal law to be mandatory Medicaid benefits in all states, physical therapy is an optional service a state may or may not choose to provide. Therefore, it is least likely to be a covered Medicaid benefit out of the listed choices.

91. A: The Health Information Technology for Economic and Clinical Health (HITECH) Act allows patients or the designees they appoint to gain access to their complete medical history in electronic format and to share that information with other medical providers. The E-Sign Act, Choice *B*, deals with electronic signatures and records as they relate to interstate and foreign commerce. HIPAA, Choice *C*, is concerned with the security and privacy of patients' health information. Finally, the Electronic Communications Privacy Act, Choice *D*, protects stored electronic communications, such as information on computers.

92. C: Pressure ulcer rate falls under AHRQ's category of patient safety indicators (PSIs). Urinary tract infection admission rate, Choice *A*, falls under the category of prevention quality indicators (PQIs). Hip fracture mortality rate, Choice *B*, and cesarean delivery rate, uncomplicated, Choice *D*, both fall under the category of inpatient quality indicators (IQIs).

93. B: The AHRQ's category of prevention quality indicators forms a foundation for evaluating community-based programs and determining where gaps exist. Inpatient quality indicators uncover risks for volumes of procedures, excessive surgeries, and high mortality in hospital settings, Choice *A*. Pediatric quality indicators focus on errors and complications that affect those in the pediatric population, Choice *C*. Finally, patient safety indicators provide opportunities for comparative public reporting and pay-for-performance initiatives, Choice *D*.

94. D: Organizations track the productivity of their case managers to demonstrate need of services, validate staffing models, and establish client acuity. Answer Choices *A, B,* and *C* are not relevant.

95. A: Utilization indicators are quality indicators that are used to evaluate the effectiveness of case management programs, along with general trends and behaviors of the population that is being served. Clinical indicators, Choice *B*, enable case management programs to evaluate the efficiency in which assessments, plans of care, and appropriate treatment protocol are being executed. Client experience indicators, Choice *C*, evaluate such items as treatment, communication with professionals, and responsiveness. Financial indicators, Choice *D*, look at measures related to cost savings and cost effectiveness, such as average length of stay and readmission rates.

96. C: To determine the newly hired case manager's measure of productivity, first determine the number of times per week the task is completed, multiplied by the time to complete the task:

$$25 \text{ intake interviews} \times 30 \text{ minutes each} = 750$$

Next you calculate the number of hours in a work week multiplied by the number of minutes in an hour:

$$40 \text{ hours in a work week} \times 60 \text{ minutes in an hour} = 2,400$$

Finally,

$$\frac{750}{2,400} \times 100 = 31.3\%$$

Answer Choices *A, B,* and *D* are simply incorrect values for the case manager's measure of productivity.

97. B: The United States Preventative Services Task Force (USPSTF) focuses on improving the health of Americans through evidence-based recommendations about services such as healthcare screenings and counseling treatments. The Agency for Healthcare Research and Quality (AHRQ), Choice *A*, provides a set of clinical guidelines to support medical professionals when making decisions. The National Quality Forum (NQF), Choice *C*, utilizes a set of performance-based standards to improve care. Finally, the National Guideline Clearinghouse (NGC), Choice *D*, provides clinical practice guidelines that are written in a patient-friendly way and are available to both clients and professionals. The guidelines outline the most effective medical treatments for conditions based on current research.

98. D: The statement that best describes that goal of the Agency for Healthcare Research and Quality (AHRQ) is "to improve the quality, safety, and accessibility of healthcare." Answer Choices *A*, *B*, and *C* are not relevant.

99. A: Healthcare-associated infections can be prevented through using toolkits and checklists to improve patient safety in long-term care facilities. Healthcare-associated infections are the most (not the least) common complication associated with patient stays in the hospital, as is stated in Choice *B*. Healthcare-associated infections are no longer known to be an inevitable hazard of hospitalization, as is stated in Choice *D;* they are just a risk. Finally, one out of every twenty-five hospitalized patients in the U.S. contracts a healthcare-associated infection, not one out of every 250 hospitalized patients, as is stated in Choice *C*.

100. C: Acute stroke mortality rate falls under AHRQ's category of inpatient quality indicators (IQIs). Bacterial pneumonia admission rate, Choice *A*, falls under the category of prevention quality indicators (PQIs). Post-operative sepsis rate, Choice *B*, and transfusion reaction rate, Choice *D*, fall under AHRQ's category of patient safety indicators (PSIs).

101. D: Self-directed care is a factor in client self-care management that includes encouraging the client's priorities and need to contribute to their treatment direction. Choice *A*, active listening; Choice *B*, establishing rapport; and Choice *C*, maintaining confidentiality, are all necessary steps in client engagement.

102. C: Case managers encourage the client in self-care management by assisting with skill development and education so the client can be better equipped and confident to help direct and participate in the direction of care. Choice *A*, ensuring the client has access to emotional and psychological services, is related to helping clients access community resources, and Choice *B*, helping build trust with the client by ensuring confidentiality, is a step in client engagement. Choice *D*, supporting clients to set their own goals, is a part of client empowerment.

103. B: Case managers should consider multiple facets of a client's life in order to provide resources that address a client's needs in each of those areas if possible. The physical domain includes basic needs, such as food and housing, while social, psychological, and emotional domains include family support, mental health care, and group support. The spiritual domain includes the spiritual needs of the client, but spiritual organizations may also be able to assist with resources in other areas, such as basic needs and social resources. Family and financial needs of the clients will fall under other larger categories such as physical and social domains.

104. D: Conflicts can arise about Choice *A*, the treatment process; Choice *B*, the way services are provided; or Choice *C*, between the client, case manager, and/or the client's support system, or the client and providers. Case managers should assist or lead in conflict resolution and utilize an effective

conflict resolution method. Conflicts between clients and law enforcement may happen but are not typical conflicts in the case management process.

105. D: The Thomas–Kilmann Instrument assesses different types of conflict resolution styles and identifies which strategies are most effective. The strategies identified include collaboration, compromise, accommodation, competition, and avoidance.

106. B: The compromise style of conflict resolution requires all participants to give a little and get a little. Choice *A*, collaboration, occurs when all participants work together to find an outcome that is in everyone's best interest and is likely the best outcome but may not be possible given time constraints and the level of conflict. Choice *C*, accommodation, occurs when one participant gets what they want because the other participant gives in and is not an effective method in most cases, as it can cause ongoing problems. Choice *D*, competition, occurs when the participants compete, and the conflict ends with the stronger person getting what he or she wants.

107. C: Choice *A*, financial issues, and Choices *B* and *D*, past or current history of substance abuse, could lead to a crisis situation. However, Choice *C*, when a client is in extreme physical, psychological, or emotional danger, is the best definition of a crisis. A client making suicidal threats would be an example of a crisis situation.

108. C: Creating a vision is the third step in Kotter's model. During this stage, the client and collaborators set goals and objectives to achieve the desired, visualized change. Choice *A*, "Create urgency," is Kotter's first step, followed by Choice *B*, "Form a coalition." Choice *D*, "Remove obstacles," is the fifth step in Kotter's model.

109. A: Focusing on a client's psychosocial needs is a component of end-of-life care. This includes spiritual needs, fears, and mental health concerns such as anxiety and depression. Choice *B*, helping the client become empowered, and Choice *C*, assessing the client's suicidal ideation, may possibly be a part of end-of-life issues but are not a typical focus. Choice *D*, working with the client to develop informed decision-making skills, is a step in client self-care management.

100. B: Withdrawal of care happens when a decision is made to remove means of artificial life support for a person diagnosed with a terminal illness. Choice *A*, hospice care, typically takes place during the last stage of a person's terminal illness with the goal of decreasing pain and discomfort. Choice *C*, DNR, is an acronym for Do Not Resuscitate. This is a legal order that requires medical personnel to refrain from performing life-sustaining measures on the named individual, such as the use of a ventilator or administration of CPR. Choice *D*, palliative care, includes all care given between a terminal illness diagnosis and death.

111. C: A biopsychosocial approach should be used with clients diagnosed with a chronic illness or disability and considers a client's medical, social, and mental health needs. Choice *A*, multicultural approach, should be used throughout services when case managers respect and accept a client's cultural background. Choice *B*, neuropsychological treatment and evaluations, are performed by neuropsychologists. Choice *D*, interpersonal skills, should be utilized by case managers with all services to ensure effective communication with clients and other service personnel.

122. D: A case manager must consider the whole person, including psychosocial, family, physical, and emotional needs in chronic illness and disability care, as all of these areas can affect clients. Choice *A*, interpersonal care, is not a main focus of a case manager. Choice *B*, hospice care, is provided at the end

stage of a client's life, and Choice *C*, end-of-life care, incorporates all care given to a client diagnosed with a terminal illness.

113. C: The Health insurance Marketplace is administered by the federal government and provides health insurance options for people with different life situations and income levels. Choice *A*, the Affordable Care Act, is a government mandate that provides laws governing various aspects of health care. Choice *B*, 211 help line, and Choice *D*, the client's employer, may offer additional resources for clients to access health care but do not match the given definition.

114. B: Case managers should respect and not discredit a client's beliefs even if they may be viewed by the client's doctor as a barrier to treatment or recommended interventions. Case managers should continue to provide education about treatment options while acknowledging the client's decisions.

115. B: Bereavement counseling provides support and assistance for individuals that have experienced a significant loss. This type of counseling helps the client navigate the grieving process in an effective and healthy way.

116. C: Especially since Simon is of sound mind, he must be the primary stakeholder in decisions relating to his care. It is very possible he could have been making a request or asking a question about his interdisciplinary team, and Jane should not have cut him off or assumed she already knew what he needed. Patients should be as involved as possible in their care, and their opinions should take precedence over most others' opinions, including family members. Case managers should keep this in mind as they relay information to the patient.

117. A: Poor communication is likely to be the most critical factor in causing medical errors during transitions that could result in improper or inadequate patient care, patient instability, and overall poor outcomes. Especially in transitioning patients between different staff members, institutions, or levels of care, organizations should ensure communication is clear, direct, and standardized to minimize possible human errors or misunderstandings in care delivery. The other options listed may support quality endeavors, but they are not shown to relate specifically to the transition of patients between caregivers or care levels.

118. C: The National Transitions of Care Coalition's sole purpose is to solve problems associated with transitions of care in specific institutions, but their general guidelines include standardization processes, performance indicators that pertain to quality in transitions of care, and efforts toward increasing the role and utilization of case managers. This coalition champions the job responsibilities of case managers and considers them an integral role in minimizing risks associated with care transitions. The Joint Commission, Choice *A*, and the Nursing Alliance for Quality Care, Choice *B*, examine standards and best practices as a whole, although transitions may make up a smaller component of their overall work. The American Pharmacists Association, Choice *D*, is a professional group for pharmacists.

119. D: Utilization management is a situational step that evaluates whether a medical admission or procedure is necessary. It examines a single procedure at a period in time, whereas case management, Choice *A*, looks at the entire patient experience holistically, from intake to discharge. Across this spectrum, case managers may take steps to ensure unnecessary treatments are not performed, while utilization managers only look at a single process step along the continuum of care. Triage, Choice *B*, is a method of categorizing admissions from most severe to least severe. Reimbursement mechanism, Choice *C*, refers to how an organization is compensated for a service performed.

120. A: The simple act of moving Nicole into another room, even though she is on the same floor and will likely be more comfortable after the change, is a major transition of care. She will be surrounded by all new equipment, a new environment, and new staff. It is during this transition that she is vulnerable to an event that could lead to a poor patient outcome, so environmental cleanliness, communication with both Nicole and her labor and delivery staff, and standardized handoffs are critical for her new attendants. This case has nothing to do with FMLA, Choice *B*, which has not been recently reformed. Utilization management, Choice *C*, refers to eliminating unnecessary steps during a medical process. Hospital hospitality, Choice *D*, is not a real term.

121. D: Medically needy individuals are eligible for a subset of the Medicaid medically needy program specifically meant for this population. It supports those who have medical expenses that reduce their earned income to where they become Medicaid eligible. This eligibility threshold varies by state and is based on the number of dependents in the household and the household income. It also has to be reestablished on a monthly basis. Middle-class individuals, Choice *A*, are most likely to have employer-sponsored health insurance. Categorically needy, Choice *B*, refers to certain demographics that are likely to have difficulty working or too many obstacles to self-sufficiency. Vulnerable, Choice *C*, is too broad of a term to apply to this question.

122. B: The correct order of procedure for developing an LPC includes interviewing the client and their family, consulting with other treatment experts to ensure the best treatment possible, and research costs and reasonable sources for any necessary treatments that come up.

123. C: Regularly visiting the doctor is an important factor in staying healthy. Other methods include avoiding substance and alcohol abuse, practicing good nutritional habits, and staying active. Choice *A*, frequent visits to a wellness coach; Choice *B*, attending religious or spiritual services; and Choice *D*, practicing effective conflict resolution skills, do not necessarily lead to maintaining good health.

124. B: Minimal amounts of self-disclosure can enhance the client engagement process; however, excessive or inappropriate disclosure can encourage blurred boundaries between the case manager and client and become disruptive to the treatment process.

125. D: Clients that are highly activated are more involved in their treatment and therefore are more likely to adhere to recommendations of the treatment and practice effective healthy habits outside of treatment. Choice *A*, empowered clients; Choice *B*, clients with effective interpersonal communication skills; and Choice *C*, clients in support groups, are not necessarily more likely to adhere to recommendations.

126. A: Helping a client learn skills that can help them navigate treatment, such as asking questions and learning to make appropriate decisions, can increase levels of activation. Choice *B*, ensuring confidentiality, is important throughout the treatment process but does not necessarily increase client activation. Choice *C*, helping clients create a crisis plan, is a part of crisis intervention, and Choice *D*, service referral, is a general case management role.

127. B: A medical exam should be completed prior to a psychological evaluation to ensure there are no medical reasons for a client's symptoms. Choice *A*, a health literacy test, is used to test a client's literacy level. Choice *C*, health coaching, and Choice *D*, motivational interviewing, are a part of wellness coaching.

128. D: The benefit of using the Delphi technique is that it enables geographically dispersed professionals to participate. This technique is not the least time-consuming data collection method, as is stated in Choice *A,* and it does not allow the participants to directly confront each other, as is stated in Choice *B.* Additionally, the technique's design does not allow it to be changed while the data are being collected, as is stated in Choice *C.*

129. A: Uncovering the root cause of process inefficiencies takes place during the Analyze step of the DMAIC approach to process improvement. Answer Choices *B, C,* and *D* are not relevant.

130. C: HCAHPS survey measurements have been impacted by the Affordable Care Act, as the results are now used to calculate government incentive payments for eligible hospitals. The survey results are still publicly reported on the internet, the opposite of which is stated in Choice *A,* and the same number of categories exists for patients to report on after being discharged, unlike what is stated in Choice *B.* Additionally, patients use a rating scale to answer questions that utilizes words such as "never" and "always," unlike what is stated in Choice *D.*

131. B: Research and development is the only area listed that is not covered by the Utilization Review Accreditation Commission's (URAC) case management standards. The standards cover a wide range of topics including: organizational structure, Choice *A,* review of marketing and sales material, Choice *C,* and clinical staff credentialing, Choice *D.*

132. D: Ensuring that Medicare pays only for services that are necessary and reasonable is one of the primary functions of the Quality Improvement Organization (QIO) Program under CMS. It does so by protecting the integrity of the Medicare Trust Fund. Answer Choices *A, B,* and *C* are not relevant.

133. A: This type of verbiage would be included by a case manager in a justification of continuation of intervention report. The focus of this type of report is documenting a patient's progress for continuation of care. The focus of a cost-benefit analysis, Choice *B,* is documenting savings as it is related to case management involvement. The focus of justifying a more costly intervention patient report, Choice *C,* is providing the rationale for a patient plan of care that is more costly than the original plan, when the original plan is no longer producing the desired results. Finally, a summary of interventions, Choice *D,* is a type of patient report that is not used.

134. C: The sentence that best explains the relationship between validity and reliability when interpreting data is "reliable data is accurate; valid data measures what is intended." If a test (data) is reliable, that does not always mean it is valid, Choice *A;* and both validity and reliability should be taken into consideration, unlike what is stated in Choices *B* and *D.*

135. A: The priority responsibility for the CCM is to verify that the client has sufficient information to give informed consent for treatment. Choices *B* (hand gestures and props) and *D* (clipart charts) may be sufficient for some portions of the admission procedure; however, every effort must be made to communicate with the client in their native language. The language departments of colleges and universities are often a reliable source of individuals who are fluent in many foreign languages. A community member, Choice *C,* that speaks the client's language would be an acceptable alternative if no other independent source is identified.

136. B: The CCM understands that the employer's plan and the client's eligibility for FMLA coverage will determine the time frame for applying for COBRA coverage. If the client is eligible for FMLA coverage, they will be covered by the employer's insurance plan until the FMLA benefits are exhausted. The

families do need to understand that COBRA fees can be as much as 102 percent of the employer's health plan coverage, Choice A. The family does not need to apply for COBRA immediately, Choice C, if the client is eligible for FMLA coverage. Also, there are limits placed on catastrophic care, Choice D.

137. D: HIPAA allows for incidental use of the client's protected health information (PHI) if the institution has appropriate safeguards in place to protect the data. In the case of the acute-care setting, paper documents are limited to the chart, which is stored securely at the nurses' station rather than the bedside. The computerized data is password protected with access limited to only the employees that need to access the data, Choice B. In addition, there are either secure shredding stations or interim receptacles to store the data scheduled for off-site shredding. The mentor's best response is to require the destruction of the copies because this action constitutes a HIPAA violation. The intended purpose of the copied information was something other than contributing to the care of the specific client.

138. A: The CCM must be aware that there are two major concerns with Mr. J.'s plan: He is risking the possible loss of his leg due to alterations in the vascular supply to the affected area, and in most cases, he will be ineligible for workers' compensation insurance coverage. The consequences of his actions should be identified and discussed with Mr. J. It is also possible that Mr. J. will make a better decision if he receives additional information from the CCM regarding his condition and recommended treatment. The terms of the employer's insurance plan will dictate the client's eligibility for COBRA, Choice B, in the event that the client refuses treatment. Choices C and D leave the impression that home care following this injury is acceptable, which in this case is incorrect.

139. B: Aggressive treatment for Meniere's disease results in the progressive decrease in hearing acuity in addition to the destruction of the hair cells of the cochlea, which results in a permanent balance disorder. Necessary accommodations would be required to address each of these manifestations. The acoustic neuroma, Choice A, is a benign tumor that can be successfully treated with surgical removal but may be associated with a risk of slowly progressive hearing loss. In most instances, the defects identified in Choices C and D (hearing deficits) are temporary and would require only minimal accommodations.

140. D: Nursing burnout is characterized by exaggerated manifestations of physical and emotional exhaustion, and providers must care for themselves before they are able to care for others. CCMs are skilled providers that are critical to the functioning of the agency, the care team, and, most importantly, the professional management of the client's care. As is the case with many complex problems, burnout manifestations may be subtle and vary from person to person; however, if ignored, the manifestations will become progressively more severe and possibly lead to somatic illness.

141. C: Although the CCM's priority concern is the protection of the client's confidentiality, Choice A, the client has given his brother permission to view the medical record. This means the CCM cannot deny the client's brother access to the record, Choice B. The CCM will also contact the primary care provider, Choice D, but contacting the risk management team is the CCM's priority at this point. Early intervention of possible issues regarding the quality of the client's care is of primary concern to the CCM after client confidentiality.

142. D: The employer, rather than the employee, is responsible for all injuries that occur due to noncompliance with the use of PPE. The CCM, as the employer's representative, is responsible for enforcing employee compliance with the use of all required PPE. Religious accommodations are made for Hindu and Muslim employees, Choice A, and employees with specific medical conditions are offered the opportunity to choose PPE, Choice B, that accommodates their requirements. Employees who refuse to use appropriate PPE even with accommodation can be dismissed, Choice C. In addition, employees

who are not able to use the required PPE due to a medical condition may also be dismissed if the employer cannot provide an alternative position for the employee.

143. D: Although the colleague has not been willing to discuss her behavior, the CCM's first priority is to discuss any concerns with the individual before progressing to the agency, Choice *A*, or the certification commission, Choice *C*, and most certainly before considering therapy, Choice *B*. The CCM's documentation of the client's complaints also requires that all involved providers be interviewed to assess the incident.

144. B: The Agency for Healthcare Research and Quality (AHRQ) is a government-sponsored clearinghouse that is focused on disseminating evidence-based research to improve clinical practice by all providers. The agency has published multiple "toolkits" that provide all of the learning resources necessary for completing educational programs related to specific concerns. The AHRQ focuses specifically on research related to the care of priority populations, which include children, elderly clients, female clients, and rural populations. In addition, the programs are focused on improving the care delivery in relation to access, cost-effectiveness, and quality in multiple settings. The CCM is aware that TeamSTEPPS includes tools to improve client safety by building all providers' teamwork and communication skills. CANDOR, Choice *A*, is focused on the proper response to an untoward event that resulted in harm to the client. SHARE, Choice *C*, is a multistep process that focuses on clients' and allows identification and comparison of all options. RED, Choice *D*, is focused on effective discharge planning, especially for diverse populations, in order to avoid readmission and post discharge emergency department visits.

145. C: The primary focus of the AHRQ is the dissemination of evidence-based practice guidelines. The agency is a government-affiliated clearinghouse that sponsors, facilitates, and increases the availability of relevant research. A partial list of areas addressed by the agency includes quality and client safety, health information technology, data and measures, and prevention and chronic care. The identification of outcomes assessments, Choice *A*, and disease-specific outcomes, Choice *D*, is commonly provided by the AHRQ; however, the overall purpose is the dissemination of research results. The AHRQ does not have prosecutorial powers and therefore does not penalize providers, Choice *B*.

146. D: The CCM understands that HIPAA requires the client's consent for sharing of PHI between providers if the client has not had a relationship with the provider, past or present. Care planning, Choice *A*, and exploration of alternative treatments, Choice *B*, are consistent with the role of the CCM and would not require the client's consent beyond the consent for treatment. The evaluation of provider outcomes, Choice *C*, most commonly uses anonymous data, which would not require the client's consent.

147. A: HIPAA allows sharing of PHI between covered entities without the client's consent when three requirements are met. Each of the covered entities must have a current or past relationship with the client. The PHI that is shared must be related to that relationship, Choice *B*, and only necessary PHI must be shared. HIPAA stipulates that the client has a relationship with each of the covered entities that are sharing the PHI; however, there may be concerns other than the current health concern that were the basis for past relationships. The client must have had a past relationship with the covered entities, but HIPAA does not specifically require previous client consent, Choice *C*, or that the covered entities and employees be revealed, Choice *D*.

148. D: The covered entities are responsible for safeguarding PHI by administrative oversight of policy development and enforcement (*III*); by physically securing all storage facilities and workstations where

PHI is stored (*I* and *II*); and by ensuring that all technology is secure with all recommended software upgrades relevant to data security (*IV*).

149. B: Active employee participation in promoting health and safety is more likely to successfully meet the OSHA outcomes than any of the other options. Choices *A* and *C* can be easily ignored because the strategies are passive with regard to employee participation. Choice *D* may be regarded as punitive, which may possibly create an adversarial climate in the workplace.

150. C: Title I of the ADA prohibits private employers with more than fifteen employees, state and local governments, labor unions, and employment agencies from discriminating against qualified clients with disabilities in all elements of the employment procedure. Title II refers to discrimination against individuals with disabilities by state and local governments regarding assignment to services and programs. Choice *C* references a lawsuit alleging that individuals with disabilities were being unnecessarily segregated in state-sponsored programs. Choices *A, B*, and *D* are all examples of title I because they reference discrimination regarding the employment process.

CCM Practice Test #3

1. Which of the following is NOT a cause of nonadherence to the care regimen?
   a. Financial limitations
   b. Limited understanding of an illness or condition
   c. Positive reinforcement of positive behavior
   d. Poor health literacy

2. Which of the following is true of adult foster care?
   a. May be used as an alternative to institutionalized living in some states
   b. Managed by volunteer caregivers
   c. Is unable to provide support for activities of daily living
   d. May not be used for the elderly

3. Which of the following is true about group homes?
   a. They are not staffed twenty-four hours per day
   b. They do not provide a permanent alternative living solution for adults over the age of nineteen
   c. They may be used for those suffering from a chronic mental illness or dementia
   d. They are set up as non-profit businesses

4. What is true of assessments done during the case-management process?
   a. Intended to only be completed once during the lifecycle of a case
   b. Not a one-time event but may be repeated to establish and/or monitor ongoing needs throughout the case-management process
   c. Only able to yield information about the physical background but not the psychosocial aspect of a patient's health
   d. Not intended to be a part of the initial steps taken by a case manager in the case-management process but rather a supplementary action item that can be done at any time during the process

5. What should happen during the planning phase of the case-management process?
   a. Case managers must work in a solo-fashioned format to develop a robust plan of care that is medically acceptable to all healthcare providers responsible for the client
   b. Case managers must leave goals as originally written despite possible changes in the patient's priorities during the case-management process
   c. Case managers must ensure that there are not multiple interventions for every goal
   d. Case managers may modify goals during the case-management process due to barriers or complications that arise, but these goals should remain individualized and specific to the patient and be monitored closely with a secondary or alternative plan in place

6. What is important for the case manager to consider when developing care plans?
   a. Should not require approval by anyone except the case manager
   b. Should only be reviewed by the patient and the case manager
   c. Should only be reviewed by the case manager and treatment provider
   d. Should capture ongoing progress of the client as well as any barriers that are preventing adherence to care

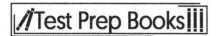

7. When can case managers close a case?
   a. When the patient has not yet fully demonstrated adherence to care
   b. When services are in place to sufficiently meet the needs of the patient
   c. When the patient demonstrates an ability to seek health support through appropriate channels
   d. Both *B* and *C*

8. Which of the following is used by mental-health professionals and other healthcare professionals, including case managers, to classify mental illness?
   a. Diagnostic and Statistical Manual of Mental Disorders
   b. International Classification of Diseases
   c. Diagnosis-Related Groups
   d. Current Procedural Terminology

9. Which of the following is a medical code that is utilized along with ICD numerical diagnostic coding as a component of the billing process?
   a. Hospital Illness-Related Diagnosis
   b. Medical Terminology Coding
   c. Diagnosis-Related Groups
   d. Current Procedural Terminology

10. Which of the following is a standard diagnostic tool that is leveraged to track epidemiology and support health management and clinical activities?
   a. International Coding of Disorders
   b. International Classification of Diseases
   c. International Disease Terminology
   d. International Procedural Terminology

11. Which of the following happens from birth to the start of an illness to the point in which the patient is either no longer ill or the patient is no longer eligible for medical or case-management services?
   a. Continuing Spectrum of Care
   b. Case Management Continuum
   c. Continuum Alliance
   d. Continuum of Care

12. What is an activity of case management that can contribute to cost containment?
   a. Identifying barriers to care
   b. Finding coupons for the client
   c. Keeping phone calls to a minimum
   d. Canceling doctor's visits on behalf of the client

13. What may be sold by an individual who is facing a terminal illness to relieve financial burdens and occurs when an individual elects to sell their life-insurance policy?
   a. Terminal illness settlements
   b. Viatical settlements
   c. Waiver settlements
   d. Contract settlements

14. What are designed to support those who lack the mental capacity to manage their own finances?
   a. Special needs trusts
   b. Disability trust funds
   c. Special needs assistance
   d. Special assistance trusts

15. Which of the following are a combination of standard medical and nonmedical services that may allow for the provision of long-term care services in the home and community?
   a. Combo service assistance programs
   b. Home health promotion programs
   c. Waiver programs
   d. Contract establishment programs

16. Which of the following are NOT goals of case management?
   a. Provide service and care coordination
   b. Promote care that is medically necessary and cost-effective
   c. Create a pathway to functional stability
   d. Impose the case manager's values onto the client

17. Which of the following may be administered at any stage of an illness or at any age on behalf of their patient?
   a. Hospice care
   b. End-of-life services
   c. Guideline-based healing care
   d. Palliative care

18. What is typically administered as a component of end-of-life care to those who are suffering from terminal illnesses with less than six months to live?
   a. Hospice care
   b. Critical pathway care
   c. Chronic illness care
   d. Palliative care

19. When should a case manager look for end-of-life care issues to be discussed?
   a. At the end of life
   b. After treatment begins
   c. Only at the request of the patient
   d. Early on in the decision-making process

20. Which of the following is administered over a period of time not to exceed two years?
   a. Long-term disability
   b. Accidental insurance
   c. Short-term disability
   d. Long-term care services

21. What is used to replace the income lost as a result of a chronic condition or illness?
    a. Long-term disability
    b. Chronic-condition insurance
    c. Long-term Social Security
    d. Long-term care services

22. What is an interdisciplinary care team?
    a. A collaborative group of healthcare professionals from different backgrounds, disciplines, and professions
    b. A group of doctors that collaborate together in treating an illness
    c. A community group of peer support for the client
    d. A group of family members and friends hand-picked by the client to support them

23. Which of the following is considered a form of long-term care?
    a. Emergency care
    b. Assisted living
    c. Outpatient clinic
    d. Vocational training

24. An insurance company sets a limit of $50,000 as the total cost that they will cover in claims, with the remaining costs above $50,000 and up to $500,000 being covered by another carrier. What is this carrier known as?
    a. Reinsurance or stop-loss carrier
    b. Health-insurance extension coverage
    c. Viatical settlement
    d. Viatical trust

25. Which of the following requires ACOs to hold providers mutually accountable for the health of their patients, offering financial incentives to cooperate and save money by avoiding services such as diagnostic tests and medical procedures that are not medically necessary?
    a. Pioneer Program
    b. Medicaid Shared Savings Program
    c. ACO Shared Savings Program
    d. Medicare Shared Savings Program

26. Which of the following does NOT require a referral to see a specialist, nor has a requirement to choose a primary-care physician?
    a. HMO
    b. IPA
    c. PPO
    d. POS

27. Which of the following is required by the Affordable Care Act to manage a minimum of 5,000 Medicare beneficiaries for a period of five years?
    a. HMOs
    b. IPAs
    c. PPOs
    d. ACOs

28. Which of the following was established with the US Medicare Modernization Act of 2003 for the primary purpose of promoting medication adherence among Medicare Part D beneficiaries through the use of education and counseling?
    a. Medicare Therapy Management Program
    b. Medication Therapy Management Program
    c. Medicare Therapy Modernization Program
    d. Medication Therapy Modernization Program

29. Which of the following serves those individuals who suffer from a chronic condition currently receiving Medicare Part A and Part B?
    a. SNP
    b. DNP
    c. PCM
    d. MGP

30. Which of the following provides active-duty family members who have a qualifying mental or physical disability with financial assistance?
    a. TRICARE Disability
    b. TRICARE Special Services
    c. ECHO
    d. SNP

31. Which of the following are NOT eligible for TRICARE?
    a. Medicare Part A recipients
    b. US Family Health Plan participants
    c. Medicare Part B recipients
    d. CHAMPVA recipients

32. What must a physician's practice pass to function as a Patient-Centered Medical Home?
    a. Standards and guidelines
    b. Criteria and pathways
    c. Tests and practice guidelines
    d. Standards and elements

33. How can case managers promote self-management in patients?
    a. Limiting the decisions patients make about their own health
    b. Solving problems for the patient
    c. Allowing patients to take actionable steps about their own health
    d. Restricting the patient-provider relationship

34. What is the most effective form of negotiation for the case manager to engage in?
    a. Aggressive negotiation
    b. Collaborative negotiation
    c. Passive negotiation
    d. Simplistic negotiation

35. What does the term *physical functioning* refer to?
    a. A client's level of physical mobility
    b. The amount of exercise engaged in on a daily basis
    c. Physical strength
    d. Activities of daily life, such as eating and bathing

36. Which of the following is true about pharmacy benefits management programs?
    a. Work strategically with self-insured companies and government programs to maintain formularies and establish pharmacy contracts.
    b. Do not have a role negotiating discounts or rebates with pharmaceutical companies.
    c. Have minimal influence over drug coverage.
    d. Do not have an active role in prescription-drug programs.

37. Which of the following provides payment of benefits to those individuals and their family members who are living with a limited income and/or resources at their disposal?
    a. SSI
    b. SSDI
    c. FSA
    d. Medicaid

38. Which of the following allows recipients of Medicare to maintain their benefits; however, a managed care organization is chosen and paid by the federal government to administer the Medicare benefits?
    a. Medicare Part A
    b. Medicare Part B
    c. Medicare Part C
    d. Medicare Part D

39. Sometimes referred to as Hospital Insurance, what covers the hospital portion of healthcare, paying for acute care and care at skilled-nursing facilities?
    a. Medicare Part A
    b. Medicare Part B
    c. Medicare Part C
    d. Medicare Part D

40. Which of the following programs provide for those individuals who have significant health needs but whose income is too high to qualify for Medicaid?
    a. Medically needy
    b. Special needs
    c. Patient-Centered Medical Home
    d. Health Home

41. Which of the following allows benefits for individuals and their family members if they have worked for enough years to receive Social Security taxes and become disabled prior to the age of retirement?
    a. Medicare
    b. Medicaid
    c. SSI
    d. SSDI

42. Which of the following is true about COBRA requirements?
    a. Employers to terminate insurance coverage upon loss of employment
    b. Employers to provide coverage for up to forty-eight months if job termination is due to disability
    c. Employers to allow their employees the opportunity to maintain their insurance coverage through the employer for up to thirty-six months when the loss of coverage is due to death or divorce
    d. Employers to allow their employees to maintain their insurance through the employer for up to thirty-six months when the loss of coverage is due to job termination or reduction in work hours

43. Which of the following is NOT included in a successful transition plan?
    a. Keeping appointments
    b. Adhering to medication orders and ongoing medication management and reconciliation
    c. Case-management goals and preferences
    d. Utilization of home visits for education and assessments

44. Case managers who work for home healthcare agencies are considered which of the following?
    a. Health-progression case managers
    b. Long-term illness case managers
    c. Provider-based case managers
    d. Community-based case managers

45. Which of the following is true about MCO case managers?
    a. Focus more on those populations that require complex management and are at the greatest risk for catastrophic outcomes
    b. Provide services to large percentages of their population
    c. Are not in a favorable position to align themselves with providers and patients
    d. Do not use best practices and guidelines proposed by NCQA

Read the following scenario and answer questions 46 and 47.

Martha is a woman in her 50s who has recently been diagnosed with some health issues related to her poor self-care in areas of health and nutrition. She is significantly overweight, has a poor nutritional diet, and does not exercise. Martha's doctor has indicated that behavioral changes are needed in order to prevent dramatic health deterioration.

46. According to Lewin's Change Management Model, which is the first step in helping Martha achieve change?
    a. Freeze
    b. Change
    c. Unfreeze
    d. Refreeze

47. During which stage of the Stages of Change Model (Transtheoretical Model) would Martha be MOST likely to begin thinking about making changes to her nutritional habits?
    a. Precontemplation
    b. Contemplation
    c. Action
    d. Preparation

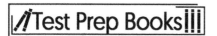
48. Which of the following is NOT a population at a higher risk of experiencing abuse?
    a. Children
    b. Elderly
    c. Young adults
    d. The disabled

49. Which of the following is MOST likely to be a characteristic of a perpetrator of abuse?
    a. History of mental illness
    b. Low tolerance for loud noise
    c. Low level of education
    d. Heart condition

50. What is a *dual diagnosis*?
    a. A conflicting diagnosis from two different physicians
    b. Occurrence of a physical illness as a result of substance abuse
    c. Presence of two mental health disorders in a person
    d. Co-occurring mental health disorder and substance abuse

51. What is the BEST definition of *client activation*?
    a. Motivating clients to engage in more physical activity
    b. A client's level of involvement in the community
    c. A client's level of involvement in their own treatment
    d. A client's ability to complete activities of daily life

52. If a case manager has a client with low activation levels, what is the BEST way to increase their activation level?
    a. Provide small, manageable challenges tailored to their needs
    b. Set high expectations that will raise their level of activation
    c. Make all decisions for the client
    d. There is no effective strategy for increasing activation levels

53. What is the goal of client empowerment?
    a. To help clients become illness free
    b. To support clients in setting and achieving their own goals
    c. To set achievable goals for the client
    d. To help the client understand their own weaknesses

54. What is the first step in client engagement?
    a. Setting treatment goals
    b. Building rapport
    c. Collaborating with other service providers
    d. Interviewing family members

55. What is *confidentiality*?
    a. The case manager does not disclose any personal information to the client.
    b. The case manager makes sure that all case notes refer to the client with a false name.
    c. The case manager instructs the client to never reveal any details of treatment to anyone.
    d. The case manager never discloses information about the client without their permission.

56. Which of the following is NOT an important element of client self-care management?
    a. Self-promotion
    b. Self-advocacy
    c. Self-directed care
    d. Informed decision-making

57. What is the result of effective client self-care management?
    a. Better overall health and less need for professional and emergency care
    b. Higher levels of client happiness
    c. Easier job for the case manager
    d. Decreased amount of medication needed by the client

58. Which of the following is the BEST referral option for the elderly or disabled who have difficulty leaving their homes to obtain food?
    a. Food pantries
    b. Food stamps
    c. Area Office on Aging meal delivery service
    d. A community cooking class

59. Which aspect of whole-person care is often overlooked when seeking community resources for the client?
    a. Physical
    b. Emotional/psychological
    c. Spiritual
    d. Medical

60. Which form of conflict resolution involves all parties working together to find a solution that satisfies everyone?
    a. Compromise
    b. Avoidance
    c. Competition
    d. Collaboration

61. In a crisis situation, what is the first and MOST important thing to do?
    a. Make sure that the client is safe
    b. Restrain the client
    c. Go to the hospital
    d. Call the police

62. If a client is suicidal, what is the MOST important information for the case manager to get?
    a. How many family members are in the area
    b. The client's food intake for the day
    c. Whether or not the client has a suicide plan or means
    d. The client's history of illness

63. What is the goal of health professionals in providing end-of-life care?
    a. To prolong the patient's life
    b. To ensure that the patient's last days of life are as painless and comfortable as possible
    c. To ensure that the patient dies in the hospital
    d. To ensure that every possible medical intervention has been fully utilized to treat the disease

64. Who should make the decision about a DNR order?
    a. The doctor
    b. A combined decision between a doctor and social workers
    c. The patient or family members
    d. Hospice care staff

65. Why is it important to have a family systems approach when providing treatment for a client?
    a. Because the client's family will likely be involved in treatment and provide significant support
    b. Because the family's wishes are more important than the client's wishes
    c. Because the client cannot make decisions about treatment without the family's approval
    d. Because doctors need the medical history of the family

66. What is the goal of motivational interviewing?
    a. To address specific symptoms or behaviors of a mental illness
    b. To convince the client to engage in medical treatment
    c. To discover the client's internal motivation and the causes of ambivalence to change
    d. To motivate the client to develop better health habits

67. In what situation would health coaching be the MOST helpful?
    a. When a person is facing the last few months of their life
    b. While a person is preparing for a marathon
    c. During pregnancy
    d. When someone has a chronic illness

68. Which of the following health literacy assessment tools have greatest validation?
    a. NVS and eHEALS
    b. SAHL and HLSI
    c. NVS and REALM-R
    d. TOFHLA and REALM

69. Which health literacy assessment tool gives the patient a list of words and asks them to read the words that are familiar?
    a. Newest Vital Sign
    b. Rapid Estimate of Adult Literacy in Medicine
    c. Health Literacy Skills Instrument
    d. Short Assessment of Health Literacy

70. Which of the following is true about interpersonal communication?
    a. It does not include phone calls and emails.
    b. It is used in personal relationships, not professional relationships.
    c. It is a very important skill for case managers to have.
    d. It consists of communication between three or more people.

71. Which of the following is an important interpersonal communication skill for the case manager to use?
    a. Assimilation
    b. Collaboration
    c. Effusion
    d. Contextualization

72. What can be a weakness of communication within a group?
    a. The room may become hot and stuffy.
    b. There will be too many good ideas from which to choose.
    c. The group leader may get overwhelmed with anxiety.
    d. The group may suppress the voice of the individual.

73. What is the first thing to consider when preparing for an initial interview with the client?
    a. The treatment goals
    b. The environment of the interview
    c. The assessment forms
    d. The confidentiality agreement

74. Which option reflects the BEST use of open-ended questions in an interview?
    a. To gather demographic information about the client
    b. To explore the client's struggles, fears, and concerns
    c. To inform the client of organizational policies
    d. To assess the client's educational level

75. What's the difference between individualistic and collectivist cultures?
    a. Individualistic cultures value independence; collectivist cultures value community.
    b. Individualistic cultures tend to be poorer; collectivist cultures tend to be richer.
    c. Individualistic cultures are matriarchal; collectivist cultures are patriarchal.
    d. Individualistic cultures are not time-oriented; collectivist cultures are time-oriented.

76. What is *cultural competency*?
    a. The ability to quickly learn new languages
    b. The ability to handle new and different experiences in different countries
    c. The ability to explain why one's own culture is better than any other
    d. The ability to understand, accept, and respect someone else's culture

77. How is a neuropsychological evaluation different from a psychological evaluation?
    a. It takes place in the client's home instead of the office.
    b. It is more comprehensive and looks at cognitive or neurological impairment.
    c. It evaluates personality and nothing else.
    d. It requires a brief hospitalization.

78. Which of the following personality tests is commonly used in psychological evaluations?
    a. Minnesota Multiphasic Personality Inventory (MMPI)
    b. Nebraska Personality Questionnaire, Short Form (NPQ-SF)
    c. American Psychological Personality Survey (APPS)
    d. Assessment for Personality Disorders (APD)

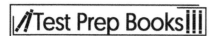

79. What is the name of the book that contains the official diagnostic information for psychological disorders?
    a. Manual to Detect Psychological Disorders, Third Edition (MDPD-III)
    b. Diagnostic and Statistical Manual of Mental Disorders, Fifth Edition (DSM-5)
    c. Diagnosis of Mental Health and Psychological Disorders (DMHPD)
    d. American Manual of Mental Disorders, Second Edition (AMMD-II)

80. What is one of the psychosocial aspects of chronic illness?
    a. The competency of the patient's doctor
    b. Mental illness, such as anxiety or depression
    c. A client's level of involvement in recreational activities
    d. Maintenance of healthy nutritional and exercise habits

81. Which government insurance program is intended to help those over 65 or with certain disabilities?
    a. Medicaid
    b. Affordable Care Act
    c. Elderly Insurance Aid
    d. Medicare

82. What is the name of the program run by pharmaceutical companies to provide affordable medications to low-income individuals?
    a. Patient prescription program
    b. Patient assistance program
    c. Patient medications assistance
    d. Patient medicine management

83. How should a case manager respond if the client's religious beliefs conflict with the doctor's recommended treatment?
    a. Dismiss the client's spiritual beliefs, and insist they comply with treatment
    b. Agree with the client's beliefs, and tell them that treatment is not important
    c. Acknowledge the client's beliefs and self-determination, but continue to provide education about the treatment
    d. Refuse to work with any clients who have beliefs that are different from the case manager

84. What is a benefit a client can experience when engaging in spiritual practices?
    a. It has no noticeable or measurable impact.
    b. It contributes to depression and anxiety.
    c. It makes the client more fearful and confused about life.
    d. It gives the client a more positive and hopeful outlook.

85. When should support groups be utilized?
    a. When the client feels isolated and does not have a strong support system
    b. When the client has a full and busy schedule
    c. At the beginning of treatment as a requirement for every client
    d. When the client stops attending doctor visits

86. What is unique about pastoral counselors?
    a. They only use the Bible and have no training in psychological concepts
    b. They disregard medical care and psychotherapy
    c. They are uniquely qualified to integrate spiritual and psychological aspects in their counseling
    d. They are unhelpful because they include spiritual elements in their counseling

87. What is the purpose of bereavement counseling?
    a. To force people to quickly get over their grief
    b. To minimize the loss the person is feeling
    c. To help people go through the grieving process in exactly the right stages
    d. To help a person grieve and adjust to loss in a healthy way

88. Why are illness prevention and wellness programs important for those with terminal or chronic illnesses?
    a. Maintenance of healthy habits can slow progression of a disease and improve quality of life.
    b. Engaging clients in these programs can distract them from dealing with their sickness.
    c. Patients with chronic illnesses are stronger and healthier than others, so it is a good time to engage in health programs.
    d. These programs can cure terminal illnesses

89. Which of the following is an early detection method that should be encouraged by case managers to promote a patient's wellness and illness prevention?
    a. Nutritious diet and daily exercise
    b. Thinking positively about life
    c. Discontinuing any unhealthy habits, like smoking
    d. Mammograms

90. Which of the following is an accurate statement about the Case Load Capacity Calculator?
    a. The Case Load Capacity Calculator may be purchased on a sliding scale fee.
    b. The Case Load Capacity Calculator may be purchased for a fixed price.
    c. The Case Load Capacity Calculator is free to those seeking to use it.
    d. The Case Load Capacity Calculator is free to government agencies only.

91. What are the four categories of the Caseload Matrix?
    a. Initial elements impacting caseload, comprehensive needs assessment impacting caseload, case management interventions, and outcomes
    b. Case management elements impacting caseload, case management needs assessment impacting caseload, case management interventions, and outcomes
    c. Quality elements impacting caseload, standardized needs assessment impacting caseload, case management interventions, and outcomes
    d. Primary elements impacting caseload, general needs assessment impacting caseload, case management interventions, and outcomes

92. Which term describes the practice of organizations looking to demonstrate the value of case management activities and services?
    a. Cost-effective comparison
    b. Health benefit ratio
    c. Medical cost ratio
    d. Cost-benefit analysis

93. Which of the following tools is an example of an industry-recognized health risk assessment?
    a. Case Mix Assessment Tool
    b. Mini-Mental State Examination
    c. Six Sigma
    d. PDSA

94. What is the practice that is commonly used by organizations to identify those people within their population who pose the greatest risk for preventable costs?
    a. Predictive guidelines
    b. Predictive forecasting
    c. Predictive analysis
    d. Predictive modeling

95. What is the average number of months used by most predictive models to review data?
    a. 6
    b. 9
    c. 12
    d. 18

96. Which programs improve the overall quality of healthcare delivery?
    a. Collaborative Quality Indicator Management Programs
    b. Continuous Quality Improvement (CQI) Programs
    c. The Agency for Quality Improvement
    d. Provisional Quality Improvement Programs

97. What practice enables organizations to monitor trends and compare "apples to apples" in their evaluation of performance and achievement of metrics?
    a. Benchmarking
    b. Metric calculation
    c. Trending management
    d. Performance management

98. Which organization operates a case management accreditation program?
    a. URAC
    b. AHRQ
    c. NQAURP
    d. NQF

99. Which agency compares its measures with other reported measures from other entities, such as AHRQ National Measures Clearing House and NQF?
    a. NCQA
    b. URAC
    c. Quality Measures Coalition
    d. National Transitions of Care Coalition

100. What action is taken by NCQA for organizations that fail to meet NCQA requirements during the Accreditation Survey?
   a. They are initially provided with a probationary NCQA status
   b. They are granted temporary NCQA status for a six-month period
   c. They are denied NCQA status
   d. They are provided a 14-day window to make changes

101. Which of the following is a level of disease management NCQA accreditation?
   a. Accredited with Qualifying Credentials
   b. Accredited with Performance Rating Standard
   c. Provisional Accreditation
   d. Accreditation with Provisional Guidelines

102. What NCQA data enables consumers to compare one health plan with another?
   a. HEDIS
   b. National Clearinghouse Guidelines reporting
   c. URAC reporting
   d. Predictive modeling data

103. Which of the following is the period of time for which an organization may receive accreditation by NCQA?
   a. One year
   b. Two years
   c. Four years
   d. Five years

104. What must Long-term Services and Support demonstrate to apply for NCQA accreditation?
   a. Perform quality assessments
   b. Use generalized plans of care
   c. Address minor incidents only
   d. Manage transitions between LTSS and behavioral health services only

105. Which statement best defines the types of performance-based measures used by the NQF?
   a. Uses a unique set of performance-based measures that are not recognized by the state or federal level of government
   b. Utilizes a set of performance-based standards that are recognized by multiple groups including states, the federal government, and private sectors
   c. Does not utilize performance measures that can be leveraged to evaluate quality of care but instead is used in determining the quality of care coordination
   d. Favors performance-based measures that align to guidelines and standards that are only utilized in the private sector

106. What did the Joint Commission create to evaluate patient safety?
   a. National Patient Safety Goals
   b. Federal Patient Safety Goals and Guidelines
   c. National Patient Safety Goals and Standards
   d. National Patient Safety Goals and Measures

107. Which agency or group provides the opportunity for healthcare improvement by sharing research information that improves the accessibility, effectiveness, efficiency, and quality of healthcare that consumers receive?
   a. Agency for Healthcare Research and Quality (AHRQ)
   b. The Joint Commission
   c. National Committee for Quality Assurance (NCQA)
   d. URAC

108. What clearinghouse provides specific patient-centered outcomes that outline the MOST effective medical treatments for a particular condition based on current research?
   a. The National Standard Clearinghouse
   b. The National Guideline Clearinghouse
   c. The Independent Review Clearinghouse
   d. The U.S. Taskforce Guideline Clearinghouse

109. How many stages of meaningful use are there associated with the HITECH Act?
   a. One
   b. Two
   c. Three
   d. Four

110. Which agency uses Quality Indicators (QIs), such as Patient Safety Indicators and Pediatric Safety Measures, to measure the quality of healthcare, and may assist in the identification of quality concerns as well as identify areas of opportunity for additional research and study?
   a. AHRQ
   b. USPSTF
   c. NCQA
   d. NQF

111. Which of the following are examples of financial indicators?
   a. Cost effectiveness and cost savings
   b. Case management tasks and activities
   c. Health risk assessments
   d. Mortality reporting

112. How is case management productivity measured?
   a. Time, tasks, and activities
   b. Length of stay, admissions, and readmissions
   c. Encounters, admissions, and readmissions
   d. Revenue, encounters, and admissions

113. Which of the following best describes the utilization quality indicator of daily census reporting?
   a. A summary of the average length of stay and number of readmissions within 30 days
   b. An overview of budgeted inpatient days per 1000 to current inpatient days per 1000 with a seven- and 30-day trend
   c. Month-to-date and year-to-date encounters information by product line for both ambulatory and inpatient services
   d. A comparison of the benchmark length of stay detail to that of a given facility

114. Who can provide an organization with the client's experience?
    a. The physician
    b. The home health agency
    c. The client
    d. The hospital

115. How are cases provided to the CCM on an inpatient unit?
    a. By periodically checking with the charge nurse on each unit
    b. Through a daily check of the hospital census report
    c. Requesting that the charge nurse of each unit page or call the CCM upon each admission
    d. By periodically checking the daily census report for all admissions throughout the day

116. Eric has sustained an injury that may require the use of a prosthetic limb. Which of the following would NOT be included in preparation for counseling the patient?
    a. Consult with a prosthetist trained and certified to design and fit the required prosthetic.
    b. Locate a support group for patients with similar prostheses and/or amputations.
    c. Advise the client that the prosthetic device is the best choice for mobility.
    d. Compile a list of available options to present to the client for consideration.

117. What is the purpose of an orthosis?
    a. To replace a missing limb or body part for both cosmetic and functional reasons
    b. To heal a limb or body part post injury
    c. To support or improve declining muscle or limb function
    d. To prevent an injury to a limb or body part

118. A case manager has been asked to work on a team to evaluate a client post rehabilitation. The client has been fitted with a prosthetic but has been unable to return to work due to what he reports as "just not feeling right." What group of functional domain assessments should be considered for individuals who are experiencing chronic pain of an unknown origin after injury?
    a. Berg Balance Scale; Balance Self-Perceptions Test; Functional Reach Test
    b. Timed Up and Go; Physical Performance Battery; Gait Abnormality Rating Scale
    c. Beck Depression Scale; Depression Scale; Mini Mental Exam
    d. None of the above

119. What types of behaviors can be expected from an individual with a frontal-lobe injury?
    a. Poor balance and impaired depth perception
    b. Promiscuity and low frustration tolerance
    c. Difficulty recognizing words and progressive blindness
    d. Poor fine motor skills and gait impairment

120. Which of the following would be considered a moderate workplace injury?
    a. Repetitive injuries
    b. Cuts and bruises
    c. Broken bones
    d. Electrocutions

121. Which of the following is true of a functional capacity evaluation?
   a. It includes an evaluation of the ability to perform basic and job-specific tasks.
   b. A team approach is not utilized.
   c. The treatment plan is created and must remain the same throughout rehabilitation.
   d. Minimal effort from the client is all that is expected.

122. Jane's husband, Tom, has suffered a traumatic brain injury (TBI). How should the CCM counsel her regarding the concerns of recovery?
   a. The caregivers must expect the client to recover quickly.
   b. The client should be placed in an institution for his own safety.
   c. Every client with a TBI will have similar symptoms.
   d. The caregiver must expect specific deficits and plan how to handle them.

123. What is ergonomics?
   a. The study of how assistive devices affect an individual's quality of life
   b. The science of creating effective ways to prepare an individual to return to their home environment
   c. The study of creating more efficient ways for people to work in their vocational environment
   d. The science of teaching a client how to adjust to the outside world

124. How should a CCM counsel a client with a total knee replacement (TKR) that does not wish to return to work despite the physical ability to do so?
   a. The CCM must advise the client that they must return to work because they agreed to do so in their treatment plan.
   b. The CCM must negotiate an alternate return to work date with the employer while attempting to help the client change their mind.
   c. Advise the client that their claim may not be covered if they do not return to work as agreed upon in their treatment plan.
   d. The CCM must discuss the client's hesitation for returning to work to determine if a slower part-time to full-time return to work is more reasonable.

125. Which of these is the MOST important factor of work-hardening programs?
   a. Making sure that the client is physically and emotionally prepared to return to work as soon as possible
   b. To provide a simulated work environment to gradually reintroduce the client to specific tasks directly associated with the position to which they will be returning
   c. Confirming that the client is still able to perform the specific work-related tasks of their job without assistance
   d. Making sure that the client is aware that they may have to return to work before they feel ready to do so

126. What is the primary goal of the CCM when working with clients requiring rehabilitation services?
   a. To work with a client to help them to return to their previous level of functioning
   b. To work with the client until they no longer need ongoing case management
   c. Making sure that the client feels ready to leave treatment
   d. To work with the client until they are able to return to work

127. Which diagnosis-related groups (DRGs) are NOT typically flagged for CCM intervention?
    a. Individuals who have sustained a TBI
    b. Industrial accident victims
    c. Amputees or possible amputees
    d. Women with high-risk pregnancies

128. Which of the following is NOT a basic rehabilitation delivery system?
    a. The self-directed-care delivery system
    b. The group-care delivery system
    c. The managed-care delivery system
    d. The fee-for-service delivery system

129. Which functional domain of assessment tools are BEST suited to evaluate a client with a cerebellar TBI?
    a. The group primarily targeting activities of daily living
    b. The group of assessment tools that target executive functioning
    c. The set of assessment tools primarily targeting ambulation and locomotion
    d. The group primarily targeting cognitive functioning

130. What is the primary goal of the PPACA?
    a. To provide American citizens with appropriate and affordable medical coverage
    b. To ensure that insurance companies are penalized for providing high-cost insurance
    c. To prevent discrimination against individuals without health insurance
    d. To provide basic essential health benefits to all children in the United States

131. Why is it important to obtain informed consent from a client?
    a. To ensure that the CCM is paid for services rendered
    b. To make sure that the CCM cannot be sued for malpractice
    c. To confirm that the client was advised regarding all aspects of the treatment plan
    d. To confirm that the correct providers were enlisted for the client's treatment

132. Which of the following is NOT an acceptable way to secure protected information in client files?
    a. Shredding nonessential patient information whenever necessary
    b. Utilizing a Document Management System (DMS)
    c. Keeping copies of all client information in the home office of the CCM
    d. Providing information only to those who need to know

133. Which statement best describes the concept of veracity?
    a. Providing compassionate care to every client
    b. Practicing in an ethically sound manner
    c. Providing options to the client that are grounded in truth
    d. Taking the vow to do no harm to any patient

134. What is the purpose of COBRA?
    a. To increase vocational training for individuals with disabilities
    b. To allow the family members of disabled persons to take an unpaid leave to care for them
    c. To strictly prohibit discrimination against persons with disabilities
    d. To allow individuals to maintain employer medical benefits in the event of loss of employment

135. Robert is a patient that has sustained an injury that requires the transfusion of blood products in order to preserve his life. Robert is a Jehovah's Witness, and his religion does not allow for allogenic blood transfusion. How should the CCM proceed?
    a. Check to see if any advance directives have been signed, and if they explicitly deny allogenic blood transfusions. If not, proceed with the transfusion without the client's knowledge.
    b. Contact the affiliated clergy and ask them to tell the client to receive the transfusion.
    c. Decline to continue as this is in direct conflict with the standard of practice for the CCM to "do no harm."
    d. Discuss the client's concerns and review alternatives with the hematologist.

136. Maria has sustained a crushing injury and is in a drug-induced coma. The physicians have deemed the client is near death and will remain on life support indefinitely. The client's next of kin, her husband, is adamant that his wife would not want to remain on life support. Which is the BEST response for the CCM?
    a. Contact the affiliated clergy and ask them to discuss the matter with the family.
    b. Decline to continue as this is in direct conflict with the standard of practice for the CCM to "do no harm."
    c. Check to see if any advance directives have been signed, and if they explicitly deny any life-saving measures, proceed according to the client's final wishes.
    d. Allow the client's husband to make the final decision regarding the cessation of life support.

137. Which statement BEST explains why it is important to maintain accurate case files?
    a. To make sure that the CCM cannot be sued for malpractice
    b. To maintain an accurate, chronological timeline of the plan of care
    c. To ensure that the CCM is paid for services rendered
    d. To confirm that the client was advised of all of the aspects of the treatment plan

138. Regarding "meaningful use," which statement BEST explains how the CCM demonstrates compliance?
    a. Providing evidence that all client records are not only properly secured and that their privacy has been protected, but that the CCM has the appropriate credentials
    b. Creating not only a clearinghouse of information that all providers can access, but also a formula that requires those providers to verify that the use of the database results in improved outcomes for patients
    c. Providing evidence that the CCM has met the standards of practice in working with clients and that all client records are properly secured and their privacy has been protected
    d. Producing records for the supervision received during each case to show the CCM has provided care

139. What is NOT considered a "bad faith" action by a CCM?
    a. The improper administration of administrative denials of benefits
    b. Failure of the CCM to explain the denial of benefits
    c. The client's awareness of the erroneous denial of benefits
    d. Personality conflicts between the client and CCM

140. Which is the BEST statement that should be added to all electronic transmissions of client records?
    a. This communication contains confidential information. If you have received this document in error, please forward to the correct individual. No additional action is needed.
    b. This communication contains confidential information. This document must be shredded immediately if you are not the intended recipient. No additional action is needed.
    c. This communication contains confidential information. If you have received this information in error, please notify the sender by phone and return the original to the address listed on the form. Any distribution or reproduction of this transmission by anyone other than the intended party is strictly prohibited.
    d. None of the above

141. Eduardo works in a meat-packing plant and recently sustained an injury that resulted in his hand being mangled and later amputated. The client is the meat-packing company and has enlisted the CCM to conduct a root-cause analysis to determine the cause of the accident. What is the primary goal of the CCM in this situation?
    a. The CCM must ensure that there are no grounds for the employee to receive medical coverage.
    b. The CCM must prove that the employee is at fault in the incident.
    c. The CCM must determine the cause of the incident in order to prevent any future incidents.
    d. The CCM must contact legal authorities to investigate the plant's procedures.

142. Which of the following statements BEST explains the primary objective of a root-cause analysis?
    a. To prevent future occurrences of a similar nature, while preserving the factors that did not contribute to the problem
    b. To discredit and deny the medical claim of the client
    c. To save the company from future financial loss
    d. None of the above

143. Which statement is the BEST response for how the CCM should counsel a family member or caregiver experiencing burnout?
    a. The CCM should counsel the caregiver to permanently institutionalize the client.
    b. The caregiver should be advised to consider antidepressant or anxiety medications.
    c. The CCM should encourage the caregiver to consider respite care.
    d. The caregiver should be counseled to consider therapy.

144. Which statement BEST explains a scenario in which a client has the capacity to consent to treatment?
    a. A client suffering from a condition impairing the function of the mind or brain.
    b. An individual that is unable to understand, retain, and weigh the relevant information provided.
    c. A client who is unable to communicate a decision.
    d. A client suffering from a condition impairing the visual field.

145. What is the BEST preparation for a CCM who has been asked to appear for a deposition regarding the outcome of one of their cases?
    a. Seek legal counsel immediately to determine how to respond.
    b. Confer with colleagues to find out what they would do.
    c. Contact the client to determine the reason for the lawsuit.
    d. Review the client's case files to uncover any areas of concern.

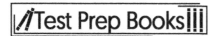

ion

CCM Practice Test #3

146. What is the BEST explanation of why self-care is important for the CCM?
a. To model appropriate self-care to clients and caregivers
b. In order to better connect with clients and their families
c. To preserve their own personal mental health
d. None of the above

147. Brittany is receiving case management regarding a workplace injury that resulted in a below-the-knee amputation. The client received a denial letter from ERISA in her post office box approximately 56 days ago and is not sure how to proceed. This denial states that she will not be given short-term disability coverage for her injuries. Under the ERISA laws, what is the BEST response for the CCM in this situation?
a. The case manager must review the denial letter for the actual date in order to determine if the legal appeal time has passed.
b. The case manager must advise the client that the employer is responsible for approving the claim, no matter the circumstance.
c. The case manager must call the insurance company to file an appeal on the client's behalf immediately.
d. The case manager must advise the client that filing an appeal will be unsuccessful and that there is no need to do so.

148. What entity governs the standards of practice for the CCM?
a. The National Society of Case Management
b. The National Association of Social Workers
c. The American Nurses Association
d. The Case Management Society of America

149. Josephine had been receiving case management services after she sustained a TBI in a bus accident. Although it was determined that the accident was not her fault, she continued to suffer from PTSD do to the injuries inflicted on other people in that accident. Josephine's husband, Andrew, was the initial caregiver, but filed for divorce 6 months after the accident claiming he could not care for his wife anymore. Before this happened, Andrew was legally entitled to receive periodic progress reports and often requested them. One year after the divorce, Josephine responded to a treatment session with extreme frustration and stormed away from the CCM crying and yelling. Andrew called the CCM to ask what had happened, stating that Josephine was inconsolable. He demanded to know what the current treatment plan for her was. Which statement below is the BEST response without breaking the patient's confidentiality?
a. Hang up the phone, as any information provided is a violation of the client's privacy.
b. Review the client's file to determine if the advance directive is current and includes Andrew.
c. Contact the client to obtain consent to speak with the estranged spouse.
d. Request that the estranged spouse and client come in together to discuss the client's case.

150. Which of the following questions is NOT typically a part of the immediate investigation following a sentinel event?
a. Who was directly involved with the incident in question?
b. When did the actual incident occur?
c. What can be done to prevent a similar incident from occurring?
d. How exactly did the actual incident occur?

232

This material is provided for exam preparation purposes only and does not indicate an endorsement of any specific scientific, political, or religious point of view. © TPB Publishing. You have been licensed one copy of this document for personal use only. Any other reproduction or redistribution is strictly prohibited. All rights reserved.

Answer Explanations #3

1. C: A lack of positive reinforcement of positive behavior by the interdisciplinary healthcare team can contribute to increased nonadherence. Financial limitations, limited understanding of an illness or condition, and poor health literacy can also contribute to increased nonadherence.

2. A: Much like long-term care support services, adult foster care provides support for activities of daily living and provides room and board for the elderly. In some states, it is offered as a component of long-term care waiver programs. It is managed by sponsoring families and paid caregivers.

3. C: Group homes provide an alternative living environment for children and adults that is staffed twenty-four hours per day. Group homes are for-profit businesses.

4. B: Assessments are not a one-time event. They may be repeated more than once to establish and/or monitor ongoing needs throughout the case-management process. Assessments form the foundation for activities associated with planning, implementation, care coordination, evaluation, and outcomes management.

5. D: The prioritization of goals may change throughout the lifecycle of a case as a patient's focus may also change due to barriers or specific needs. The case-management process is a collaborative process that can utilize multiple interventions to address a single goal.

6. D: Care plans are evolving documents that should be updated throughout the lifecycle of a case to reflect the ongoing progress of the patient. Care plans should be designed and collaborated on by the patient, payer, treating physician, and any others indicated.

7. D: Cases should only be closed when certain criteria are demonstrated within the life cycle of a case. Once services are sufficiently in place to support continued improvement or stability of a patient and the patient demonstrates the ability to independently obtain appropriate health status, the case closure is an appropriate next step.

8. A: The DSM is used by mental-health professionals and other healthcare professionals, including case managers, to classify mental illness as well as collect data and bill clients.

9. D: CPT codes are used to help identify medical, surgical, and diagnostic procedures and services to entities such as physicians, health-insurance companies, and accreditation organizations.

10. B: ICD codes are leveraged to track epidemiology and support health management and clinical activities.

11. D: In case management, patients are at greatest risk during the transition points of care—specifically, when they are transitioning from one level of care to another. The continuum of care (CoC) requires case management of patients in multiple settings. It happens from birth to the start of an illness to the point at which the patient is either no longer ill or the patient is no longer eligible for medical or case-management services.

12. A: If the case manager can identify barriers to care then services will become more effective, ultimately reducing the need for additional services and the costs that will be incurred.

13. B: Viatical settlements are used during a terminal illness to relieve financial burdens. An individual can choose to sell their life-insurance policy for a percentage of the face value.

14. A: Specifically, special needs trusts are designed to benefit the disabled or mentally ill. SNTs are designed to support those who lack the mental capacity to manage their own finances.

15. C: Waiver programs may include case management, a home health aide, personal attendant care services, adult day health services, respite care, and residential care. On occasion, states may choose to include additional value-added services.

16. D: It is not the job of the case manager to impose their value system onto the client. Rather, the case manager should empower the client in self-directed care and support the client's priorities even when contrary to those of the case manager.

17. D: The characteristic that distinguishes palliative care from hospice care is the time at which palliative care may be offered. Case managers may advocate for palliative care to be administered at any stage of an illness or at any age on behalf of their patient.

18. A: The goal in providing hospice care is not to provide a cure but to ensure that the patient's remaining days are as comfortable as possible.

19. D: This should be discussed early on in the decision-making process since having a plan in place makes the patient's wishes clear and reduces the level of stress for the individual, the family, and the patient.

20. C: Short-term disability is not intended to be long term. There are a set of benefits leveraged to provide coverage for an individual during a time in which they are deemed disabled.

21. A: As the label indicates, long-term disability is used for chronic conditions with the intention of replacing income that is lost as a result of a chronic condition or illness.

22. A: What is unique about the interdisciplinary care team is that it consists of professionals from many different backgrounds, including nurses, doctors, social workers, dieticians, and family members. They all work together in order to best meet the needs of the client and develop an effective plan of care.

23. B: Assisted living is considered a form of long-term care because it assists those who struggle to care for themselves and to function independently.

24. A: Reinsurance, also known as stop-loss insurance, is a method used to reduce risk or net liability or loss in catastrophic cases that could put an insurance company at risk for losing an amount of money that is so significant that it could cause them to go bankrupt.

25. D: Under the Affordable Care Act, ACOs and providers are mutually accountable for the health of their patients. They receive financial incentives to cooperate and save money by avoiding services such as diagnostic tests and medical procedures that are not medically necessary.

26. C: PPOs are more flexible than HMOs and do not require referrals as seen with other programs.

27. D: This is a component of the ACO framework. Currently, more than 12 million Medicare beneficiaries are enrolled in an ACO.

28. B: This is the definition of the Medication Therapy Management Program. Medication Therapy Management Programs (MTMP) were established with the US Medicare Modernization Act of 2003 for the primary purpose of promoting medication adherence among Medicare Part D beneficiaries through the use of education and counseling.

29. A: SNPs are available in specific regions/service areas. Special needs plans (SNP) serve those individuals who suffer from a chronic condition and are recipients of Medicare Part A and Part B.

30. C: This is the purpose of the Extended Care Health Option under the TRICARE program.

31. D: TRICARE and CHAMPVA are two distinct programs.

32. D: A physician's practice must pass a set of nine standards and ten elements to become a designated PCMH.

33. C: Self-management entails empowering the patient to solve problems and make decisions about their healthcare, identifying potential resources, taking actionable steps, and maintaining the patient-provider relationship.

34. B: Collaborative negotiation is the most effective form of negotiation in the case-management context. It is built on relationships of trust and seeks to have everyone come away from the negotiation having gained something.

35. D: Physical functioning refers to basic activities of daily life (ADLs), such as eating and bathing. ADLs also include the activities that help a person maintain independence, like driving, shopping, or cooking. Physical functioning and behavioral health can be closely related.

36. A: PBMs work strategically with self-insured companies and government programs to maintain formularies and establish pharmacy contracts. PBMs also have a role in negotiating discounts and rebates with pharmaceutical companies.

37. A: Supplemental Security Income (SSI) provides payment of benefits to those individuals and their family members who are living with a limited income and resources (e.g., home, car, land) at their disposal.

38. C: Established as a result of the Balanced Budget Act (BBA) of 1997, Medicare Part C was created to serve as the Medicare managed care option.

39. A: Medicare Part A, sometimes referred to as Hospital Insurance, covers the hospital portion of healthcare, paying for acute care and skilled-nursing facility care.

40. A: States may establish *medically needy* programs to provide access to care for people who earn too much income to qualify for Medicaid.

41. D: Supplemental Security Disability Insurance (SSDI) provides payment of benefits for individuals and their family members if they have worked for enough years to receive Social Security taxes. People who become disabled before the age of retirement can apply for SSDI.

42. C: This is a requirement associated with this particular qualifying event. Coverage is allowed for up to thirty-six months in those instances where there is a loss due to death, divorce, legal separation, acquisition of Medicare, change in a child's dependent status, or other *qualifying events*.

43. C: A successful transition plan includes scheduling and keeping follow-up appointments, utilization of home visits, medication orders, and medication management that includes ongoing medication reconciliation.

44. C: Case managers who work in the home healthcare setting are provider-based case managers. In addition to home healthcare, provider-based case managers work within organizations and facilities such as IPAs, rehabilitation centers, hospitals, and behavioral-healthcare locations. Choice *A* is not a specific type of case manager, although all case managers (including those who work in home healthcare) should focus on health progression. While home healthcare case workers may provide care for patients with long-term illnesses, Choice *B*, they are not considered long-term illness case managers. Choice *D*, community-based case managers, work with nonprofit agencies as well as local state departments. Their core population consists of those communities that are low income or Medicaid and Medicare recipients.

45. A: MCOs look to reduce the risk for catastrophic outcomes; however, they have the unique opportunity to align the payer's, physician's, and patient's interests to achieve the best possible results.

46. C: Unfreeze is the first step of change according to Lewin's Change Management Model. The stages of change are compared to an ice cube changing shape. In order to make change, a person has to first unfreeze, recognizing the need for change and becoming willing to challenge the status quo.

47. B: Contemplation is when a person first becomes aware of the need for change and is willing to begin thinking about it. It comes after precontemplation, when a person is unwilling or unable to see that there is a problem and is not thinking about change. After contemplation comes the preparation stage, when a person is more actively preparing for change and making plans. If Martha is beginning to think about making changes, she has passed the precontemplation stage and moved into the contemplation stage.

48. C: While abuse can happen at any age and to any population, the three groups most likely to experience some form of abuse are the elderly, children, and the disabled. Young adults are not considered a population at higher risk of abuse.

49. A: A history of mental illness is one of the main factors correlated with abuse. Although a low tolerance for noise or low level of education may contribute in some cases to abusive situations, neither of them is the best answer here. A heart condition is not correlated with perpetrating abuse. Other factors would be substance abuse or a tendency of a caregiver to get easily frustrated.

50. D: Dual diagnosis refers to the phenomenon of both a substance abuse disorder and a mental health disorder present in the same individual, so this would be the best response. Either one may be influenced by the other. It does not have to do with conflicting diagnoses from different physicians, nor does it refer to two mental health disorders or a physical illness resulting from substance abuse.

51. C: Client activation refers to the level to which clients are involved in their own treatment and able to meet their own health needs. Client activation is not static: clients can increase their levels of activation as encouraged and educated by the case manager. Client activation does not specifically refer to a client's involvement in the community, physical activity, or ability to perform activities of daily life. However, all of these things may play a role in clients being involved in their treatment.

52. A: For clients with low activation, the best strategy is to provide them with manageable challenges that meet them on their level. This encourages them as they are able to meet these challenges and

motivates them to take even bigger steps. If clients are pushed beyond their current level of activation too soon, they may become discouraged by failure. It is not helpful for the case manager to make all decisions for clients, as this will disempower them.

53. B: Client empowerment is when the case manager supports clients in accessing their own strengths and resources and setting their own goals for treatment. Empowerment focuses on the client's strengths and resources, rather than problems and weaknesses. While the case manager can work in collaboration with the client, it should be the client who ultimately sets the treatment goals and decides what is best for their life.

54. B: Building rapport is the first, and one of the most significant, aspects of client engagement. The successful provision of services will be based on a positive relationship between the client and case manager. If a client does not feel comfortable with the case manager, they may decide not to engage in treatment at all. Setting goals, interviewing family members, and collaborating with other service providers may be important parts of treatment, but none of these are the first step.

55. D: Confidentiality refers to a case manager's responsibility to maintain the privacy of the client and to protect all information that is shared with them. Information may be shared with others collaborating in the client's treatment, but this should never be done without the client's permission. Confidentiality should always be maintained, except in cases where the case manager has received a court order. While self-disclosure on the part of the case manager is an important issue, that is not what confidentiality is referring to, nor does it have to do with what information a client chooses to share about their treatment.

56. A: Self-promotion is not a notable part of self-care management. Self-advocacy, self-directed care, and informed decision-making are all important aspects of self-care management. A client should be provided with the information and encouragement to manage their own treatment and health care needs.

57. A: Effective self-care management will increase a client's overall health and will decrease the need for emergency and professional care. If a client is taking charge of their own health needs, they can become more independent and maintain better health. The primary goal is not necessarily to make the case manager's job easier or to increase the client's happiness, though these may be secondary benefits. While clients may be able to take medications themselves, unless there is a change in health status, self-care management will not necessarily decrease the amount of medication they take.

58. C: A recommendation to the Area Office on Aging for meal delivery programs would be the best option for home-bound elderly or disabled people. While food pantries or other food resources may help those who have transportation, they are not the best option for this population.

59. C: While much effort is often put into accessing financial, psychological, or medical resources for a client, their spiritual needs are often overlooked. For many clients, their spirituality is an integral aspect of who they are, and spiritual or religious resources may provide a great support for them.

60. D: Collaboration is when a conflict is resolved in a way that satisfies all parties. In compromise, everyone has to give up something in order to get something and settle the issue. In competition, the most powerful person wins. In avoidance, the conflict is avoided altogether. Collaboration is the best strategy for resolving conflict, though it is not always easy to solve a conflict in a way that makes everyone happy.

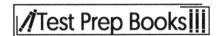

61. A: In a crisis, the most important thing is safety. The first step is to ensure that the client is safe, and not a harm to themselves or others. While calling the police, going to the hospital, or restraining the client may be necessary steps to take, and may be aspects of achieving safety, they are not necessarily the first step. Safety is always the first step that needs to be achieved.

62. C: The most immediate concern is to determine if the client has a plan for suicide and the means for carrying it out. This indicates a high level of suicide risk, and the client may need to be hospitalized. The other answers contain either insignificant or less important information than this.

63. B: The main goal of end-of-life care is to ensure that the client's last days are as painless and comfortable as possible. Decisions around which treatments to use to prolong life are up to the patient. The main goal of end-of-life care is not to make sure the patient dies in a hospital; this should be a decision made in collaboration with the patient.

64. C: The decision about a DNR order is entirely up to the patient or family members. There should be no coercion on the part of the doctors or social workers, but they should provide information so that the patient can make an informed decision.

65. A: In most cases, the family of the client will be involved in treatment and play a supportive role for the client. In some situations, a family member may even serve as the caregiver. Whether the family dynamics are positive or negative, clients function within the context of family, so it is important to understand the family as much as possible. This does not mean that the client cannot make decisions about their own treatment, or that the family's opinions are more important.

66. C: The goal of motivational interviewing is to discover and explore a client's intrinsic motivation and belief in their ability to change. It also tries to identify any barrier to change and the ambivalence a client may feel about change. Motivational interviewing does not focus on specific behaviors or symptoms, but rather on underlying causes.

67. D: When someone has a chronic illness, they may need extra coaching and support to develop and maintain healthy habits. A healthy lifestyle can slow progression of a disease, minimize the symptoms, and improve quality of life.

68. D: The Test of Functional Health Literacy in Adults (TOFHLA) and the Rapid Estimate of Adult Literacy in Medicine (REALM) are the two most validated and tested tools for health literacy assessments. TOFLA is a thorough and comprehensive test, while REALM is shorter and easier to complete.

69. B: The Rapid Estimate of Adult Literacy in Medicine (REALM) provides patients with a list of words to read. They are instructed to read the words that are familiar to them. Words that are mispronounced or not read are not scored.

70. C: Interpersonal communication is an important skill for case managers to have, as most of their work involves interpersonal communication. Interpersonal communication is the process by which people exchange ideas, meanings, thoughts, and feelings with each other. It is a part of all personal and professional relationships and is used during phone calls, emails, and in face-to-face interactions.

71. D: Contextualization is an important skill for the case manager to use when communicating with clients. There will be a barrier to interpersonal communication if the case manager is not able to use words that will be best understood by the specific client. Education and cultural background are two things to consider when communicating with different clients.

238

72. D: While there are many positives to group dynamics and communication, it is possible for the group to suppress the voice of the individual. Some people in a group may not feel comfortable enough to freely share their opinions and may just accept the apparent opinion of the group, leading to group think or conformity.

73. B: Even before meeting a client, the case manager should consider where the interview will take place. Depending on the needs of the client, it can take place in an office, the client's home, or another location. If the client is involved in this decision, they will immediately feel some control and empowerment in the treatment process.

74. B: One of the main purposes of using open-ended questions is to explore the client's fears, concerns, and struggles. Good open-ended questions will give the client the opportunity to share whatever they feel is important. For simple demographic information, close-ended questions may be more helpful.

75. A: Individualistic cultures tend to place more emphasis on independence, privacy, and individual decision-making. Collectivist cultures place more emphasis on the community and family. Decisions are often made as a group, not by an individual. Whether a client comes from an individualistic culture or a collectivist one will probably affect how involved the client's family and community will be in the treatment process.

76. D: Cultural competency in case management is the ability to understand, accept, and respect a client's culture and religion. The case manager must also recognize their own cultural biases and understand how they may influence treatment.

77. B: Both psychological and neuropsychological evaluations examine a person's personality, intelligence, functioning, and potential psychological disorders. However, neuropsychological assessments are more in-depth assessments of everything related to cognition and the brain. If there are physiological reasons behind a client's symptoms, such as a brain injury or dementia, they may be referred for a neurological evaluation.

78. A: The Minnesota Multiphasic Personality Inventory (MMPI) is very commonly used in psychological evaluations. It is an objective test that can be scored on the computer and can help with psychiatric diagnosis. Built into the MMPI are questions to test whether someone is lying or faking answers on the assessment.

79. B: The Diagnostic and Statistical Manual of Mental Disorders, Fifth Edition (DSM-5) contains the official and current criteria for diagnosing psychological disorders. The DSM was updated to the fifth edition in 2013, and there were several changes to categorizations of disorders as well as diagnostic criteria. The multiaxial diagnostic method was also eliminated in the new edition.

80. B: There are many psychosocial aspects of chronic illness and disability, including mental health concerns, such as anxiety, depression, isolation, hopelessness, and stress. A medical illness must be viewed within the context of whole-person care and not treated in isolation. A chronic illness or disability will affect a person's social, emotional, and psychological well-being.

81. D: Medicare is the government insurance program for those over 65 or people with certain disabilities. Medicare can sometimes also be used in conjunction with Medicaid to cover medical costs.

82. B: Patient assistance programs are run by pharmaceutical companies to provide affordable medications to low-income patients. Patients should ask their doctors or pharmacists about these

programs. There are also other state-run programs and nonprofit organizations that help with medical costs for the uninsured or underinsured.

83. C: A client's beliefs and self-determination must be affirmed and acknowledged. Ultimately, it is the client's decision about what treatments to pursue. However, the case manager can continue to provide information and education about objectionable treatments.

84. D: Spirituality can play a positive role in the life of someone suffering from a major illness. Some benefits of spirituality may include adding meaning to life and providing a hopeful outlook for the future. Spirituality may also decrease stress levels, prevent depression and anxiety, and lead to greater overall health.

85. A: It is not necessary for every client to join a support group, especially if they are already busy and have a strong support system. For clients who feel isolated and hopeless in their illness, it could be beneficial for them to join a support group with other people who have similar struggles.

86. C: Pastoral counselors are unique in that they combine both spiritual and psychological aspects into their counseling and are trained in both areas. For clients who are struggling spiritually, and for whom spirituality is especially important, pastoral counseling may be what they need.

87. D: Grieving after experiencing a loss is a natural process. No person experiences grief in exactly the same way as someone else, so bereavement counseling should be tailored to the needs of the individual. The goal of bereavement counseling is to help someone grieve and adjust to the loss in a healthy way.

88. A: While it may not be possible to cure chronic illnesses, illness prevention and wellness programs can help to slow progression of the disease and improve quality of life. No matter what the sickness is, maintaining healthy habits will always contribute to overall well-being.

89. D: While engaging in a routine of being mindful and having a positive outlook on life, consuming a nutritious diet, engaging in daily exercise, and eliminating unhealthy habits all contribute to positive health and wellness. The only option listed that is considered an early detection health measure is Choice *D,* mammograms. Case workers should encourage all their patients to seek medical care. Early detection measures like cancer screenings and mammograms are part of preventative health and can potentially catch diseases before they have spread or become a severe problem.

90. C: The calculator is free of charge. The remaining answers are incorrect based on any reference to the calculator having a cost associated with it.

91. A: The four categories of the Caseload Matrix are as follows: initial elements impacting caseload, comprehensive needs assessment impacting caseload, case management interventions, and outcomes. The remaining answer choices are incorrect because they do not fall into the four categories as defined by the CMSA and NASW concept paper.

92. D: Cost-benefit analysis is the term that refers to how well an organization can show the value of a case management program. The remaining answer choices are incorrect. Health or medical benefit ratio (sometimes noted as the medical loss ratio) refers to the amount of premium revenue spent on medical care and services. Cost-effective comparison is not a term commonly used to show the value of a case management program.

93. B: The Mini-Mental State Examination is an example of a health risk assessment that is currently in use within various organizations. It is used to assess for cognitive function. The remaining options are incorrect. PDSA and Six Sigma are examples of quality improvement measurement strategies. The Case Mix Assessment Tool is not a standard assessment tool.

94. D: Predictive modeling is a tool that many organizations use to identify those people within their population who pose the greatest risk for preventable costs. The remaining answer options are incorrect. None of these terms are nationally recognized terms.

95. C: Most predictive models prefer to leverage 12 months of data to handicap the model. The remaining answer choices are incorrect. While 6 months is an option, it is not the preferred time frame, nor are the other answer choices.

96. B: CQIs improve the overall quality of healthcare delivery therefore allowing for an identification of factors that affect healthcare outcomes. The remaining answer options are incorrect. They are not industry-recognized quality improvement programs.

97. A: Benchmarks can enable organizations to monitor trends and performance metrics in a consistent manner. The remaining answer options are incorrect because they are not terms commonly associated with monitoring the overall performance of a program.

98. A: URAC operates a case management accreditation program with a primary focus on enabling health plans to build a program that is actively capable of managing transitions. The remaining answer options are incorrect because they are not accrediting bodies.

99. B: URAC compares its measures with other reported measures from other entities such as AHRQ National Measures Clearing House and NQF. The remaining answers are incorrect. NCQA has HEDIS and NTOCC primarily focuses on transitioning patients between multiple healthcare settings and identifying common gaps that affect outcomes.

100. C: Organizations that fail to meet NCQA requirements during the Accreditation Survey are denied accreditation by NCQA. The remaining answers are incorrect based on this NCQA practice.

101. C: NCQA provides three categories of disease management accreditation: Accredited, Accredited with Performance Reporting, and Provisional Accreditation. Provisional accreditation alerts the industry that a disease management team does not meet all of the NCQA guidelines or standards, thus the remaining answers are incorrect.

102. A: NCQA utilizes HEDIS scores to measure the performance of managed care organizations. The remaining options are incorrect because HEDIS is the NCQA measure available to consumers to compare the performance of one health plan with another.

103. B: Organizations may be accredited for a three-year or a two-year duration by NCQA. The remaining options are incorrect based on this NCQA practice of a two- or three-year guideline.

104. A: Organizations that demonstrate the ability to achieve NCQA defined standards of managing transitions between levels of care or LTSS settings, performing quality individualized assessments, and the capacity to handle critical incidents may be eligible for NCQA accreditation. These are standards defined by NCQA and performed by LTSS organizations that would enable them to meet LTSS eligibility. The remaining options are incorrect. Care plans are not a component of eligibility defined by NCQA and

organizations must demonstrate a capacity to handle complex or critical situations commonly experienced within the LTSS population.

105. B: National Quality Forum uses a set of performance-based standards that multiple groups, including states, the federal government, and private sectors, recognize and utilize in the evaluation of the quality of performance and overall contribution to improving care. The remaining answer options are incorrect because they negate the overall role of the NQF as defined in the preceding statement.

106. A: National Patient Safety Goals (NPSGs) are created by the Joint Commission. These are standards that have the intention of improving patient safety across the healthcare continuum. The remaining answer options are not appropriate selections because the NPSGs are the only standards that are created by the Joint Commission.

107. A: The Agency for Healthcare Research and Quality (AHRQ) provides the opportunity for healthcare improvement in that it provides research information to the public and healthcare professionals. The remaining options are incorrect. NCQA and URAC are accrediting bodies. This is not the role of the Joint Commission.

108. B: The National Guideline Clearinghouse provides specific patient-centered outcomes and defines the medical treatments that are a best practice for a particular condition based on current research. The remaining options are incorrect. These guidelines do not exist.

109. C: There are three stages of meaningful use and providers must demonstrate the ability to function within each of the stages before they can move to the next one. The remaining answers choices are incorrect based on the requirements of the HITECH Act for three stages.

110. A: AHRQ uses Quality Indicators to measure the quality of health care that supports the identification of quality concerns. The remaining answers options are incorrect because they are not the owners of the QI process. It is a function of AHRQ.

111. A: Cost effectiveness and cost savings are two common financial indicators used by organizations as quality measures to examine overall impact of services provided. The remaining answer options are incorrect. Neither of these are financial indicators used as a quality measure for an organization. Health risk assessments help to provide the patient's history, and mortality reporting is an outcome, not a financial indicator.

112. A: Data collection of productivity indicators for case managers may concentrate heavily on time, tasks, and activities. The remaining answer options are incorrect because they are more commonly associated with utilization indicators.

113. B: Utilization indicators are tracked to evaluate the effectiveness of case and disease management programs and to note the general trends and behaviors of the population that is being served. Industry-recognized utilization indicators that are measured include (but are not limited to) average length of stay, emergency department visits, readmissions within 30 days, and outpatient service utilization. Daily census reporting is a common utilization indicator. It provides an overview of budgeted inpatient days per 1000 to current inpatient days per 1000 with a seven- and 30-day trend. Choice *A* lists two other utilization indicators but does not describe the specific utilization indicator of daily census reporting. Choice *C* describes encounters data, another utilization indicator, while Choice *D* describes the utilization indicator of average length of stay, not daily census reporting.

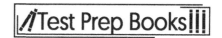

114. C: Client experience information can only come from the client or caregiver, although it may be collected by various entities such as the physician, hospital, or home health agency. The remaining options are incorrect because client experience information can only come from the client or caregiver.

115. D: This answer is correct because this strategy allows the CCM to periodically review the census report for new admissions, physician orders, and diagnoses related to prolonged admission. This way, the CCM can plan which units to round on and create a plan for how to follow up with each specific patient. Choice *A* is incorrect because the charge nurse is typically made aware of an admission within thirty minutes to one hour beforehand. This strategy also interrupts the continuity of care for other patients on the unit. The charge nurse has many other duties and likely patients to care for as well. Choice *B* is incorrect even though running the census report is the best way to determine which patients in a given DRG have been admitted. It is necessary to run this report periodically throughout the day to check for new admissions. Choice *C* is also incorrect (see rationale for *A*).

116. C: This answer is correct because the CCM must not impose what they believe to be the best option onto the client. Once informed consent is obtained, the CCM must allow the client to determine which option they feel most comfortable choosing. It is the client who must live with the results. Choice *A* is incorrect because the CCM must utilize the most highly trained and best equipped technician to design, align, and fit the prosthetic. This professional will use the client's medical, personal, and professional profile to design a device best suited for the client to use. Choice *B* is incorrect because the client may benefit from speaking with others with similar diagnoses, other amputees, or those with specific personal and/or work environments who can empathize with the client and help to normalize their questions and concerns. Choice *D* is incorrect because the client is entitled to choose the course of treatment that they prefer. Creating a list of appropriate devices and treatment plans will afford the client the information necessary to choose well.

117. C: The goal of an orthosis is to improve the functioning of any body part, and treatments may include but are not limited to shoe inserts, slings, and braces. Choice *A* is incorrect; this is a definition of a prosthetic. Choice *B* is incorrect because the orthosis does not heal any body part. Choice *D* is incorrect because the orthosis is not designed to prevent injuries.

118. C: This answer is correct because the client appears to be suffering from depression. The associated inventories are designed to gauge the client's mood and determine the level of depression. Choice *A* is incorrect. Although the client has sustained an injury that would likely affect their balance, the issue in this case is more related to a nonphysical cause. Choice *B* is incorrect. The client in this scenario does not report an ill fit, decline in mobility, or any changes in physical functioning. Choice *D* is incorrect.

119. B: This answer is correct because a frontal-lobe injury is an assault to the brain's primary emotion control center. The client will experience difficulties modulating emotions and struggle with inhibition. Choice *A* is incorrect. The behaviors noted in this selection are indicative of an injury to the temporal lobe. Choice *C* is incorrect and indicates an injury to the occipital lobe. Choice *D* is incorrect because it is indicative of an injury to the cerebellum.

120. C: Broken bones are considered a moderate workplace injury because, while they necessitate a hospital visit, they only require a short amount of time for recovery once treated. Choices *A* and *B* are incorrect because these types of injuries would be categorized as minor or mild. Choice *D* is incorrect because electrocutions are severe/calamitous occupational injuries.

121. A: This answer is correct because completing an evaluation of the ability of a client to perform basic and job-specific skills is the first step of a functional capacity evaluation. Choice *B* is incorrect. An interdisciplinary team is brought together to collaborate on the evaluation. Choice *C* is incorrect because treatment plans can be adjusted as necessary during the rehabilitation process. Choice *D* is incorrect because maximum effort is expected from the patient.

122. D: Working in tandem with the neurologist, the CCM must help the caregiver to understand the brain functions and the consequences of damage to any specific area. Choice *A* is incorrect because any client who has sustained a TBI will experience myriad symptoms and will likely never fully recover to their previous level of functioning. Choice *B* is incorrect. The client and caregiver must make this decision. The choice to permanently hospitalize a client is a delicate matter and, although it should be added to the plan as a viable option, the CCM must consider the needs of the patient and family as a unit. Choice *C* is incorrect. Depending on the specific area of damage, the client will experience many symptoms. Each area of the brain is responsible for a specific function; damage to any specific area will have a particular set of physical and/or emotional reactions.

123. C: Ergonomics is the study of creating more efficient ways for people to work in their vocational environment. Choice *A* is incorrect. Devices can be used within ergonomics to positively impact the client's life, but ergonomics is not defined as the study of assistive devices. Choice *B* is incorrect. Clients' return to their work environments is the paramount goal of ergonomics, rather than returning to home environments. Choice *D* is incorrect. Ergonomics is not the science of teaching a client how to adjust to the outside world, but rather to their work environment.

124. D: The CCM must discuss the client's hesitation for returning to work to determine if a slower part-time to full-time return to work is more reasonable. Choice *A* is incorrect. The client can adjust their treatment plan as needed. Choice *B* is incorrect. The CCM must allow the client to determine the best pace for treatment. Choice *C* is incorrect. The client's treatment plan must consider slow progression or setbacks in treatment.

125. B: The CCM must reassure the client that the employer has agreed to allow the employee to be reintegrated into their previous work environment. Choice *A* is incorrect. The client will be assured that there will be sufficient time for them to relearn all of the hard and soft skills necessary to perform their job functions. Choice *C* is incorrect. Assistive devices will be utilized if necessary. Choice *D* is incorrect. The client will NOT be forced to return to work unprepared.

126. D: The goal of the treatment plan is to guide the client's return to work. Choice *A* is incorrect. The client may never return to the level of functioning prior to their injury. Choice *B* is incorrect. The CCM is not to continue an intervention indefinitely, but to refer the client for ongoing services once their need for specific intervention has been satisfied. Choice *C* is incorrect. The client may never feel ready to leave treatment; the CCM must periodically advise the client on their progress and plan for the contract to end.

127. D: Although these clients will benefit from CCM intervention, they are typically referred to an obstetrical specialist. Choices *A, B,* and *C* are incorrect. These types of clients are typically referred to a CCM due to the high probability of needing post hospitalization case management.

128. B: There is no rehabilitation delivery system of this nature other than support groups, which are not a primary source of treatment. Choice *A* is incorrect. This delivery system allows for the client to care for themselves as often as possible, directing the course of treatment. Choice *C* is incorrect. This

response refers to the insurance company acting as the primary gatekeeper of benefits. Choice *D* is incorrect. This type of care occurs after a face-to face interaction with a provider.

129. C: A cerebellar injury typically results in an interruption of coordination, fine motor skills, ambulation, and the ability to grasp objects. Choice *A* is incorrect. These tools are designed to gauge balance. Choice *B* is incorrect. These tools are designed to gauge damage to the frontal lobe, where initiation, motivation and inhibition are housed. Choice *D* is incorrect. These tools are designed to gauge damage to the frontal lobe.

130. A: The PPACA was created to ensure that all Americans receive essential medical benefits at an affordable rate. Choice *B* is incorrect. Although specific sanctions are levied against insurance companies that fail to comply, this is not the goal of the act. Choice *C* is incorrect. Discrimination is strictly prohibited against persons without health coverage, and this legislation does address that issue by providing health coverage. This is not, however, the primary goal of the act. Choice *D* is incorrect. Although the PPACA is providing essential health benefits to children, that is not the focus of this legislation.

131. C: It is crucial that the client's awareness of the plan of care be confirmed in writing. Choice *A* is incorrect. Although the fee schedule is also negotiated with the client and the cost of services both with and without CCM intervention must be presented (if applicable), the informed consent is for treatment purposes, not for payment. Choice *B* is incorrect. The CCM can be sued for malpractice for any reason. The presence of a signed consent form does not prevent the CCM from facing legal action. Choice *D* is incorrect. Although this information is included in the client's case file, the actual informed consent document must include the client's awareness of the plan of care.

132. C: Files may be kept in a separate location but must always be secured under lock and key. Choice *A* is incorrect because any nonessential paper documents must be shredded whenever possible. Choice *B* is incorrect. The DMS's are designed to protect patient information. Choice *D* is incorrect. It is the best practice to provide protected health information only to those that need to know in order to continue the care of the client.

133. C: The CCM must ensure that interventions are truthful and presented plainly. There must be no use of jargon, technical language, or unnecessary information. Choice *A* is incorrect. Although it is always appropriate to maintain a sense of compassion while caring for clients, this is not the formal definition of veracity. Choice *B* is incorrect. Ethical treatment is a tenant of the basic standards of practice for all CCM's, but this is not the formal definition of veracity. Choice *D* is incorrect. Every clinician must ensure that their interventions do not bring harm to their clients, but this is not the formal definition of veracity.

134. D: Specifically related to rehabilitation, this act allows for the employee, spouse, or dependent children to continue to receive medical coverage for a minimum of eighteen months and a maximum of thirty-six months. Choice *A* is incorrect. This response describes the Workforce Innovation and Opportunity Act of 2014. Choice *B* is incorrect. This describes the Family Medical Leave Act of 1993. Choice *C* is incorrect. This is the purpose of the Americans With Disabilities Act of 1990.

135. D: It is always appropriate to utilize the physicians when presenting the options for treatment. Doing this will ensure that the client has the correct information to choose their preferred treatment. Choice *A* is incorrect. This is a violation of the client's rights. If the client is lucid and able to provide informed consent, the CCM cannot override the client's decisions. Choice *B* is incorrect. Although it is a

good idea to contact the affiliated clergy of the client's religion for support, the client should decide the proper course of treatment. Choice *C* is incorrect. It is unethical to abandon a client during treatment unless there is an emergent and unavoidable need to do so. The CCM must adhere to the client's wishes, even if the CCM does not agree.

136. C: It is incumbent upon the CCM to locate any advance directives to confirm the patient's final wishes and ensure that they are followed. Choice *A* is incorrect. Although this is an appropriate response, this is not the best answer. The CCM must take the lead on this case and attempt to confirm the client's wishes. Choice *B* is incorrect. The CCM cannot abandon a client during a case simply due to the client's decision not to pursue the options presented by the clinician. Choice *D* is incorrect. The appropriate action would be to first check for any advance directives and follow them if they do exist.

137. B: Case files must be accurate in order to confirm the exact treatment plan agreed upon by the client. Choice *A* is incorrect. The maintenance of accurate case files cannot prevent the CCM from facing a lawsuit. Choice *C* is incorrect. The maintenance of accurate files does not guarantee payment for services. Choice *D* is incorrect. Although this is correct, it is not the best answer. Case files must be accurate in order to confirm the exact treatment plan agreed upon by the client.

138. B: The meaningful-use clause requires all providers to show that their work is both appropriate and impactful. Choice *A* is incorrect. Meaningful use does not directly refer to the confidentiality of client files. Choice *C* is incorrect. This is not a definition of meaningful use. Choice *D* is incorrect. Meaningful use does not refer to supervision received by the CCM.

139. D: Although the rapport between the client and CCM is crucial to the process, it is not necessary for the client and CCM to be friends in order for the treatment plan to succeed. Choice *A* incorrect. Bad faith involves the improper administration of administrative denials of benefits. Choice *B* is incorrect. Bad faith also involves the failure of the CCM to explain the denial of benefits. Choice *C* is incorrect. This is the third and final aspect of bad faith.

140. C: All of the language in this answer provides specific instructions as to how the document must be handled. Choice *A* is incorrect. The document cannot be forwarded by a third party; this is a violation of HIPAA. Choice *B* is incorrect. The CCM cannot guarantee that the documents have been shredded. It is imperative that the correct fax number be confirmed prior to sending the transmission. Choice *D* is incorrect.

141. C: The case manager is tasked with investigating the incident to operationalize the best way to prevent a recurrence. Choice *A* is incorrect. The CCM is not to act in an unethical way. Choice *B* is incorrect. The CCM has not been enlisted to find any party to be at fault, but to determine the root cause of the incident. Choice *D* is incorrect. Through a systematic investigation, the CCM will be able to determine the cause of the incident and identify all contributing and noncontributing factors.

142. A: The CCM must seek to determine the primary cause of the incident and all contributing factors in order to enact any necessary policy or procedural changes. Choice *B* is incorrect. The CCM may be acting as an agent of the company, but the primary goal is to prevent future accidents of a similar nature. Choice *C* is incorrect. Although implementing the necessary policy or procedural changes will result in little or no financial loss for the company, this is only as a result of the prevention of similar incidents. Choice *D* is incorrect.

143. C: It is important for the CCM to remind the caregiver of the importance of caring for themselves just as they do their family member. Choice *A* is incorrect. The decision to admit their ill family member into an institution is a delicate matter. The discussion must also include the client and should not be considered as the only option. Choice *B* is incorrect. Although it may be necessary to consider medications, the medications cannot alleviate any physical stress involved in caring for a family member. Choice *D* is incorrect. This is also a viable option but is not necessarily going to allow for the caregiver to completely disconnect from their role in order to care for themselves.

144. D: A client who is blind is still able to hear and comprehend and retain the information presented. That client is also able to weigh the relevant information provided and communicate their decision to consent to treatment. Choice *A* is incorrect. A client unable to utilize their mind cannot form the rational thought required to think clearly. Choice *B* is incorrect. This client would not be able to appreciate the differences between the options presented and would not be able to provide informed consent. Choice *C* is incorrect. The client in this situation may be able to hear the information but is unable to communicate that understanding; therefore, they cannot consent.

145. A: The CCM must immediately consult an attorney to determine the best course of action. Choice *B* is incorrect. Although it is tempting to discuss the case with a colleague, this has the potential to violate the clients' privacy. Choice *C* is incorrect. The CCM is never contacted by the client but is usually served notice of the lawsuit. Contacting the client may only serve to escalate the situation and lead to professional sanctions. Choice *D* is incorrect. Although this is necessary, the first response must be to seek legal counsel; the case file will be pulled and reviewed once the attorney can determine the best course of action.

146. C: The CCM must work diligently to guard their own well-being in order to provide appropriate care to clients. Choice *A* is incorrect. Although it is important for the CCM to model appropriate self-care, the most important reason is to preserve the well-being of the clinician. Choice *B* is incorrect. This is one of the results of the CCM making self-care a priority. As the CCM effectively manages stress, they are better able to empathize with their clients. Choice *D* is incorrect.

147. A: According to ERISA, an appeal can be filed if the 180-day time frame has not expired. Choice *B* is incorrect. Under the ERISA guidelines, the employer does not have to honor an appeal received after the 180-day time frame has expired. Choice *C* is incorrect. According to ERISA, all appeals must be received in writing. Choice *D* is incorrect. An appeal can be filed if the 180-day time frame has not expired and there is no one to be sure if the appeal will be denied or not.

148. D: Case managers adhere to the practice standards of the CMSA. Choice *A* is a fictional entity. Choice *B* is incorrect. This entity governs the standards of practice for social workers only. Choice *C* is incorrect. This entity governs the standards of practice for nurses only.

149. B: Prior to disclosing any protected information, the client must either obtain a release of information to do so or determine if one already exists. If none exists or it has expired, the CCM cannot reveal any information to a third party. Choice *A* is incorrect. It is not a violation of the client's privacy to respond to the caller. The CCM is not allowed, however, to confirm or deny the names and/or treatment plans of clients. Choice *C* is incorrect. A client with a TBI is unable to provide informed consent to sign a release of information or an advance directive. Choice *D* is incorrect. A client with a TBI is unable to provide informed consent to sign a release of information or an advance directive.

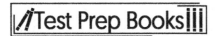

150. C: This question is asked later in the investigation, during the root-cause analysis. The purpose of this question is to determine how to solve the problems identified in the initial investigation. Choice *A* is incorrect. This is one of the initial questions asked during the postmortem of a sentinel event. Finding out who was involved will guide who the investigator must interview. Choice *B* is incorrect. This question is also integral to the investigation of the sentinel event. The answer to this question will direct the investigator to any physical cause of the incident. Choice *D* is incorrect. The answer to this question will determine if a human error, mechanical error, or procedural error was the likely cause of the incident.

Index

Dear CCM Certification Test Taker,

We would like to start by thanking you for purchasing this study guide for your CCM Certification exam. We hope that we exceeded your expectations.

Our goal in creating this study guide was to cover all of the topics that you will see on the test. We also strove to make our practice questions as similar as possible to what you will encounter on test day. With that being said, if you found something that you feel was not up to your standards, please send us an email and let us know.

We have study guides in a wide variety of fields. If you're interested in one, try searching for it on Amazon or send us an email.

Thanks Again and Happy Testing!
Product Development Team
info@studyguideteam.com

FREE Test Taking Tips Video/DVD Offer

To better serve you, we created videos covering test taking tips that we want to give you for FREE. **These videos cover world-class tips that will help you succeed on your test.**

We just ask that you send us feedback about this product. Please let us know what you thought about it—whether good, bad, or indifferent.

To get your **FREE videos**, you can use the QR code below or email freevideos@studyguideteam.com with "Free Videos" in the subject line and the following information in the body of the email:

    a. The title of your product

    b. Your product rating on a scale of 1-5, with 5 being the highest

    c. Your feedback about the product

If you have any questions or concerns, please don't hesitate to contact us at info@studyguideteam.com.

Thank you!

Made in the USA
Las Vegas, NV
02 April 2023

70022463R00144